ARMED AND DANGEROUS

LONDON GANGSTER'S PATH TO MULTIPLE MURDERS AND 45 YEARS IN PRISON

JOHN HILTON

To my dear friend Julie,
Thank you for all your help and advice,
love and respect

To Victoria,
This book could not have been completed
without your input and skill.

This book is dedicated to the memory of
Charlie Tozer and Mickey Murray.
Rest in peace my friends.

SPELLING DIFFERENCES: UK V US

This book was written in British English, hence US readers may notice some spelling differences from American English: e.g. color = colour, meter = metre and jewelry = jewellery

CONTENTS

CHAPTER 1

"GOD MUST HAVE KEPT YOU ALIVE FOR A REASON"

I lay in my warm, cosy bed. The sound of bombs exploding in the darkness, blasting and rumbling away, had almost become a nightly musical event. I would listen intently to the sounds; you could hear a small hissing as they fell through the air. On impact, the bombs would sound like a shotgun, followed by a sustained roar. The shrapnel would shower over the houses like metal droplets of rain and I would often count the taps that hit nearby buildings, trying to work out how close the bomb was to our house.

The Second World War broke out when I was ten years old. The day it was announced, I ran out onto the street and expected loads of aircraft to be flying above and lots of commotion. But to my dismay, it was quiet. The thought of the war brought pure delirium and made my imagination run wild. I craved the excitement of danger and the unknown. In reality, the war was a slow process, but Hitler's men eventually delivered what I had expected and soon reached our shores, causing carnage on our streets. As a naïve young boy, I did not realise the implications and destruction war brings. At first, I felt like war in my land would bring new adventure and possibilities, but reality soon set in when people were dying around me and the world I once knew was no longer safe.

At the time, I was living on Brixton Road with my mum, dad and sisters. Before the war came and disrupted our existence, I had a wonderful childhood, doing all the activities a boy would be doing back in the 1930s. Playing outside, tinkering with toys, going on adventures through the brambles of the park, playing without a care in the world. Enjoying sibling banter, being mischievous, falling over and being careless, but never a problem child. Before the war, there was a plan for most; we had an idea of what our future looked like, where we would work, where we would live. But the war stripped us of our education, it impacted our mental health and stripped us of hope.

My parents, Mr and Mrs Arnold, already had two daughters when I was born. Francis was two years older than me and attended the same school as I did, and Lily was the oldest. Francis was a cheerful girl and we had a wonderful relationship, most likely because we enjoyed the same activities and were of a similar age. She was a bit of a tomboy, loved the great outdoors, enjoyed climbing trees, kicking a football, always ready to rough it with the boys. She often came home with stained clothing, getting muddy in the fields and getting her hands dirty at any chance she could. Having a lot in common, we spent our younger days together, passing the time in small and enchanting adventures.

Lily was the oldest daughter; she was ten years older than me and was always reading true romance stories, which she used to hide under her mattress from our mother, who disapproved of such things. I remember when Lily went out on a date, she would sneak back into the house through a window. She came into my bedroom with a bag of warm, salty chips and we would sit on the bed scoffing down this greasy but wholesome food. We had to keep quiet, so as not to wake anyone, giggling as we sat up, eating in the darkness. I didn't realise, but at the time, these small encounters were a bonding moment, small acts of kindness, laughing together, eating together. They bring you closer to your loved ones, and this memory sticks out to me as one of those fond moments. I admired Lily for breaking the mould of a conventional woman of that time; she was ready to take risks and let her heart rule, rather than her head.

We lived in a large Victorian house, 112 Brixton Road, which is still standing, in all its glory today. It had a large, grassy garden with flower beds to the side and an oak tree at the bottom, which was ideal for climbing and messing about with and using as part of kids' roleplay. Next door had the same size garden with an orchard; the girls would keep watch and I would sneak over the wall and steal some juicy apples. That was always a thrill; the sneakiness of it, the anticipation and the thrill combined made me feel alive. I think the neighbour knew but he never said anything. If he had done, we would have been in serious trouble with our mother. Back in the 1930s, stealing even an apple wasn't acceptable. Any form of theft would bring shame upon the family, which I think made stealing even more appealing to me.

The rear of the house was covered in a rambling grape vine, which stretched all over the brickwork. Francis would hang onto my shirt, and I would lean out the window as far as I dared and pick as many grapes as I could. The thrill of trying not to get caught picking the fruit was just as exciting as eating it. Sometimes, we would pick and eat the odd bad grape, which gave us sharp pain in our stomachs, followed by the runs. But it was worth the belly ache, just to taste such sweet, beautiful fruit, a rarity in the 1930s. Especially as rationing meant we were restricted on food.

In the centre of the house, there was a huge kitchen on the ground floor with a long wooden table and a large black enamelled stove. I remember it vividly as it was the heart of the house, the hub of our meetings and where we were united as a family at mealtimes. Mum was a small slim woman with dark red hair, who always seemed to be bustling around the kitchen, which was full of delicious aromas. She was always cooking, rustling up tasty meals for us. We looked forward to her delicious meals and her warm embrace at the end of a long school day. My mum was a house-proud woman and made sure we did our bit to earn our keep. Every weekend, we had to scrub the kitchen with salt and woe betide us if it wasn't gleaming by the time we finished. Though we had chores, which we would never look forward to, it kept us on the straight and narrow and I appreciated the structure, discipline and routine my parents instilled in me.

The war cast an ominous shadow over most, but I found the bombs and chaos quite exciting, almost like an alternative world of danger, and the element of surprise kept me on my toes. My parents, on the other hand, were extremely worried, and rightly so. We were near the heart of London, and they were desperate to get out of the danger zone to keep our family safe.

There were all types of attacks on London at the time. The Blitz, known as the 'Lightning War,' savagely took out large areas, resulting in many injuries and deaths. Bombs were dropped randomly, no one knowing where they could land next, and most of us would scurry to the bomb shelters and wait out the onslaught of nightly explosions. There was one type of bomb, known as a doodlebug, with mini wings, which fascinated me. It looked like a small aeroplane with no pilot, similar to a cruise missile but slightly bigger. If you could hear this bomb, then you knew it was nowhere near you, but if the bomb sound cut out, you would pray that it was not your day to be blown up. This is what we got used to; living like this became the norm and before you knew it, you knew nothing else but the threat of bombs and death.

On the 1st of September 1939, two days before war was declared, the government began evacuating children from towns and cities. It was the largest movement of people ever seen in Britain. Most travelled by train and went to live with other families, who would foster them. My sisters and I stayed with our parents, which I was grateful for. I would have missed them terribly if we had been shipped off to an unknown destination and a strange family. Evacuation was an adventure for some, who had never seen the countryside, but others were homesick and unhappy. Foster parents were often shocked by the lack of hygiene and poor diets of inner-city children.

A variety of food was not as easily accessible as today, with sprawling supermarkets on every corner. Today, with a tap of a button, you can get cuisine from all over the world, while we had rationing. This was a controlled distribution of scarce resources and food. Strangely enough, richer families discovered what it was like to go hungry, whereas the poorer families found rationing left them better fed than before. Equally, some city children found themselves staying in isolated farming communities with no electricity, running water or food. It was hit or miss or pure luck where you ended up staying and what type of childhood you were destined to have. Even though we stayed with our parents, we still had to deal with the threat of gas attacks, air raids, rationing, changes at school and complete disruption to our daily life. This disruption, as well as shortages of food and everyday necessities continued after the war. The post-war period saw changes that would make a lasting impact on everyone for years to come.

Every school day after an attack, we would all gather round and pray for the families and children that had been killed the night before. It became a common occurrence to lose people we knew, every single day. There was always someone we knew of that had died; a neighbour, a distant relative or an old family friend. Death and destruction became the new normal. The war desensitised many to loss and pain; it toughened the masses, and brought with it a distorted view of pain and death. But alongside the negatives, it brought some positives too. The war brought people together; in the hardest times, we became a loving and nurturing community. Everyone looked out for each other; the destruction of the city and the deaths of so many brought out warmth and love from people, which would normally not have been seen in everyday life. Trauma and pain bring the humanity out in many, and we became known for our defiance and stiff upper lip.

When I was twelve, my parents thought it would be safer to move a little further out of London and they managed to snag a house in Harrow, which is out in Middlesex, bordering the city, trying its best to be a countryside village. We lived in the middle of a row of five houses and knew all our neighbours. We were a close-knit little community; the smaller size of the town meant you knew everyone, and parents felt their children were safer in this environment. As time went on, bombs continued to shower down on London and the rest of the cities across England. Hitler and his men were not giving up; the onslaught was now in full swing. Moving to Harrow meant we would be out of the direct line of fire. For the city, it was a numbers game, a chance of bad luck where the bombs landed. My parents had the right idea, and we were all elated to be starting a new chapter of our lives in the leafy suburbs.

Harrow was idyllic, with far more trees and greener parks and many a playground. We settled in with no trouble at all. There was more space to play and, again, the neighbourhood was super friendly. We all were going through the war together; each family had its own story and struggle. People wanted to lift each other up in the darkest of times and they did this with great determination and strength. I, on the other hand, just saw the excitement and danger of it all. I found the madness of the war riveting and I would often collect the shrapnel or shell cases of any military ammunition I could find. I was fascinated by the mechanics and how it all worked. I would admire the intricacy of the machinery and study it in great detail. Being a young boy, I didn't understand the magnitude of a war. It was only when I was older that I could reflect and see the war for what it was.

One neighbour of mine had returned to the street; he was a service man, on leave from the army and he was back visiting his family. His arrival was common knowledge and held some excitement, bringing stories from the feet on the ground. We children were fascinated by his war stories and domineering stature. Getting a first-hand account of the fight across the water was better than any play or radio report. I would sit and listen to him for as long as he would talk, staying rigid in my spot, soaking up his every word.

One night, a night like every other, we went to bed as usual and all of us were fast asleep, tucked up in bed. What seemed an average uneventful evening became one that would change the course of my life to a completely different direction. I came to, half-conscious and under rubble, dust smothering me. I was lying there with no idea with what had just occurred; stunned and confused, I couldn't move and there was piercing ringing in my ears. The whole five houses on the strip had been demolished, no longer standing where they once were. I could not see anything in front of me; there was a fog of thick dust whirling in the air and it became impossible to breathe. Each breath I took clogged my lungs and I felt like I was suffocating, gasping for oxygen that was no longer available. A stick of bombs had been dropped and all the houses were gone, including everyone living there. My entire family was killed on impact, along with everyone who lived on my street.

I remember shouting, "Mother, Mother, Mother!"

The last thing I remember was being amongst the rubble, crushed and unable to move, wondering what had happened, struggling to catch my final breath, dust circling me and a deafening ringing in my ears before I fell unconscious again. Just before I did, I heard a faint voice saying, "It's alright, we're coming…"

I woke up in Harrow hospital with a bandage round my head. Having no idea what had happened to me, I looked around at the unfamiliar surroundings, wondering how the hell I had ended up there. I was lucky to have survived with few injuries; it was almost a miracle that I came away unscathed. All I came away with was a depressed fracture to my skull. Other than that, I was in pretty good shape. The doctors came round and had to break the news to me that my whole family had died, along with everyone living on the street. It felt unbelievably surreal; how was it possible I was the only survivor?

Being twelve, I didn't really have the vocabulary to express my emotions or really understand the impact of losing my family. I don't think I ever really processed it or grieved properly. You just didn't show emotion in those days and who did I have to cry to? Nobody else loved me in this world. I only had my immediate family, and they were all gone. Children are resilient, especially ones growing up in the war. Without knowing it, I had already been prepared and groomed for my loss. I had witnessed many people die already, so I had become desensitised to death and feeling sad. I had to just get on with the cards I had been dealt. There was a mindset I applied to most situations; pick myself up and dust off my shoulders. This attitude kept me in good stead in future years.

Whilst I was in the hospital, I used to wander round for hours and watch the doctors and nurses in action. I would go to the laundry department and chat away with the ladies; they used to make me cups of tea and looked after me for the short time I was there. I enjoyed my time in hospital; I got a lot of attention and love from the nurses, which pleased me greatly. They showed empathy for my plight; knowing I was now all alone in the world made them more caring and loving towards me.

One Irish lady said, "God must have kept you alive for a reason."

Her comment stayed with me for the rest of my life, the memory always popping to the forefront of my brain whenever I found myself in sticky situations. Why had I been chosen? Why had I survived? For me, it was hard to understand that I was the only survivor. Was there some kind of destiny I needed to fulfil?

My recovery was a swift one and there must have been lots of whispers in corners as to what would happen to me now my parents were gone. I was an orphan in the government's eyes and was now a burden to society. I didn't fancy living in an orphanage; that would have been a real shock to the system. They were going to have to work out where I was going to live. As far as I knew, I didn't have any other family to go to. But the hospital must have done some digging as I had a surprise visitor. One morning, I was lying in my bed, getting restless and bored in the hospital wing when a woman appeared at the foot of my bed. She was an attractive lady and had an odd air about her. Her appearance was striking, and I wondered why she was standing there glaring at me intensely.

She said to me with a matter-of-fact tone, "I am your birth mum and I've come to take you home."

It was then that I learned Mr and Mrs Arnold, Lily and Francis were my foster family. I had no idea at the time that they were not my blood family. I had never been made to feel any different, so in that respect, they did a great job of making me feel like I was one of their own. I had mixed feelings about this revelation; I had a moment of questioning my existence and who I really was.

Finding out I had a living birth mother was a shock, to say the least. But in what I had lost, I thought to myself, there was possibly a gain and there was someone now to potentially look after me and love me once again, as one of their own. I'd never met her before; I didn't have any memory of her at all. Questions and concerns buzzed through my head, but I went along with being re-united with her as a positive and miraculous occurrence. The authorities must have contacted her to tell her what had happened to me and my family. She must have had a pang of guilt and felt sorry for me, to come and take me back. I got myself ready and was led blindly by this stranger, calling me her son.

Over the time we spent together, I soon realised my hopes and dreams for our mother-and-son relationship would be shattered. Our relationship was awkward, distant and confusing. I didn't feel much like she was happy to have me back in her life. In fact, I felt more like a burden than a joy. She wouldn't talk to me much, so I would stay out of her way, so as not to irritate her or be in her eyeline for too long. I could see it would bother her if I was hanging around her or even in the same room.

We lived at 51 Belgrave Square. I woke up screaming one night, thinking someone was in the flat. I must have had a night terror, or a bad dream; I couldn't remember why I was screaming. My mother could see I was visibly shaken, but she came bursting into my room, furious that I had woken her up and for making such a noise. This incident must have really pissed her off as, next thing I knew, I was being shipped off to Derby to stay with a family there. For my mother, I was just a nuisance; any little thing I did would set her off into a foul mood, which would have me on tenterhooks. I often wondered if she had mental health problems;

that was probably the reason she gave me up in the first place.

At the time, I didn't understand why she sent me away again; her behaviour was confusing and hurtful. Every time she rejected me, I think a part of me died. All I was really looking for was love and care, like any child needs to flourish in this cold and unforgiving world. Unfortunately for her, my stay in Derby didn't last for long. Part of my coping mechanism to deal with her behaviour was to lash out and grab attention the best way I could. I stole a bike and hid it behind the back of a church, causing mischief in the quiet village. Derby was not ready for my behaviour, and they sent me swiftly back to my mother, who had, in my absence, moved down to sunny Hove.

The house in Hove was on New Church Road; a lovely house, spacious with a balcony from my bedroom and a grand piano in the lounge. It was a gorgeous house, but it was not a home; there was no love in it. The house was cold and felt clinical, almost like it should not be lived in. I could sense my mother didn't want me around, more than ever, so I was constantly walking on eggshells. I felt like I was an inconvenience and I avoided her has much as I could, spending the majority of my time at school and getting a part-time job in the dairy. I did anything to avoid the house and would often wander the streets to kill time. We had an uneasy relationship and, as I got older, it became more strained. I found joy and happiness instead in my interests and hobbies. I fell in love with bikes and tinkering with them for hours gave me great pleasure and escapism from my miserable reality.

CHAPTER 2

APPROVED SCHOOL

I spent endless days tinkering around with my bike. I would often only stop messing around with it when there was no more daylight to see by and I was forced to put down my tools until another day. I painted my bike bright red and was always trying to change the gears so I could go faster. If I could modify it in any way, I would. I remember thinking I needed more tools to keep my hobby alive and to be able to tinker away at other parts of the bike. I was limited in what I could do with my tinkering with the tools I had; therefore, little progression or extended knowledge could be achieved. I decided to venture to the local shop, which had a large collection of various tools, one of which was just what I needed; an adjustable spanner. I hovered around the tool section for a while and contemplated stealing it. I was in two minds at first, but the desire to have it overtook me. Even knowing right from wrong, I still couldn't fight the urge to pocket it and take it home.

After a long battle in my head, I finally plucked up the courage and took it, placing it neatly into my pocket, as secretly and calmly as I could. My heart was racing, my armpits were dripping wet, and I found myself getting hot under the collar, feeling like the whole world was staring at me. Next thing I knew, a large hand grabbed my shoulder and aggressively spun me around. I saw the shopkeeper hovering over me, and he told me to hand over the spanner. My heart sank; I knew I was in serious trouble. I had obviously been acting suspiciously and had lingered too long in his shop, catching his watchful, beady eye. He took great pleasure in reprimanding me, with a long-drawn-out speech and, without hesitation, he called the police. I waited in absolute fear for them to turn up.

I couldn't believe what was happening; how did stealing an adjustable spanner escalate to me being in trouble with the law? I would have expected to get a slap on the wrist instead. The policeman approached me with a stern look on his face, gave me a long-winded speech about how stealing was wrong and how disappointed my mother would be. I was put in the back of the police car, with my head lowered with shame. I could only sit there with knots tightening up in my stomach and I felt sick at the thought of what was in store for me. On the car journey home, my stress was heightened. I was panicking, full of anxiety and tremendous worry. This was the first time I had been in trouble with the police, and I had no idea what sort of reaction to expect from my mother. She answered the door, and I shook my head in an apologetic manner. I saw her face drop and watched the disappointment appear and stay firmly etched on her face.

"I don't want to see you until the morning," she said sternly. Turning her back on me, she slammed the front room door and left me to wallow in pity and shame.

I desperately wanted to tell her why I had stolen the spanner, but I knew it was no use. She wouldn't understand, and I felt like any explanation would fall on deaf ears. So, I sulked up to my room, tail between my legs, feeling desperately sorry for myself. I lay down and contemplated my fate and the wrath of my mother. If she didn't like me much before, then she would definitely hate me now.

Unfortunately, in the 1930s and 40s when I was a youth, petty theft was a serious offence. Charged, I was whisked to Hove Juvenile Court. The shop manager and policeman gave evidence against me; caught red-handed, I had no choice but to plead guilty. I was ordered to pay two shillings as a fine, which in today's money is the equivalent of ten pence. It really wasn't much at all and I was quite happy with the fine, thinking that would be it. The judge asked if I had a previous record and, as I was not known to the police, he believed I was unlikely to re-offend and that I had made a terrible, stupid mistake. Coming from a good home, they thought I had no reason to behave again in such a manner and it was a daft decision I had made, without thinking of the consequences. They thought going through the ordeal of the court would be enough to put me off stealing for life.

At that moment in time, I swore to myself I would never steal again; I had been shaken and shocked that I had ended up in court and vowed to myself never to return. At the time, I was starting off my working life, doing an apprenticeship to be a typesetter. I was worried I had fucked up my future and was praying I would not be kicked off the course. I had made a silly mistake and now I was paying the price. In my heart, I was fearful of ever re-offending and had the full intention of never getting into trouble again.

The judge asked if there was anyone else who would like to give evidence, and the probation officer said, yes, the defendant's mother. She came to the stand and my heart leapt a little, as I thought she would give me a good character reference. My mother was there to protect me; that's what families do, they look out for each other in a crisis, and this was one of the times to do so. This was a moment where she could show me her love and loyalty.

I think the judge was also expecting my mother to stand up for me, so he was slightly taken aback when she said, "I feel my son would benefit from a period of discipline, as he has grown completely out of control."

I looked at her in surprise and with utter disappointment and disbelief. I couldn't understand her reasons for going against me. How could she say these awful things about me? I wasn't a bad kid; I was still finding my way in the world and she threw me to the wolves, the first chance she got. Heartbroken, I watched my mother sit down, with a vacant look on her face, and waited for my verdict. The probation officer was taken aback too; the look on his face gave me knots in the pit of my stomach. He must have thought the worst of me, as I was being made out to be a monster. The magistrate fixated his eyes on me.

"I'm taking the advice of your mother. I'm sentencing you to eighteen months of approved school, as I feel this would be the best thing for you."

I looked over to my mother, pleading for help. She completely ignored me. I wanted to shout at the top of my lungs: why have you done this to me? But deep down, I knew why; she was using this opportunity to get rid of me. It was better for her that I was out of her hair, and I knew it. I was taken down the stairs and put into a grubby whitewashed cell with rusty, iron bars against the window, shutting out the outside world. When the door banged shut, I stood in the middle of the cell, absolutely shattered. I had a flashback, thinking about what the Irish nurse had said to me: "God must have kept you alive for a reason." In that moment, I didn't feel this way. I almost wished I had died with my foster family, rather than suffer this terrible betrayal.

A few hours passed by, and the probation officer came down to my cell and told me I was going to an approved school in Red Hill. An approved school was a type of residential institution, where you could be sent by court, or were sent if deemed to be beyond parental control. My mother's input had thrown me to the gates of hell.

The probation officer tried to assure me it was not too bad there and not to worry too much. But he could see I was devastated; we sat in his car and drove there in complete silence. I was a bundle of nerves; I didn't have a clue what to expect and anticipated the worst possible outcome as we sped along the country roads. Red Hill Approved School was three large blocks, set in sprawling, spacious grounds. At first glance, it looked like a huge, friendly farm. From the outside, you would never have known it housed sentenced youth. I was led into the reception; the probation officer left me in the care of the reception officer. He wrote down my age, date of birth and my present address. I was then frog-marched to the headmaster; I stood in front of him as he scanned my paperwork. He stood up, towering over me, with the intention of intimidating me with his large frame.

He stated, "You will obey the rules at the approved school, and you will have to behave yourself for the eighteen months you are here."

Without any facial expression whatsoever, he seemed so bored and separated from himself. He told me to wait outside, and someone would come and collect me when they were ready. I sat patiently; this world was alien to me and I had no idea what was in store. All I could do was hope and pray I would survive.

Eventually, an older boy came and took me to my house block. First, though, he took me to the clothes store and gave me basic clothing and bedding. I was led upstairs to a large dormitory, where there were about fifty beds and minimal furniture. I was shown to my bed; the dormitory was completely empty, not one person in sight. I decided to make my bed and put my clothes away in the cupboard, taking my time, processing my new environment. I was then taken downstairs, where there were only a few boys lingering in the foyer. All the other boys were out on the farm working. No one said a word to me. I sat in the yard and could smell the wafts of cooked food; I was now quite hungry. On realising the food was ready, I followed the boys to the dining hall. It was a huge room; wooden tables stretched out, the echoes of our footsteps bounced off the cold walls and never-ending ceilings. We were not allowed to talk whilst eating our food, which felt awkward and unnerving. We would throw occasional glances at each other, as if to reassure ourselves we were not going mad. There was only the sound of clinking knives and forks being clattered against the plates and the chewing of overcooked, stale food.

After we had eaten the bland food, we were allowed some leisure time, so I made my way back to the yard. Two boys approached me; I was new blood and they were eager to find out where I was from, my length of time at Red Hill, and most importantly, why I was there. They were a friendly bunch; I seemed to make friends easily and was asked if I liked football. I used to play football all the time when I was a little kid, so I was happy to be asked and agreed to play football with them every Saturday. In the days that followed, I made friends from all different areas. I was like a social chameleon; I could mix and blend with the best of them. It helped to be popular in these situations and I was settling in with confidence and ease. The approved school was a working farm that seemed to never sleep. My job during the day was mucking out stables, feeding horses and general farm work. It was intensive labour, not to mention a smelly, filthy job, but it wasn't the worst thing I could be doing. At least the farm work kept me occupied, was strenuous exercise and gave me time to think about my future, as I moved hay around in the beating sun.

One boy I grew close to whilst at the school was a boy from Cornwall. We got chatting one evening and he said he was thinking about running away. I didn't say anything. I took in the magnitude of this; what would be the repercussions of escaping? Once the seed was planted in my head, though, I thought there was a possibility for me to do the same thing. I managed to scrape together ten shillings and decided I would run away back to London. I just had to wait for the right moment.

Some of the older boys were bullies; they would force the younger ones to do their work for them and, if you had no backbone, you were getting taken advantage of. I actively avoided them like the plague. I wasn't scared of them; I just didn't want any trouble. However, trouble always managed to find me somehow. One day, one of the boys tried to make me do his work. I had two choices: either do what he asked or get beaten up. I refused. He was not used to anyone saying no to him and I could see he was shocked. He started ranting and raving at me, trying to impress his followers and hangers-on. Thinking he could intimidate me, he began ranting that he was going to bash me up, being animated and loud, drawing attention to himself.

I told him, "If you fancy your chances against me, then go for it."

By this time, the argument had gathered some momentum

and a lot of the boys had gathered around, wanting to see a fight. They were jeering and egging us on. No way was I going to be bullied and I was not prepared to back down. I leaned forward and punched him three times in the face. He was startled, as he wasn't expecting me to make the first move. He sank to the floor, holding his head. He had been stunned, disorientated and clearly his ego was bruised. He stayed down for a while, before he could manage to see straight and find his legs. The other boys were laughing at him and pointing. I knew then that I was in for a good beating. Once the boy had massaged his wounds and gathered his mindless minions, they would be back with a vicious retaliation. It was in that moment of realisation of what was to come that I decided to act upon my thought of escaping.

I ran, faster than my legs had ever done before. I darted across the fields and reached a small, rickety gate that led to the cobbled street. Full of adrenaline, I made my way to the train station and bought a one-way ticket. I was pacing up and down, waiting impatiently for the train, bursting with energy and hope. I was desperately wishing the train would turn up before they found out I had escaped. It had only been minutes, and I was sure I would make the train before they got there. But alas, it was not to be. Suddenly busting round the corner, three of the senior staff came running towards me. They grabbed me with force and bundled me into a van. I had been caught, and I knew there was a severe punishment in store for me back at Red Hill.

I was straight back into the headmaster's office. "Why did you run away?"

"I was homesick," I replied.

"That's no excuse. There are lots of boys here who are homesick, but they don't run away!"

I was told I would receive my punishment in due course, so I waited anxiously. Time seems to stand still when you are living in fear. I was taken down to the dining hall, where I was told I would receive my punishment after our evening meal. I could barely eat anything; I was sitting there, wishing the day to be over so I could put my head down and sleep. Once the finished plates of food were cleared up, a wooden horse was pulled out, and all the boys were told to gather round whilst they had me bend over it. The housemaster produced a long thick cane and gave me six strokes. The lashings were so painful, I had to muster up all the strength inside me not to scream in agony. The sting was unbearable, and I tried my best not to flinch with each subsequent lash. I was determined not to show any emotion or pain, as I knew all eyes were firmly fixed on me. The boys were watching me intently to see my reaction. I returned to my seat and sat down gingerly. My backside was burning and throbbing; I was in excruciating pain. I was in shock and was mustering all the energy I could to act unbothered by the lashings.

The boys came up to me, asking me, "John, did it hurt?"

Obviously, I lied and managed to fake a smile, making out it was no big deal. In reality, I was dying inside.

Before bedtime, I pulled my trousers down and took a look at my wounds. My bum was red raw, and I could see the welts appearing where the cane had struck. I lay down in agony that night, unable to get comfortable; the pain was so excruciating, I barely slept. I knew it would take a while for the lashes to heal; they were wide open, and blood was still seeping from my wounds for days after. It was impossible to sit or even lie down at certain angles. The healing process was slow and agonising; I just had to wait it out and deal with them day by day. I bathed them and took care of the lashes as best I could. In total, it took over a month for them to fully heal. They would re-open if I moved too quickly or even sat down in the wrong way. I was over the moon when they finally started to scar, as I could finally sleep in comfort.

I had learnt a couple of valuable lessons; one was never show people any fear and the other was always to stand up for myself, no matter what. Showing weakness was a no-no. The bullies left me alone after that and I gained many a friend in standing up to them. Maybe they felt safe in my presence, but I earnt a lot of respect for my bravery and gained some fair-weather friends.

Even at fourteen, I knew these people would come and go. But I also learnt through this experience that there is safety in numbers and making alliances with people is a must, especially in an environment like this one. Maybe approved school did me some good for me after all!

CHAPTER 3

APPLES AND PEARS

I continued working on the farm and, in my free time, I played a lot of sports, which kept me occupied, stopped me overthinking and, most of all, kept me out of trouble. Before I knew it, my time at Approved School was over. I had done eighteen months and was asked to come into the headmaster's office and was handed my ticket home, back to Brighton. I waited eagerly at Red Hill station, anticipating my return and how my mother would receive me. I walked briskly to my street, New Church Road, and found myself standing outside my home. I was full of anxiety and excitement to be back in familiar surroundings. It felt like a lifetime and now I was back in my home town. I felt nervous and exhilarated to knock on the door. I lingered outside for a while, contemplating what to say to my mother, but managed to bring myself to knock after a few minutes. She answered straight away, the door flung wide open, and I saw the horror and distress on her face.

The first thing she said was, "Have you run away?"

My heart sank; she was not in the least bit happy to see me. Not even a flutter of happiness. I handed her my discharge paper; she read over it and then reluctantly let me in.

She said, "Your room is just the same as you left it," and disappeared into the kitchen, not even asking how I was.

I walked through my bedroom door, and I must say it did feel good to be back in familiar surroundings. The one thing I was really looking forward to, was going for a bike ride. I had missed my bike more than anything else. After placing down the few belongings I had, in my small, neat room, I went to look for it, only to find it had disappeared. Hastily and with sheer panic, I asked my mother where my bike was. She said she had sold it, in a matter-of-fact tone. Her reasoning was that she thought I would not need it again. Maybe she thought I would not return home after her display of disloyalty at the court room.

My heart sank. I could not believe she would do that; I saved up the money myself to buy the bike and she had no right to sell it. I was absolutely gutted; I remember looking at my mother, thinking what a rotten thing to do. But I showed no emotion, as I didn't want her to see she had upset me. She didn't deserve the satisfaction of knowing she had gotten under my skin. As time went on, I came to realise she got a kick out of hurting me; her eyes would glisten over and a subtle, but noticeable smirk would appear, as if she wanted to get a reaction out of me.

With no means of making money, I wandered around aimlessly for a while, thinking of what this next chapter of my life would be. I was in limbo, happy to be free, but with no prospects and no goals. I was at a loss as to what to do with my life. One day, I was hanging around the fruit market and a local lad I knew came up to me and asked me if I fancied working on the stalls. I jumped at the chance. At the time, the markets were thriving, the place to go for whatever you needed. It was the heart of consumerism, visited by people from every walk of life. He said I would get paid daily and, to be fair, I was in need of the cash. I started off sorting out the fruit and veg for the customers into their orders. I was mainly in the underground cellar, arranging the orders into the right crates and then carrying them up the stairs to the customers' vehicles. I had a friend who would often help me, especially when it was busy. Then, when the market shut for an hour for lunch, we would go to the local pub for some food and have a good drink before returning for the last stretch of the day.

I had not thought about stealing since leaving Approved School. I genuinely thought I was a changed man, until I was presented with an opportunity. My stealing brain come back into play when my friend suggested a way to take cash from the shop

I worked in; he had worked there before and knew the layout well. I saw a quick way of making cash and decided to act upon it, even though I had promised myself to stay out of trouble. The prospect of lots of money excited me more than being good, so I was willing to take the risk.

The plan was, when everyone else left for lunch, I would hide in the shop and wait for my friend to arrive. He would bang on the shutter and I would let him in, then he would take the cash from the office. At the time, there were not any cameras around; CCTV was not in place at the time, so as far as we were concerned, if we were not spotted, no one would know it was us. When the time came, I walked down the stairs and hid behind a humungous sack of potatoes, waiting patiently for everyone to vacate the premises. The manager came down the stairs, looked around to see if anyone was there, but I stayed silent and still behind the potatoes, so he had no clue I was there. Like clockwork, he strolled back up the stairs and pulled the shutters down so he could go for his hour's lunch break. Minutes passed; next thing I knew, my pal banged on the shutters to signal he was there. I opened the door for him and, together, we went into the office, forced the drawer open and scooped the money up. Taking the money was over in a flash and was a simple affair. We left sharpish and found a nearby park to share the money out. It came to two hundred and fifty pounds, so one hundred and twenty-five each, which was a lot of money back in the 1940s. When the hour was nearly up, we scurried back to join the rest of the workers coming from their lunch break and strolled in like normal. I carried on packing the fruit and veg, keeping my head down in the cellar. I was buzzing that I had finally acquired some money to set me straight for a little while and thinking I had pulled off a successful robbery.

Next thing I knew, the manager started shouting, "I've been robbed!"

The whole store crowded round to the office to see what had happened. I acted the way one should, with shock and some interest in the antics around me. The police arrived and took statements, but the trail of the thief went cold as there were too many workers there to find the culprit. Plus, it could have been a random attack on the shop; it would have been hard to prove who it was without any evidence.

Yes, I thought with pure glee, we had gotten away with it.

I couldn't wait for the weekend to come, so I could go and spend my money. Saturday came, and I was up bright and early, eager to go shopping. I had been pining over my old bike, so the first thing I did was replace it with a better model and then treated myself to some smart clothes. I felt like I was rich, and I still had seventy pounds left, so I decided to stash it until I could make good use of it. Who says money can't buy you happiness? It certainly bought me some.

Thinking I had gotten away with my robbery, I carried on at work as normal. One morning, the manager called me into his office, and standing with him were two plain-clothed officers. Apparently, I had been recognised by some other workers leaving the building, but they didn't recognise my friend. They nicked me and took me down to Brighton police station; I didn't say a word in the car. I was so sure our plan was fool-proof; I was racking my brain over who had seen me? They took my picture and got my fingerprints, and I was charged for stealing from the workplace. I was locked in the police cell and eventually I was taken to the sergeant's desk and charged formally. This was a different situation now; I was sixteen and I knew they would come down heavy on me. I was taken upstairs to the magistrates' court; I pleaded not guilty and was told I would be held on remand until a trial date. Knowing I was going to prison, I felt sick; why did I take the money? I couldn't really understand this overwhelming urge to steal. I was overcome with adrenaline when I was stealing, and the buzz was too much for me to ignore.

After a long wait in the cells, they took me handcuffed in a police van with two other men; it was about an eight-mile drive to Lewes prison. We came to a halt outside the prison gates, waiting for them to be unlocked. The prison had a medieval look about it, with an intricate design over the brickwork and an oval door. I wondered if it had always been a prison, or if it had been an old relic of a building. All the convicts were taken out of the van in pairs and ordered to line up. We arrived outside the reception block and were ushered inside it, where our handcuffs were removed and I could finally get my circulation back, the blood pumping swiftly back into my numb hands. The policeman left us, and the screws took us to a wooden bench to sit on. One by one, our names were called out so we could be processed. When it came to my turn, I was told to strip off, hold my arms out and open my mouth, so they could check to see if I was hiding anything. They asked me to run my fingers through my hair to see if I had any contraband stowed away. The next step was to bend over and spread my cheeks for a quick examination. Being sixteen, this was highly embarrassing; I was glad when it was over.

I thought to myself, this is an extreme violation of my privacy and human rights.

Little did I know, this would be one of the least significant violations. Then I was told to wrap a towel around me and to get into a lukewarm bath. They must have thought I needed a good scrub or were worried about contamination. I was given my clothes back; all prisoners at this time were allowed to wear their own clothes.

They gave me a cheese sandwich and a mug of warm tea, all of which I was grateful for. Whilst being locked in a small cell for what seemed like an eternity, at least my belly was full and my thirst quenched. Eventually, they came and collected me and took me to the main prison, where I waited about six hours. When they came for me and gave me my bedding, they told me I was being moved again to the remand block. By this point, I was knackered, barley keeping my eyes open and just wanted to get my head down. The screws unlocked the steel doors to the remand wing and then I was led to my wing, up the iron stairs and along to the landing to an empty cell. The screw produced a white card with my name and prison number on it and placed this into a wooden holder on the door.

He gestured frantically with his arms in an animated fashion and said, "in you go!"

He told me that somebody would come and turn the lights off, then he slammed the door shut with a loud bang. All this information overwhelmed me; really, I still couldn't believe I had ended up in this place.

Finally, I was on my own, and now had the time to process the whole saga. I had a good look around the cell. There was a small, high, barred window, set deep into the wall. At the far end of the cell, there was a wide plank of wood, which served as a frame for a bed. On top of this was a grubby, lumpy straw mattress and a thin, disintegrating straw pillow. Beneath the window stood a wooden washstand, on which stood a wooden wash basin with a water jug and soap dish. Under the washstand was a foul-smelling chamber pot to do my business in. On the opposite side of the cell, there was a small wooden table with a knife, spoon and a white china mug. Forks were forbidden since they could be used as deadly weapons.

By now, I was physically and mentally exhausted. I just made my bed, lay down and stared intently at the sixty-watt bulb set in the terribly slap-dash, painted white cell, with black marks of filth scattered around it. I could not fathom what had happened to me in such a short space of time. It was a whirlwind of emotion, and I could not seem to process any of it. I heard a click, and the cell was plunged into darkness. Exhausted and feeling all alone, I turned over on my side and fell into a deep sleep.

Bang! Bang! I was rudely awakened by somebody kicking the door. The flap on the spy hole was turned back and I could see an eyeball glaring at me, popping out of its fat head.

"Get out of bed!" bellowed the screw.

For a moment, I could not remember where I was; then reality hit me, I was in prison. I quickly jumped out of bed and got dressed. Someone shouted for the door to be unlocked; there seemed to be a kerfuffle from outside and, after some time of pandemonium, the door was opened.

"Slop out!" the screw barked.

I picked up the chamber pot and water jug and joined the endless line of convicts waiting to empty their slops into a large china basin. It had a running tap so you could rinse your chamber pot out and there was also a small tap where you could get your drinking water. The stench in the air was foul, a mixture of urine and faeces. It was overwhelming, and I found myself holding my breath whilst trying to clean my chamber pot as quickly as I could. All the while I was cleaning, I could hear all the screws shouting orders and the echoing of the doors slamming shut. This place was a sensory overload, so many noises at once. I was taking in every moment of my new surroundings and thinking, this is fucking hell on earth.

Before breakfast, we had to make our bed and it needed to be neat, ready for inspection. We did not have the luxury of lying in and sleeping the morning away. You needed to be up and out once the bell was rung at seven-thirty am. Failure to do this promptly would mean you were placed on report. I heard another loud bang and the doors opened with breakfast in tow. The breakfast consisted of a bowl of cold porridge and a mug of cold tea.

I thought to myself, if only I could go back to Approved School, this place is disgusting and dehumanising.

When the door finally shut in the evening, I was always pleased to be in my cell alone. The peace that came with being in my own company was immeasurable and I felt like I could let my guard down, even if it was only for a little while. I would be held here on remand for a few weeks until my trial. I spent my time reading books and working out in my cell. I wrote numerous letters to my mother, asking her to send me clean clothing and also asking her if she would come to court and say something positive on my behalf. I felt like I needed all the help I could get, and she owed me that at least. One final chance to redeem herself. She never responded in writing; however, she did send me fresh clothing, so I was optimistic that she may turn up to my court date.

The majority of the inmates were older than me, so I felt like we didn't have much in common. Being so young, I was over-whelmed by the environment. I kept myself to myself, and tried my hardest to remain focused and be positive about my sentence. I thought the courts would be less aggressive with me, considering my age.

Finally, the day came, and I found myself in reception, patiently waiting to be taken to Lewes Assizes Court for my trial. I was handcuffed to another man before being let out to a prison coach bound for the court. Once we were there, I was put into a holding cell, still in handcuffs, tightly gripped to my wrists. There were quite a few convicts waiting there to go on trial. Nobody spoke much. Maybe they were all nervous; I know I was. We silently waited for our name to be called out. I left the cell and was escorted by two screws into the dock of the court, where a screw stood on either side of me. The judge looked at me and then nodded to say the prosecution may proceed. The barrister rose to his feet and read out the charge. They asked how I pleaded. I had thought carefully about my plea, and considered the fact I had two witnesses against me. They were one hundred percent certain they saw me leave the shop with my mate and they also claimed they saw me splitting the money in the park. Knowing this, I had no option and pleaded guilty.

The shuffling of papers seemed endless; court felt like such a long-winded, time-consuming process. I grew more and more restless, waiting for my sentence. The judge asked if anyone there wished to speak on the defendant's behalf.

"Yes, my lord, the defendant's mother wishes to speak."

My heart skipped a little beat; this was the help I was seeking, and I fluttered with excitement, thinking she was here to save my bacon. Finally, my mother had come through for me.

"Bring her forward!" the judge bellowed.

My mother came to the witness box, and my heart started to race even more. I was elated she was here to defend me.

Instead, she told the court that she couldn't control me, and I had brought shame on the family. She said she felt I needed some discipline, and she would like the court to send me to an institution, which apparently I needed badly because of my outrageous and uncontrollable behaviour. I couldn't believe what I was hearing; she was supposed to be on my side, but instead she was throwing me to the wolves once again! My own mother; I was meant to be protected by her, for her to have my back in any situation, but instead she was my enemy. I felt sick as she spoke and just wanted to run as far away as I could. I remember quite vividly that she never looked my way once. I was distraught; my body was getting hotter, and anger surged like bolts of electricity through me. She left the box and disappeared, still not once looking my way.

The judge asked me if there was anything I wanted to add. I replied, "No."

I didn't care about my future for those few minutes; sadness filled every cell of my body and I swore to myself never to trust her, or anybody, again.

The judge went on to say, "I am sentencing you to three years of borstal training, which may put you on the straight and narrow."

He nodded to the screws, meaning for them to take me downstairs and put me in another holding cell. I was shattered; what a miserable, hopeless day. All I could think about was my mother's betrayal. I vowed I would never ask her for help again, and I felt as if our relationship was beyond repair after this last episode of disloyalty. Stabbing me in the back twice was enough for me to severe the cord. I will never forget that moment; I had lost both my mother and my freedom that day.

CHAPTER 4

WORMWOOD SCRUBS

The door banged shut and I just lay on the bench in the holding cells, waiting to be returned to Lewes prison. Unfortunately, I learned I would not be going back there to stay. It was 1946 and I was just over sixteen; being of age, I was told I was going to be transferred to Wormwood Scrubs, a much harsher and more extreme environment than the one I was in. Being on remand in Lewes was a doddle in comparison. I was in for a real shock to the system; after all the horror stories I'd heard of Wormwood Scrubs, I mentally prepared myself for what was to come. The screws came for me a couple of hours later, handcuffed me to another prisoner and led me to the yard, where a long bus was waiting for me and the other prisoners who were on the move. Once we were loaded on to the bus like cattle on its way to market, the screws checked the bus was secure and then seated themselves at the back of the bus to observe us throughout the journey. I felt like a naughty schoolboy, being watched constantly. The doors were locked, and we began making our journey to Wormwood Scrubs.

By this point, it was night-time and I remember vividly the bright lights of the other cars whizzing by and the shop fronts all twinkling away. Pretty girls walking the streets, dressed up for the evening, throwing their heads back, laughing, excited for their big night out. I sat slumped in the van, thinking to myself, the first chance I get to escape from prison, I will. I knew in a real prison I was going to have a real tough time, as I was aware most of the prison staff were ex-service men. Ex-service men with an axe to grind, who liked nothing more than exercising their power. Not only that, I was going to be in with some real tough villains, and I was going to be tested and provoked. Being young, the other convicts were going to try it on with me, and I was going to have to stand my ground to survive. The journey seemed to take forever and, even though I was dreading my long sentence, I was quite grateful when we finally arrived at the infamous Wormwood Scrubs. The outside of the prison was a sight to behold; two towers either side of the gate, with white square panels dotted around the brickwork. It felt less inviting than Lewes; it had an eerie feel to it. I was starving, dying of thirst and had a raging headache; all I wanted was to get my head down and put this miserable day to bed.

The normal formalities went ahead; papers handed in and being observed by the prison guards with scrutiny. Then the steel gates swung open, and we were inside and, once again, I was at the reception block, led in handcuffs and taken in to be processed. I was chatting with the other boy I had been handcuffed to and I could sense we were made of similar cloth. The same interests, same outlook on life, I could sense we were going to become friends. This place was slightly different; there was a lot of fuss and it felt like I was amid organised chaos.

I turned to the youth I was cuffed to and joked, "This place is a madhouse."

He laughed in acknowledgement and proceeded to put out his hand for me to shake. "I'm Pat Murphy," he said in a thick Irish accent. He had a warm and friendly face, and a likeable character.

"John Hilton," I responded.

We started talking. I disclosed why I had been sentenced and he told me he was from Slough and had been sentenced for burglary. All the while, drama was escalating and unfolding in the reception block, pieces of paper were flying about everywhere, prisoners were screaming and phones were ringing off the hook. Half-naked boys were running around, revolting against being processed. The screws were shouting, trying to take control of the situation and then an altercation broke out. Fists and feet were flying about and I could not tell who had started what; all I can remember was that it was like a Kung Fu movie. It was complete mayhem, and I got a sense of what this place was going to be like from the get-go.

When my name was called out, I approached the high wooden table, eager to get this over and done with. The screw looked up at me after reading my paperwork and asked me to confirm my name and length of sentence.

"You have been to Borstal, you know the drill," he piped up. He obviously had read my paperwork thoroughly.

Once again, I was subject to humiliation, firstly being told to strip off and have a towel wrapped round my waist. I was then told to hold my arms out and open my mouth for inspection. This took a much longer time than I had anticipated, and saliva started to drool out; he must have thought I had a secret compartment in there. Next was the spreading of my butt cheeks, which takes some getting used to, and was no more pleasant than the last time. Then we walked into the bath house and were ordered to clean ourselves. We were told to meticulously scrub ourselves before we would be allowed into the main prison. After receiving clean clothes and fresh bedding, I sat down and was fed a dry, corned beef sandwich and given a mug of tea, which was exactly what I needed after such a stressful day. As soon as the last bite went into my mouth, I was hurried into a holding cell, waiting on my transfer into the main prison.

"How long will it take?" I asked impatiently. By this point I was knackered and anxious to get to bed.

"However long it takes, pet," the screw replied with a curled-up smile.

He seemed to take joy in the process being so long-winded. Another mind game they played with convicts, always a ploy to make us snap, even the wrong look could wind you up. It was one of the most boring and frustrating times I have spent. Just waiting and waiting for what seemed like hours. I am sure they keep you waiting on purpose, a kind of winding-up strategy to get you enraged and agitated. Another sick and pathetic way to exercise their power.

"You're going to the Borstal wing," he said.

Finally, I thought and exhaled a sigh of relief.

I picked up my bedding and followed him to the wing. Murphy was in toe too; he had been brought out of his holding cell at the same time and was joining me on the same wing. I was pleased he would be with me; at least I had already made a friend and wasn't completely alone. The screw we were with left us with a Parole Officer and we were once again confronted with our paperwork. I thought this was completely unnecessary, as if the paperwork had changed miraculously in the last few hours of watching the paint dry on these dreary walls.

"Hilton, your cell is twenty-one and Murphy, your cell is seventeen. Off you go and get settled." He then hurried off.

Making my way through the wing, the other inmates were shouting and banging the doors. There was lots of horseplay and scrutiny as we were fresh blood entering the wing. We were fresh meat in the lion's den, ready to be ravaged, any chance they got. They were sniffing out the fear, the weak from the strong. Trying to intimidate and gauge what sort of inmates we were. I just ignored it; I'd had more than enough of people and their shit for one day. Looking around, I would say the average age of the inmates was sixteen to twenty, so at least we would be with men of a similar age. We made our way to our cells and I unpacked my belongings. I was so relieved to be in my cell and get my head down. Sleeping was all I could think about. Doing fuck-all, all day, really wears you out.

Murphy and I stuck together; we seemed to have similar interests and I felt comfortable around him. We would eat together and stayed on our own; we chose not to interact with the other inmates, letting them come to us if they wanted to. After a little while, curiosity got the better of the other inmates. One day, a couple of boys came to our table, and I could see they had been thinking about approaching us for a while. We asked the normal questions, such as where are you from? One replied North London, the other South. I could see the rival gangs, the normal situation in the city. Different areas, with points to prove, postcodes to protect. I could see they were weighing us up. Once they could see what type of boys we were and that we couldn't be bullied or intimidated, they left us alone.

Murphy said they were just a bunch of mugs, and the prison was full of them. People trying to prove themselves and massage their own egos. They wanted us to be a part of a clique or gang within the prison. I didn't want that; I was happy staying on my own. Less trouble when you're not involving yourself in everyone's business and I was not there to be popular or to gain new friends.

Our routine in Borstal was simple. Every morning, we would be out in the yard; we had a physical training instructor, who would put us through a thirty-minute routine of physical training exercises. They were quite intense, and most of the boys didn't look forward to it, but I did. I loved exercising, as pushing my body to the limit gave me a huge thrill and a rush of endorphins. I always felt good once we had finished exercising; a positive mindset would come flooding in and made prison far more bearable. After the training, we would go to work, sewing mail bags. You had to bring your chair from the cell down to the ground floor and set them in rows. You would sit and sew all morning until lunch time. The work was mundane and monotonous; your fingers and hands could cramp up with using your fine motor skills for so long. It was hard graft and time seemed to stand still, sitting in silence, sewing endlessly. The food was awful, no taste and out of date, though you would eat it because you would be starving by the time midday arrived. It was mostly watered-down soup with potatoes and a crop of bread. Not much for growing boys; your stomach would still be loudly rumbling after lunch. You stayed constantly hungry, never fully satisfied, which in turn can make anyone quite irritable. I was always thinking about food, I dreamt about a good meal, and to have the feeling of a full belly once more.

Once lunch was finished, it was another thirty minutes of

exercise, where we could go and stretch our legs and fill up our lungs with as much clean air as we could. We mostly walked around the yard and spoke to each other, passing on relevant information, gossiping and bitching about the institution. Then it was back to the dull and repetitive work of sewing mail bags until four pm. Once finished, we would take our chairs back to our cells and wait for tea. I quickly had enough of being hungry all the time, so I decided to volunteer for a job in the wing kitchen, washing the dirty dishes and trays. I didn't like the job at all, but it was the only way to access more food. I would scrounge any leftovers, as I was always hungry. I was still a growing boy and none of the meals we were getting cut the mustard. The lack of food was an issue for all the boys in the prison; they were wasting away, the convicts becoming desperate. One day, a boy came over to me and asked if I could get him some extra food.

I shook my head and responded, "Sorry, mate, we don't find much extra and me and Murphy have whatever we can get."

There weren't enough scraps to go round. If he wanted extra food, he should find it himself.

He looked at his pal, then back at me and said, "I don't give a fuck, I want some food!"

He stepped towards me in an aggressive manner, and I could see things were going to escalate. Seeing how things were about to play out, I took the first step and headbutted him. He staggered back and then I gave him a good right hook to the jaw; he fell to the ground with a thud. Making sure he couldn't get back up, I kicked him savagely in the face. I could see the other boys were shocked, but they didn't interfere. The fight happened so quickly, it was over in a flash. I walked away and sat next to Murphy. Adrenaline was still coursing through my veins, but I felt confident I had won the war. I didn't want to have a fight; I never looked for trouble, but if it came my way, I was sure as hell going to defend myself. I learnt the lesson at Approved School to nip all sort of intimidating behaviour in the bud before it escalated and that's exactly what I did when I was at Wormwood Scrubs.

These boys were as hungry as we were, but it was a dog-eat-dog world, and only the strongest would survive in these situations, so I wasn't about to be taken advantage of.

We weren't in Wormwood Scrubs for long. Murphy and I received a written notice, saying we were being moved . Maybe it was due to the incident with the other inmate. I was not best pleased, as I had only just got settled into the routine. But at least I had my pal with me, which made me feel confident about the move. I was hoping to go to an open prison, where at least I would have an opportunity to run away. One bright and early morning, Murphy and I were back on the bus driving past normal life, which seemed so surreal, as I had not seen normal existence for a while and had near enough forgotten about the world outside. I looked out of the window and saw normal day-to-day life and craved my freedom, more so now because I could see the outside world once again. We were off to one of the toughest Borstals in England, with an eighteen-foot fence and the strictest of rules. We were carted off to Rochester. A stricter regime and a harsher environment, so I was fuming they had moved me. Though it had an awful reputation, Rochester looked less intimidating from the outside; instead of towers, two pillars stood either side of the gate and it seemed much smaller and less intimidating than Wormwood Scrubs.

Many of the prison staff, including the governors, had seen an abundance of action during the war. Knowing this, that the prison acted like an extension of military life and was run with a strict regime, there was no room for error in Rochester. On arrival, the guards barked orders and were intimidating from the get-go. The screws dressed in military-style clothing with shiny black boots; their clothing seemed to add more confidence to the way they conducted themselves. As if they were acting out a sick fantasy or role-play. They were engulfed in the joy of the power they had over us and we were fully aware of the pain and anguish they were inflicting. We were now exposed to the reality of prison life and it was an ugly, wicked affair.

CHAPTER 5

A FEW LESS FINGERS FOR FREEDOM

Rochester reception block was like all the others I had been in. We were processed with the normal routine of being searched and dehumanised; then we were given our usual cheap bundle of bedding. We sat around for a while in agonising boredom until it was time for me and Murphy to be moved. Murphy and I were told we were being moved to Rodney House; we were pleased we were being moved together. Having each other around was like a comfort blanket, a familiarity that we needed. Nothing is worse than being in a block and not knowing anyone. At around five-thirty, we were led across the yard and told to go to the end of the wing and wait by the dining area. It was a large room, separate from the rest of the wing, with a glass-fronted screen, boiling hot in the summer and freezing in the winter. The rectangular room consisted of long, stretched chipped and worn-out wooden tables; about a dozen boys sat at each one.

We were to learn later that at the head of each table sat the table leader. The table leader was the most feared; the theory behind it was that they could keep the best order. Beside them sat their friends, then the further down the bench you were, the lower down the pecking order you were. The newly-arrived receptions were the lowest of them all. When we were seated, the kitchen orderlies would serve trays of food to the table leader. He would help himself first, then pass the food down the table to the next person and so on. By the time the food reached the end person, there was barely any food left, just scraps and crumbs. We couldn't believe the injustice of it all; if we carried on like this, we would wind up starving to death. In my opinion, it was inhumane and, as far as I was concerned, it didn't matter who you were, you should still be able to eat a decent meal. I approached the table leader, who was a well-built tall boy.

I asked him, why the food couldn't be shared out more fairly. I explained our concerns that there was hardly any food left for us.

He laughed and said, "That's just the way it is, if you don't like it, fuck off to another table," and turned his back on me dismissively.

I was furious; the disrespect and rudeness of this boy got the fire in my belly fully alight. It felt like it was Wormwood Scrubs all over again. The Borstal ethos was 'might makes right.' I wasn't afraid of him, but I knew if I forked him and lost the fight, I would look weak, and my life would be made a living hell. I decided to discuss the situation with Murphy, and we agreed we had no choice, we had to do something. Whatever we did, we couldn't fail. The plan was, I was going to attack the table leader in the communal washroom. The washroom had a row of sinks in the middle of the room and on the tiled walls were a row of dirty, stained and un-scrubbed toilets. I thought the best time to get him was after the pre-breakfast morning rush had died down. All that remained was to choose my weapon; I needed something that would do the job properly.

Murphy had an idea to unscrew one of the iron legs from the beds. It was about three feet long and quite heavy. Heavier than I had anticipated. Heavy enough to make a painful impact, it would be perfect to get him with. The idea was, after it was all over, we would clean the bed leg and screw it back on and nobody would be any the wiser. It was a great plan and a perfect weapon.

The next morning, I waited for the rush to be over and made my way over to the washroom with Murphy's bed leg wrapped in an old towel. Murphy stood outside to keep watch and nodded over to indicate the table leader was inside the washroom, washing his smug face. The table leader glanced at me and sneered, then looked away. Thinking he was the bees' bollocks, that look he gave me was a big mistake. His arrogant face only spurred me on and made the blood rush to my head in rage. I walked up behind him, took the bed leg from the towel and smashed him over the head three times. Hard and with full force, I pummelled him. Blood spurted from his head, splattering the walls like a paint effect on a jazzy t-shirt. He fell unconscious to the floor with a thud; he went down like a sack of potatoes. Job done, I felt satisfied he had got what he deserved. I quickly washed the bed leg as thoroughly as I could, wrapped it in my towel and gave it back to Murphy. He immediately hurried back to his cell and screwed it back onto his bed, like nothing had happened.

I made my way casually to the dining hall for breakfast. As I sat down, I shook my head at what I had just done. All for a fair ration of food. The lengths you had to go to, just to prove a point in this place, were ridiculous; no one would behave like that in the real world. But you had to do what you thought necessary to survive. I couldn't show him I was weak and allow him to speak to me like that. That was a no-no. Word soon spread amongst the boys that I had done in the table leader, who was now in a hospital ward recovering and could be there for weeks. I never said a word about the incident, but later that day, a couple of the boys asked me if I wanted to be a table leader. I point-blank refused the table leader's job; that was not why I attacked the boy, not for power or reputation. It was the last thing I wanted; all I wanted was our fair share of food. I could see some of the boys couldn't understand my stance on this. But I couldn't care less about their opinion. I didn't want to be ruling the prison; I wanted to be left alone and be able to eat enough that my belly was full and satisfied.

Despite the seriousness of the attack, only a half-hearted attempt was made to find the culprit. As far as the housemaster was concerned, us prisoners were just another number. They weren't bothered about our safety or our welfare; they just wanted to get on with their job and go home. I had gotten away with battering and hospitalising someone, yet I was in there for stealing a bit of money; the whole system made no sense. Surely violence against another human was worse than stealing a few quid? But the system will punish you for fraud or stealing money, far worse than anything else. Society holds money in the highest regard, and I soon realised how little a human life actually meant.

Murphy and I got a job picking up rubbish. It wasn't a bad job; we had to throw the rubbish out of the window into a heap in an unused yard, which was quite peculiar. But we did as we were told, no questions asked. We had the freedom to roam all over the place, which gave us an opportunity to stumble over and explore new parts of the prison, which other prisoners had no access to. We found a yard that stored ladders, paint pots, shovels and bundles of equipment. Some of this looked like tools to repair the tired, worn-out prison, as and when needed. All this equipment was behind a six-foot metal fence, and when Murphy and I saw the ladders, we both had a light-bulb moment. We turned instantly to each other and grinned, like Cheshire cats who had caught the cream. We now had an opportunity to escape. We could get out of the wing under the cover of darkness; it would be a simple matter of clambering over the fence and taking a long ladder, making our way to the wall with it. We couldn't believe our luck; all we needed was to make rope with our bed sheets to let us down to the ground, providing we could get out of the windows.

I took some time to inspect the windows thoroughly; they were set deep into the wall, with a thin metal conduit pipe running to the top of the wall and, under the air vent, was a window. All I had to do was tie the end of the rope to my belt, climb up the conduit pipe and put my foot inside the vent to support my weight. I then would bend the steel mesh in front of the window. Once that was done, I could break the glass, climb through and tie the handmade rope to the window. Then I would slide down the rope and we would make our way into the ladder store. Then we would take a ladder and prop it up against the wall. We would climb up the ladder as high as it reached and then scramble, like rock climbers, to sit on top of the wall and pull the ladder up. Lastly, we would lower it down the other side of the wall, climb down the ladder and away we would go, home free. The plan we had in mind seemed simple enough and we thought could be executed with ease. As confident as we were, we did not consider other anomalies that would come into play.

Things didn't go quite to plan. As Robbie Burns once said, 'The best laid plans of mice and men often go astray.' Meaning even careful designs or projects do not always succeed. This plan happened to be one of them. The next day, Murphy and I raided the laundry room and stole enough sheets to make a rope about twenty feet long. We smuggled the rope into the dining area and hid it inside a large, unused dustbin. We decided to wait until after tea had been served, as the housemaster would be occupied checking the boys out in the gymnasium. When the time was right, I grabbed the rope from the dustbin and ran upstairs, out of sight of the housemaster. Murphy kept watch and I attached the rope to my belt and clambered up the conduit pipe. Feeling like Spiderman, I stuck one foot into the air vent as planned and grabbed the steel mesh to bend it back from the window. Suddenly, without warning, it gave way, which I had not anticipated, and I fell fifteen feet or so onto the landing below. The steel mesh came falling after me and clattered with a loud bang on the floor next to me, causing an echo to ripple throughout the prison.

I had landed on my back, and was unable to move for a few seconds. I lay there, most likely with concussion, wounded and confused. How I survived the fall, I do not know. Stunned, my flight mode kicked in; I tore the rope from my belt and jumped up, heart racing and disorientated. In complete shock and without thinking, I jumped up, as if a bolt of electricity was surging through my body. I got up and ran to the dining area and sat down at the table, my heart firmly in my throat. Everyone was looking in my direction, wondering what the noise was all about. I held my hands on my lap, and I realised they were tingling. Then I looked down and realised my third and fourth fingers had been completely torn off. The tops of my fingers were missing. The white bones gleamed up at me through the jagged flesh on my left hand. Then I looked at my right hand and saw my index finger was hanging off. My shirt and trousers were now covered in blood and my hand continued to ooze out the dark, red liquid. In a panic, I tried to use my shirt to stop the bleeding, but it was no use. Blood was spurting out from both hands, like an uncontrollable hose pipe; it was impossible to stop the bleeding. I was feeling weaker, the more blood I saw.

Seeing the state of my hands, Murphy turned pale and looked like he was about to vomit.

He said, "Mate, you need to get to hospital."

I stood up and said, "Stay here, Pat."

By this point, I was not thinking straight. Lightheaded and delirious, I walked to the wing office. As soon as the housemaster saw the extent of my injuries, he phoned the hospital, and I was taken out of the wing, straight to the medic of the prison. They put cotton wool on my stumps and then wrapped them loosely in bandages. Which was ridiculous; they needed pressure on them to stop the bleeding and, at the rate the blood was streaming out, I thought I would soon have no blood left. But I was in too much pain to make a fuss. I was taken to the front gate and stood there with a screw, waiting for an ambulance. By now, the shock had started to fade and I was coming to a realisation of the extent of what had just happened. I felt sick and was in immense pain. It seemed to take ages for the ambulance to turn up; every minute waiting for the ambulance was as agonising as the next, and I had never felt pain like it. Once I got to St Bart's hospital in Rochester, I was given injections for pain relief, which took the edge off and was a welcome relief, before being wheeled into the operating theatre.

I was taken in on the Wednesday night and then operated on in the early hours of Thursday morning. As soon as the operation was over, I was taken from the hospital on to a stretcher and thrown into a dirty, old work van with nothing to rest on and no support for my hands. I was in so much agony, but they didn't give a damn about any aftercare. There was no course of pain relief or advised rest from the doctor. I was a nuisance, as far as they were concerned; an animal would have been treated better. One of the screws reluctantly sat with me in the beat-up van, whilst I was escorted back to Rochester Borstal. I knew I was in a lot of trouble, and I was not looking forward to the greeting awaiting me.

I was taken straight to the punishment cell and placed on two reinforced tables; the door banged shut behind me and the lights were turned off. I was left in the pitch black for twenty-four hours. Alone, cold and in absolute agony. My hands were covered in blood-soaked bandages. I had never experienced pain like it; the pain seemed to worsen over time. I felt like I was on the verge of death and thought there was no way I could endure this suffering any longer. I urinated over myself as I could not use my hands to unzip my trousers; without pain relief, my hands were useless. I was unable to do anything but just lie there, twisting and turning in the dark, wishing death upon me, just to take away the excruciating and unbearable pain. In those ghastly twenty-four hours, I realised how cruel humanity was. I was left to rot and wriggle around in my own filth. In that space of time, I had an enlightening moment; I knew how alone I was in this world. This lack of empathy from the screws and the doctors stirred up a different emotion within me, and in turn a change of character. I vowed from that day never to show any emotion. To button up and present a quiet and calm façade, even if I was raging or frightened, to never show it. I took this barrier against the world with me throughout the rest of my life and, after this incident, it was easy to maintain. I came back to this moment, and it gave me great strength in the years to follow.

In the morning, I woke up in the punishment block, rolling around in excruciating pain. My hands felt like they were on fire, the pain overpowering every thought and every movement. Not one person came to visit me; not a screw, a doctor or a nurse.

I thought, surely my injuries warrant someone to check on my wellbeing.

Suddenly, a boy spied through my peephole; he was being taken up to normal population. He must have been shocked at the state I was in, because I later found out he told the boys upstairs about my predicament and they went to the principal and threatened to smash the place up if I wasn't taken to hospital to get the care I desperately needed.

Thankfully, the governor listened to the pleas of the convicts, and I was taken to the hospital and looked after for about three weeks. I had a good rest in the hospital, getting the chance to recharge my batteries and heal from my extensive injuries. Whilst I was there, I had a visit from the president of the committee; he came to charge me for trying to escape the Borstal. The three magistrates stood at the foot of my bed and asked me how I pleaded. I responded guilty and was told four months would be added to my sentence. Which, looking back, was not much of an extension to my time at all. If an attempted escape happened these days, a lot more time would be added. I was just relieved and thankful that they fixed my hands up and I finally had some medication for pain relief. I never wanted to feel pain like that again.

On my return to Borstal, I still needed to complete my punishment, so they also decided to put me on only water and bread for days upon days, until I was so weak, I could barely move. I would go to bed hungry and wake up in the same state, fragile and depleted of energy. Food was the only thing on my mind; it consumed my every waking thought. The screws took away my privileges too, one of which was my recreation, the one thing I loved dearly. But without any proper food, I was unfit to exercise. When that food punishment was over, they continued to stifle me of any recreation.

Months passed, and I had had enough of missing out on my Sunday walks through the woodlands with the boys. So, I plucked up the courage to go to the housemaster and asked for the 'root march' privilege back. This meant I would be back on the Sunday walks with all the boys, exploring the woods and all that nature had to offer. He stupidly agreed to it, and I went on my merry way with the boys, stumbling through the undergrowth and the dense forest of trees. Finally, I was out of the prison walls; I was now fed up of being in this hell-hole and planned to get away, the first opportunity that arose. On the walk, when no one was looking in my direction, I decided to go and hide in a bush. It was large enough to hide my whole body and I was well concealed under the lush, green leaves. This caused absolute carnage, as the screws went into a frenzy, trying to find me. The only thing on my mind was to escape. I stayed in the bush for hours; they all got their whistles out and were searching manically to find me. One of the principal training officers was right next to the bush, and got so frustrated, he ended up catching his trousers on the brambles where I was hiding.

I heard him say, "If I catch that little bastard, I will kick his arse all the way back to Borstal."

I stayed rigid in that bush, so as not to be detected, until they all gave up and trotted back to rotten Rochester prison. Finally, after what seemed like forever, I was able to leave the foliage and run. I didn't look back. Instead, I found myself wandering the streets of Bethnal Green...

CHAPTER 6

CUT FROM THE SAME CLOTH

In his infinite wisdom, Murphy also decided to hide in a bush, not too far from my foliage, and escape with me. We were a team and it wouldn't have felt right escaping without each other. Our original escape plan, though well-thought-out, went disastrously wrong and yet an escape on a whim worked perfectly. Who would have thought a great escape would be as simple as hiding in a large bush? How stupid these screws were, was beyond belief. How could they not look in the surrounding area? I could only imagine, in their rage, they were not thinking clearly, in turn making poor decisions. But their stupidity worked well for us. We caught a train to London; I just looked out at the passing scenery, watching green fields passing me by. I sat and appreciated the scenery unfolding; I had forgotten how beautiful and mesmerising the outside was. It felt strange but amazing to be on a train again amongst free people. Sitting on the train, I glanced at the everyday citizens going about their daily business. One man was sitting, reading his daily newspaper and I thought to myself, these people don't have a clue about prison life and probably never will. They wouldn't care about the conditions convicts live in; why would it concern a law-abiding citizen? After all, we were considered the scum of society, a bitter aftertaste in most people's mouths. As far as society was concerned, we didn't deserve our human rights. I remember, as we drew nearer to the outskirts of Victoria station, I smelled the familiar smoky smell of London. Factory fumes and pollution filled up the dense air. It felt good to be home.

As we passed through the ticket barrier, Murphy turned to me with a huge grin on his face, and said, "It's good to be back in the smoke again."

I nodded in agreement; it did feel good to be back around the buzz and excitement of London. It was 1949 and I was now twenty years of age. I was now a free man in his prime, raring to live, explore the world around me and have a good time. London had been battling years of the Great Depression after the war. It was only around 1949 that Britain began to move into an exhilarating new era. Food and clothes rationing ended and there was more of a buzz of life and enthusiasm on the streets. A variety of goods were now readily at our fingertips. Money seemed to be more readily available, which for us was a win-win situation. The more money circulating, the more opportunity.

We decided to catch the tube to Bethnal Green. We jumped off the tube with joy, enthusiasm and life pumping through our veins. We got to Bethnal Green Road, reached the top of Brick Lane and turned right down a small, enclosed path into the Boundary estate. The estate was darted with buildings, sprouting off in different directions. It would be easy to get lost amongst them as each brick building looked the same. We climbed the never-ending, concrete stairs up to a third-floor flat and Murphy knocked on the door a couple of times. We waited for a while and I thought maybe no one was in. Thankfully, a small, dark-haired woman answered the door; it was Murphy's Aunt Vera. She gave Murphy a long, heartfelt hug and a massive smacker on the cheek and hurried us inside, avoiding the nosy neighbours. She had obviously missed his company and was making a huge fuss of him. I think she knew we had run away from Borstal, but she didn't say a word about it. She was hospitable, and I felt welcome in her presence.

"Are you hungry?" she asked, a warm glow radiating from her.

"Starving hungry," replied Murphy.

She nodded and smiled. "I thought you would say that."

She led us through to the kitchen, which was small, but well looked after, clean and quaint; she obviously liked to run a tidy house. I sat down slowly; my aching body from last night's antics was now making itself known. I plonked myself down, tired but happy, and I sat there and watched her as she cooked us a huge breakfast. The smell of frying bacon after such a long time of not smelling its sweet and smoky aroma was a sensational moment for me. My first bite of my breakfast sent my taste buds into a spin; all the flavours bursting in my mouth was heavenly and divine. I sat and savoured that moment, reminding myself that the small pleasures in life can bring you the most joy. It didn't take us long to eat every morsel on our plates. That breakfast was one of my most memorable meals. Finally, there was some flavour and love thrown into our food, a stark comparison to the vile prison garbage.

"Where are you staying?" Aunt Vera asked inquisitively.

"Nowhere yet," Murphy replied. "We were wondering if we could stay in the spare room until we can get ourselves sorted out, Aunt Vera?" he gushed at her, with a cheeky smile.

She looked hesitant and doubtful, but I don't think she had the heart to say no. When she replied, I realised she must have been thinking of her husband and how he would feel, having two extra men in the house.

"You'll have to see what Sam says. Why don't you go down the Roman Road? If he says yes, then it's alright by me."

We got up, tired from our late-night escapade. My belly was so full, I was having trouble digesting the beautiful breakfast. My body was not used to feeling satisfied, and I could have slept right there on the spot. Instead, I pulled myself together and made the short journey with Murphy to the Roman Road.

"What do you reckon Sam will say? Do you think he will let us stay?" I turned to Murphy; I was really hoping we would have somewhere safe to lay our heads for a while. I wasn't up for trying to find somewhere else to go and was looking forward to staying with his aunt, as she seemed like a pleasant enough lady.

"We should be alright; he's a good old boy," Murphy responded with reassurance.

I was worried we were going to have nowhere to stay and the thought of trying to find anywhere else made me anxious. I also wondered if there would be a search party looking for us, thinking the prison would be furious that we had managed to escape.

We arrived at the Roman Road; the hustle and bustle of the market was madness, but it was enjoyable to see such life coursing through the streets. The place was so crowded, I couldn't see in front of me. It took us a while to navigate through the sea of heads, who didn't care for one moment that we were trying to get through, all wrapped up in their own worlds. The market was swarming and the noise of chatter and market men shouting with their thick London accents made me feel right at home.

"There he is!" Murphy pointed over to the right-hand-side and I could see a large, flush-faced man of about fifty, wearing a checked cloth. He was weighing up some apples for a customer. After he had finished, he turned to us and grinned with a cheeky twinkle in his eye.

"I might have guessed you would run away," he said with a smile. We nodded and gave a small, curled smile of triumph. "Well, I can't say I blame you; I'd have done the same myself. Where are you staying then?"

"Nowhere," replied Murphy. "We were hoping we could stay in the spare room, until we get ourselves fixed up. Aunt Vera said she doesn't mind if you don't. And don't worry, Sam, we will behave ourselves."

Sam gave a warm smile.

Murphy paused for a moment, then said, "Do you still handle suit lengths?"

Sam lit a cigarette and smirked. "As many as I can get." He put his hands in his pockets and gave Murphy two pound notes. "Right, off to work."

Murphy handed me a pound note and we walked away smiling; things were looking good.

"What's a suit length?" I asked. I had never heard of this before and was curious as to what he meant.

Murphy laughed. "It's easy; all you do is break into a warehouse or a tailor shop and steal the best rolls of suit material, about ten pound per role, depending on how good the quality is."

Sounded good to me! As far as I was concerned, it was good money, as the average working man was only earning ten pounds a week. If we could get a few rolls a night, then we were quids in. We spent the next couple of weeks walking around Bethnal Green, searching for and looking at local warehouses and tailor shops. We had no choice but to work on the manor, as we had no transport, and any cloth we stole we would have to carry out on our backs. Eventually, Murphy and I decided on a warehouse that would suit us, (no pun intended). It was situated in a quiet area, with little traffic and we worked out the easiest route to get back. We waited till about eleven o'clock at night and made our way to the warehouse. Then we broke a window at the back of the building, covering the window with piece of cloth so as not to make a noise, and proceeded to climb inside. The warehouse was pitch black; we navigated through it with torches, creeping around in the darkness. We stole rolls of the most expensive suit material and then made a swift exit, making sure we were quiet, moving in the shadows of the streets.

In those days, once the public houses were closed after ten, the streets in the East End were virtually deserted. Except for the odd pedestrian stumbling around drunk in the roads and the odd policeman patrolling the backstreets. There were dimly-lit gas lamps lining the streets, which meant there were plenty of shadowy parts of the streets we could hide in. If someone appeared and it came on top, we could simply drop the rolls and run for our lives. I never realised how heavy these rolls of material were. By the time we got back to Boundary estate and dumped the rolls into the back of Sam's lorry, covered with empty sacks, my back and arms were aching all over. I underestimated how difficult they would be to manoeuvre and transport. By the end of our mission, I was sweating profusely, out of breath and boiling up. This was hard graft. I thought there must be an easier and more efficient way of nicking these rolls and getting them to where they needed to be. So, we decided we would have to get a van. This would allow us to cover more ground and speed up the process tenfold, without breaking our backs in the process.

We went into the flat and told Sam what we had done.

"You don't waste no time, do ya?" He heaved himself out of his patchy, green armchair and went downstairs to inspect the goods. After which, he remarked, "That's not a bad bit of gear. I'll give you thirty quid for it." He was well pleased with the produce, and we were overjoyed to finally have some decent money in our pockets. This would be the beginning of mine and Murphy's cloth enterprise; we were on a roll...

That was that; taking from warehouses and tailors became our new job, all over the East End. Murphy and I got a white van and went to any factory and warehouse we could find. We were moving fast, making lots of money, and even had custom-made tailored suits to accompany our newfound wealth. We now looked the part, and were turning heads when we went out on the town. We got a reputation for ourselves as big spenders, especially in the West End, where we mixed with the rich and elites. We spent our free time in numerous bars and clubs, pulling endless numbers of women. We were young and enjoying life to its fullest. Consequently, we were welcome everywhere. Money talks and we were flying high, attracting all the right attention in the up-and-coming areas. Vera and Sam never asked us to leave, as I think they secretly liked us living there. They had no children and I think they enjoyed the company and, to be honest, we enjoyed theirs. Good solid, salt of the earth people and, as a team, we were unstoppable.

We decided to rent a small flat as another base. We held parties there and took girls back there instead of Vera's and Sam's out of respect and to keep the two lives we lived separate. We lived like this for about a year and everyone one was pleased with the arrangements; money was pouring in, and we were all happy. We had a party gaff and a home; what more could you ask for as young lads in our prime? Everything in our lives was falling into place and we felt like we were on top of the world. We felt unstoppable and invincible; it was an era of our lives that was fresh and new, and we welcomed every minute of it with open arms.

We would go on the rob a few nights a week. To maintain our lifestyle, we had to constantly find new targets and keep our ears to the ground. One foggy night, we robbed a tailor's shop in Stepney and were making our way back to the van with four rolls of premium, quality cloth, when we saw two blue-suited figures coming towards us. At first, it was hard to see clearly if they were policemen or not, as the fog was so thick, you could barely see a metre ahead of your face. Murphy thought they were fireman coming off duty, but something told me different. As they drew nearer, I could see who they were.

I dropped my rolls and shouted, "Let's go!"

I ran as fast as my legs could carry me. I could hear the shrill sounds of whistles being blown and shouting, "Stop! Stop!" I looked over my shoulder and could see them closing in on us.

"Split up," I shouted at the next corner.

Murphy turned left and I turned right. I skidded round the corner and dived into someone's front garden. Thinking I would not be caught if I found a good hiding spot, I threw myself into a small, prickly hedge. I hugged the ground and lay there in a huddle, hoping and praying I had got away with it.

Then I heard a voice shouting, "He's in the garden!"

One of the residents was quick to be a helpful civilian when she heard the sound of the piercing whistles. Sticking her nose in where it was not wanted, she looked out of her window, saw me in the well-groomed garden and alerted the policeman without an ounce of hesitation.

The torch shone down on me.

"Rise to your feet," the panting officer wheezed. He clearly wasn't used to running and could do with shaping up.

I stood up and tried to make a run for it, but he grabbed me by the arm and gave me a clip round the ear. This dazed me and

I ended up being unable to wrestle out of his grip. He marched me to a police station; all I could think was, fuck, this can't be happening. He took me to the front desk and then swiftly took me into an interview room, where I was questioned by a plain-clothed police detective.

"Who's your mate that got way?" he probed.

"I was on my own," I replied.

"No, you weren't, two of you were seen!" he barked. You could see he was getting frustrated and hot under the collar. He obviously was in no mood for games.

"If you know so much, then why are you asking me?" I retorted.

The detective gave me a clip round the head for being cheeky. Another blow to the head; the bastards never kept their hands to themselves. I refused to make a statement but was eventually charged with breaking and entering a tailor's shop and charged for the theft of four rolls of suit material. I was locked in a cell for the night, feeling extremely depressed. I had that sinking feeling I was going back to Borstal. That night, I barely slept and thought about the life I was missing outside, hoping Murphy had managed to get away. We had made an error of judgement and now I was paying the price once again.

The next morning, I appeared at the London court; they sentenced me to three years' Borstal training, saying they would get me on the straight and narrow with some tough training and rigid discipline. Like hell it would change me; I am who I am, and it's in my blood to be a robber. I was good at it and it was all I knew. The more the system tried to stop me, the more it spurred me on. No amount of Borstal training was going to change my character. But from handling suit lengths to doing another length inside was quite a turnaround in two days...

CHAPTER 7

DRUMMING

I wrapped myself in the thin, old prison blankets and lay down on the filthy, cold concrete floor. I thought, fuck them. I couldn't believe I was back in Borstal; I really didn't think I would get caught and I was pining for the life I had outside. It was just my luck. I was hoping Murphy had gotten away and was somewhere safe, but I wouldn't know, not until I had left this God-awful place. I decided I wouldn't allow them to get me down and tried my best to get to sleep. But it was near-on impossible to sleep on the floor. I could only think that animals, even rats and mice, received better treatment than this. I was being punished for escaping; no prison likes a prisoner getting the upper hand. I had put two fingers up to the institution by escaping and they were now going to make sure I well and truly paid for it.

One of my punishments was having my mattress taken away. I was left to sleep on the cold, hard prison floor, with some hard-back books as a pillow. Oh, how my body ached, and trying to get comfortable was no use. All my human rights were stripped from me, as a way of breaking my spirit or driving me insane. But of course I wouldn't allow their mind games to break me. This wasn't a punishment; this was something different. Sleep deprivation is a form of torture. Food withdrawal was another form of punishment they decided to inflict on me. They gave me fifteen days of bread and water. The Navy uses this type of punishment, usually over a three-day period, which for that length of time is bad enough. But fifteen days causes havoc in the body. Fifteen days was far too long for anyone; eventually, the body would run into nutritional deficiencies and likely you would end up getting extremely sick and delirious. The bread and water diet made me feel weak and gave me heart palpitations. I was sick of the sight of bread; holding it down was painful, and even finding the energy to chew the hard bread was a struggle. Towards the end of the punishment, my body and mind started to give up. In the last few days, I could feel myself fading away and all my thoughts turned into one big blur.

Once the gruelling fifteen days were over, I started the next stage of my punishment. I had forty-two days of a number two diet, which was porridge, potatoes and bread, three times a day. I had to do this for twenty-one days straight, then I had a break for seven days of an ordinary diet, which included all my vital nutrition, except I wasn't allowed puddings, jam or sugar. After the seven-day break was over, then it was back to a number two diet, for the last fourteen days. Towards the end, I could not face eating any more potatoes, porridge or bread. The stodgy carbs ended up not agreeing with my body; I felt sick and had the runs for days. There was little nutrition in the diet and, for such a length of time, it must have been severely detrimental to my body. How they got away with treating prisoners like this, I don't know. In the forties, there was hardly any regulation when it came to the welfare of a prisoner. No outside governing body came to check on our wellbeing; we were literally left to rot. The screws were doing my body and mental health as much damage as they could. I just nibbled on bits and pieces to survive; all I really craved was a mug of sweet tea. I was really suffering towards the end, but I was determined not to let the screws see it.

When my ordeal was over, I was taken back to the Borstal wing and put back into my old cell. I'd never thought I would be pleased to see the four walls of a crumbling and isolating cell. Finally, I had a bed to sleep on; a mattress, however thin and lumpy it was. I found it was pure bliss to finally be in a bed. I had never appreciated such a small luxury until then. That night, I slept like a king in a dungeon.

About a week later, my body had started to recover. The aches and pains were fading, and my mental health was snapping back. After so long without the nutrition I needed, a fog had loomed over me, but now I was eating regular food, I was thinking clearer and was fully focused. It was at this time the wing principle came to my cell and told me I was being transferred to Portland Borstal, after four months of being here, which was quite a surprise for me. For some reason, they had reduced my sentence; now I would be serving only fifteen months out of the three years. I found their decision an odd one, but I didn't argue; at least the end of the sentence would be closer than anticipated. I had just done four months, so once I arrived in Portland, I would only have twelve months left, which I was super happy about. I would be out in no time.

Arriving in Portland Island, I soon realised the place was always windy, as gusts of wind were constantly circling it. It was like the place created its own freak weather. The Borstal was an old shell of a place, grey in colour, extremely cold and damp but, despite the severe weather conditions, the prison was not too bad. I was given a job as a cleaner, which kept me busy, and the days always seemed to pan out differently. I even got to enjoy some leisure time; I played some football, and I had the great pleasure of going swimming and boxing. It surprised me that such activities were available to prisoners. The place was like a fitness club rather than a Borstal. By the end, I started to enjoy my routine. I was always keen to stay active, so the Borstal's focus on fitness suited me to no end.

I kept to myself and avoided trouble, and before I knew it, my time was up. I was going to go back to the only place I had ever called home. I was back on my way to London, again travelling by train and appreciating the view once more. I went straight to Aunt Vera, who gave me a big kiss and a wide, welcoming smile; she was more than pleased to see me. She cooked me a huge breakfast, which I was immensely grateful for, and she told me all the news since I had been away. Sam's market stall was doing well, and money was rolling in. I was keen to hear how Murphy was; apparently, he had left London and moved up to Birmingham. This was because the police wanted him for a string of burglaries and his presence in London was making things hot for him. He had been lucky to get away, as the police just missed catching him before he left.

I was pleased that Murphy was free. I would miss his company, but I didn't fancy my chances in Birmingham and wanted to stay in London. My most pressing need now was to get some money and I knew London was ripe for the picking. Aunt Vera said I could have my old room back for as long as I needed it. I was overjoyed; for me, this was like a second home and I settled back in quickly. My first night of proper sleep, I was gone before I even hit the pillow.

Later the next day, Sam arrived home. He was delighted to see me too. A twinkle caught his eye, and I could see he was overjoyed I was home and I could feel he had something up his sleeve. We went for a drink that night at the local pub, and he was keen to find out what my next move was. I shrugged, as I hadn't really thought that far ahead. I knew I needed to do a few burglaries to get some money together. I gazed at Sam for a while; he was looking old now, he must have been in his sixties, but I could see age catching up to him. Deeper wrinkles were forming on his forehead and around his eyes. He was still a powerful man, not frail at all, just with more wrinkles than before and a sagging face. Time just seemed to have a way of showing itself suddenly and, before you know it, age catches you and life has passed you by in a heartbeat. He still wore the same checked cap and I wondered if he ever washed it. It felt as if it was permanently stuck on his head, like an extension of his body. He scratched his face and looked like he was deep in thought. He took a long gulp from his pint.

"There's someone I know. He's older than you, but you would be better off with him than alone. He can teach you a thing or two. You'd be wise to take up the offer."

In the forties and fifties, crime consisted mostly of burglaries and occasionally the odd smash-and-grab. A smash-and-grab was when a firm pulled up outside a jewellery store; three of them would get out of the car and three of them would be carrying pickaxe handles to threaten any passerby if they tried to interfere. The fourth man would smash the shop window with a hammer and steal the jewellery, then they would pile into a car and drive away as fast as possible. Burglaries in those days were known as drumming, as houses were referred to as drums and burglars were known as drummers. Another phrase used for us were creepers or creeping, which implied we waited for everyone to go to bed before making an entry. The early hours of the morning were always the best time to enter a house. Once inside, you would creep through the house as quietly and as delicately as you could, stealing anything worth taking. If this was your preference, you would be known as a creeper. And the last phrase that was used is the term climber, whereby you climb up a drainpipe, making your entry through a bathroom window or a bedroom window. All of the robbers I knew had their own preferences of how and when they liked to rob and the style of robbing they chose.

Public houses were also popular amongst thieves in the forties and fifties. The pubs used to shut at ten pm on the nose. The landlord would shout last orders around nine forty-five. There would be a mad rush for everyone to buy their drinks; there would be sensational queues to get your last fix of your desired poison for the night. Whilst the landlord and bar staff were rushed off their feet, you would climb up the drainpipe through the bathroom window and have a quick search through the premises and take what was valuable. I always used to pray there were no dogs, as the last thing I needed was to be rolling around the floor with an angry mutt, barking and making a scene. They would make your presence known, so you would have to do your homework on the landlord before attempting a move. Usually, you would find money and jewellery and that was enough to get you by for a little while. These types of robberies would rarely bring in the big bucks, but were a steady stream of income.

Sam said he could hook me up with an older guy. According to Sam, he was one of the best drummers out there. He had done his knee in though, jumping out of a window on one move. But according to Sam, he could still get about. In the meantime, Sam said he would give me some money to tide me over. I thanked Sam; he was a good friend to me and had helped me out a lot in such a short space of time. I got up and went to the bar to get the next round of drinks. I thought to myself, things were looking up. Drumming wasn't my favourite thing to do, but I was happy to take on any work that came my way and this opportunity landed in my lap, just when I needed it the most.

Two days later, I met Sam in the pub on the Roman Road, and he introduced me to Fred, a tall slim man with a thin, wiry moustache. He looked like he was in his late forties, and was originally from Manchester, but had lived most of his life in London. As Sam had mentioned, this was the professional burglar he wanted me to team up with. We shook hands and sized each other up; first impressions can normally give you a gut feeling about someone. He seemed like a decent character from the get-go. He said Sam had told him I wanted to do some drumming.

"Well, Sam has given you a good name, so if you're up for it, I am looking to take on a new partner."

It was as simple as that; there was no interview or invasive questions, I was now on the team. That was the beginning of our blossoming working relationship.

Fred really knew his stuff. The first thing he taught me was how to fit and open a mortice lock. In those days, most of the mortice locks were shaped like the letter 'e'. Fred taught me to take any normal key and, using a small grinder, grind the key down thinner. Then I would use a file to smooth out the edges all over the key. If you did this with six keys, you would always get at least two out of the six that you could put into the lock and have a fiddle about with until you could unlock the door.

If there was a Yale lock on the door, which every door did have, he would show me how to open it without a key. We got a length of Celluloid, which you could usually buy from a motorcycle shop, cut it into four-inch strips and round both ends off. Then all you would have to do was insert the rounded edge between the door jam and the lock. Then shake the door gently back and forth. Put the Celluloid into the Yale, which would eventually make the door pop wide open. It was all so simple to do. In the drumming business, we called it loiding. Most people never bothered to lock the mortice, relying on the Yale lock to keep their house safe. People were far too trusting in those days; they had no idea how many criminals were out there, waiting for an easy opportunity.

There were a couple of ways to know if the mortice was on. One way was to put a lighter in front of a lock to see if dust had landed on it or not; therefore you knew if it had been used. If you wanted to know if the mortice was on, all you had to do was slip in a small length of film strip and wiggle it up the door. If it stopped, the Yale lock was on, but if it went past the lock, then it wasn't on. A great trick and so simple.

I was a fast and good learner, and Fred was a great teacher. He taught me many tricks and was patient with his teaching; we would laugh and not take the day too seriously. Most days felt like a new adventure, and I got a buzz out of every successful robbery. We ended up becoming good friends and spent most days together, robbing as many empty houses as we could. I called him Manchester Fred and would often take the mickey out of his accent. As far as I was concerned, we were a good team. We worked together for about ten months, which flew by.

We were good, efficient burglars. We were only robbing high-class flats; we never robbed council houses, we never robbed from our own. I used to ring the bell in my suit with a briefcase and I'd have a fake name, Mr Sinclair. I would use this name if anybody would answer the door, saying I was there for a car or something of a similar nature, to avoid causing suspicion if the target house did have someone in. We always had a cover story ready for any situation, for example if we were caught loitering or if someone was unexpectedly at home.

I remember doing three or four tie-ups many years later, which is where you make an entry into the house or knock on the door and frighten the life out of everyone on the premises. You would steam in and tie everyone up. The reason for doing this was that I had what I thought was reliable information, that there was a good amount of cash and jewellery on the property. Only, a lot of the time, I would find out this was false information. After doing several tie-ups in a row and coming away empty-handed I thought, fuck doing the tie-ups. They were more trouble than they were worth. So, I went back to robbing; at least you could see what you were nicking, and your own information and research is far more reliable than someone else's.

I always found drumming easier and a safer way of acquiring money; the fewer victims the better. We would go up to the door, see what type of locks they had and what was on. To see if there was a lock on, we would shake the door. The process was quite a meticulous one. If no one was in, we would clear them out, taking jewellery, silver, money, whatever we could get our hands on. We would only go on the rob between twelve and four in the afternoon. That was the time when most people were out and, when four o'clock came, we would stop robbing, as most people would be arriving home from their daily jobs. In one day, we were robbing four or five houses. We didn't have time to stop and reflect; our only concern was making as much money as we physically could. We were living a good life and earning enough to support a healthy lifestyle. This meant I had enough spare cash to socialise; when I did, I would go out up the West End once a week and flash the cash, but never spend or flash the cash on the manor. That would be the kiss of death. On the manor, if people could smell your money, you would be a target and they would know it wasn't from an honest living. When I went up the West End, I was booted and suited to the nines. We would go to Jack of Clubs or the Swallows; anywhere people had money, we were there, mixing with the best of them.

Like all good stints, they come to an end and, of course, our lucky roll eventually ran out. One day, it all got on top; we were doing a robbery in Middlesex and the woman of the house came home. We fled the scene; in doing so, we jumped over a wall and Fred's knee gave way. I managed to carry him to the car and we got away by the skin of our teeth. I wasn't sure what to do, so I drove to Aunt Vera's in Bethnal Green and the first thing we did was have a look at Fred's knee. It didn't look too clever; it was inflamed and swollen. Aunt Vera wrapped a cold compress round the knee, but I could see Fred would be out of action for some time. In fact, this injury led Fred to retire; he said he was too old for the game and didn't want to end up in Dartmoor. He had managed to save a few quid over the years and could live comfortably. Sometimes, you know when your luck has run out. It was a sad time for me, as Fred was good company; he loved a laugh and a good drink, and he was a master of the job. Knowing all that he had taught me, I thought I would be able to make it out there on my own. We shook hands and parted ways; he was one of the old-time burglars and the last of his generation.

I decided to go robbing on my own. Now Fred had passed on his knowledge, I was more than ready to move in the shadows and go on burglaries without assistance. Sam told me I was getting a name for myself in the East End and there were whispers of me being on the Old Bill's radar. Sam suggested I leave the manor to take the heat off, even if it was only for a while. I really didn't want to leave Bethnal Green, but I knew Sam was right. It was gut-wrenching leaving, as I had come to look at Aunt Vera and Sam as a surrogate family. But he was right, it was time to move on. I didn't want to get nicked and ending up in Wandsworth prison. So, I packed my bags, moved over to North London and rented a flat in Northumberland Park Road, Tottenham, where I would once again be anonymous...

CHAPTER 8

MEETING THE FIRM

I settled into North London life and soon got to know the area like the back of my hand. However, I still liked to visit my old haunts from time to time. Familiarity suited me well and I enjoyed seeing old faces, catching up, and getting information I needed. I was also always scouting for potential work. One night, I was over in Walworth, South London, having a drink in the Good Intent boozer. At the time, it was run by an ex-boxer, who was a good laugh and a welcoming landlord. It was situated in East Street market; there was a mixed crowd of market workers, assorted thieves and office workers. I was drinking on my own and got chatting to a couple of thieves. They knew of notorious Manchester Fred and I proceeded to tell them he had retired and I was now working alone. As I was leaving, a thief named Bob Connelly asked me what I was doing now. I said I would carry on drumming and said I could do with a partner and asked him if he was interested. He shook his head, saying it wasn't his game. However, he said he had some work coming up and explained he was short of men, that's why he asked me. He went on to explain there was an engineering firm in North London and every Thursday they collected the wages for the engineering workers.

"How many of them collect the wages?" I asked.

"Well, there's the wage clerk who carries the money and his four minders. They're big lumps; that's why we need another man to be four-handed, to make sure we'd get the prize." He gave a keen indication I would be the fourth.

I'd never been on a robbery of this calibre before, but I knew full well what they were talking about. If the money was right, I would consider any type of robbery.

"What's my whack?" I asked, hoping It was considerably more than my usual drumming money.

"You should get a grand at worst," he responded, looking eagerly for my reaction.

I could see he was keen to get me on board. A thousand pounds, I thought to myself, that was an impressive amount of money. I didn't want to come across as too impressed, so I maintained my composure. In the 50s, this was good money.

"What do I have to do?" Now he had my full attention.

"Well, the entrance to the firm is in a side road off the main drag. They collect the money from the bank, the cashier carries the money and is minded by the four burly geezers. We originally fancied taking the bag as they come out of the bank. But there's too many people about and the bank's right on the main street. Anyway, they collect the money and then drive straight to the firm, and they pull up straight outside. They all get out and take the bag inside. We will be in the van as they pull up. We will stop right behind them and, when they are out in the open, we will be four-handed. Two of us will have pick axe handles and one will have a Fairy Liquid bottle, filled with ammonia. While two of us steam into the minders, the other one will squirt the cashier, grab the bag and away we go."

A detailed plan, I thought to myself, and reflected for a moment. To be truthful, I was a bit dubious; two against four was not my idea of good odds and they were all big men, who could more than likely put up a good fight.

"We could put two down and that still leaves two more. You've got to assume they have all got a bit of arsehole. They could make it hard for us."

I didn't want to be out in the open, fighting for a bag. The more attention we drew to ourselves, the more likely the Old Bill would be called. The robbery needed to be as smooth and as quick as possible.

Bob nodded. "You could be right there; I can see your point. The last thing we want to do is to get the bag of cash and still be fighting when Old Bill arrives."

We stood in silence and then I said, "I'll tell you what we could do. We could make the driver work harder. He can have some squirt, he leaves the engine running, jumps out with us and squirts everyone in sight. Three against four, most likely they will back off when they realise what we are squirting on them."

Bob nodded in agreement. He told me he would tell the others, meaning the rest of the firm and we could meet back there tomorrow lunchtime.

"What about the motors?" I asked.

Again, we needed at least two motors, an arrival car and a getaway car. The police would be able to track us if we only had the one.

"Don't worry," he replied. "We have got a van and another motor, which will be popped up to change. They have been rung, so there's no problem, they are ok."

A rung car, or a ringer, is a stolen car that has had its number plates replaced with a set from another vehicle. Usually from a written-off car, which in turn changes the car's identity, basically making the car untraceable, especially back to us. Bob seemed to have everything covered, which made me feel assured that we would be able to pull this job off without any hiccups. I was confident this firm were professionals, and I don't mind working with anyone who knows what they are doing. We parted ways on the understanding that we would meet at the Good Intent pub the next day and I would meet with the rest of the firm.

The next day, I walked into the smoky pub; the cleaner must not have come as I could smell the stench of stale booze as I walked through the door. The bar was quite packed, and we blended in nicely. I could see Bob standing at the bar, with three other men. Bob was an Irishman; he was about five foot seven, tall and slim built, and in his day he had been a good amateur boxer. His nose had been broken a couple of times and he had massive hands with knuckles full of scars and signs of a well-lived life. He was a quiet man and only spoke when he felt he needed to. But when he lost his temper, he was a hard man to control, and everyone would get out of his way. He was a good driver and a hard worker; he stayed focused and was an ambitious man, always looking for the next bit of work. I looked over at the other two men and proceeded to walk over. One of the men was a good six-foot tall, solid build, dark hair and a huge scar over his left eye. His daunting exterior was later to be softened by his great sense of humour. My first impression of this tall and overbearing man, Gus Thatcher, or George, was that he was a serious man and I thought he wouldn't take too much shit from anyone. As things turned out, he was a good man to have on your side, especially in a sticky and heated situation.

Bob then introduced me to Philip Kelly, who was a shorter, stocky man with a permanent grin on his face and a thick length of dark blonde hair falling over his forehead. He was someone who had a good nature, easy going and up for any job. I later found out he was a keen gambler, which would be his downfall later in life. My first impression was that he looked alright to me. He had a friendly and warm nature about him, and I felt comfortable in his presence. They all seemed to be money hungry, which I related to, and they were serious and efficient robbers, who knew their stuff. All of their strengths, I liked. I could see good potential with this firm.

We ordered some drinks and started to discuss the robbery; they had a good getaway route mapped out, and all that remained was to decide who was doing what. We decided me and Gus would steam into the minders with the coshes. A cosh is a thick or heavy bar used as a weapon; we used this term back in the 50s a lot. Bob would take the bag and Philip had the car and van in two garages in Lewisham. We all planned to meet at the garages at nine am on Thursday morning. Once the vehicles had been collected, we would drive over to North London, park the car and then change over to the next one. We would stay in the van and drive over to the bank and park up as near as we could. Then it was just a case of waiting until the engineering firm arrived to collect the wages. We'd take off and arrive ahead of them, parking at the top of the road that led to the firm. Everything was now planned and ready to go. I love a good plan, thoroughly thought out, leaving no stone unturned. It made me confident that this would be a successful robbery. If you are lazy and slap-dash, things can go wrong and the last place I wanted to end up was back in prison. This would be the first robbery of this nature for me. I had a mixture of excitement and anxiety flooding my head; this was to be a brand-new venture and the prospect of some real money. But I was also nervous as this was a pavement robbery, out in broad daylight, with more risks and potential problems with the public.

The day came around quickly. That morning, I had my breakfast and mug of sweet, syrupy tea as usual and got ready for the robbery. The waiting part is always the worst; the adrenaline is coursing through your veins and the anticipation is unbearable. We sat in the rear of the van, all of us dressed in black. Balaclavas on our heads, ready to pull down over our faces, and black gloves on our hands. As we left the van, we gripped our pickaxes; the handles were taped over with black electrical tape for a better and tighter grip. As I can recall, everyone was tense; this was a big job, and we all knew the stakes were high, but the reward was worth it. However, no one was smoking furiously or sweating heavily. Nobody needed a sudden trip to the toilet or was having doubts about going ahead with the job, like they have portrayed in movies. The movies always portray a seed of doubt with at least one robber, but we were all on the same page. This was my first time on the pavement, my first robbery of this kind, so I was a little unsure of how it would go and slightly nervous that I could fuck it up and let everyone down.

Suddenly, Philip said, "The car is here."

As the car passed by, Philip started the engine and rolled slowly down the road. I remember Bob holding the squeezy bottle and a faint whiff of ammonia was in the air. Gus and I tightened our grip on the coshes. The North London engineering firm's car came to a stop; as they did, Philip accelerated and screeched to a halt. We all piled out. Gus and I rushed across the pavement, and I smashed the nearest minder in the leg, which gave way, I hit him over the head and down he went with a massive thud. Spark out on the floor. I saw Bob squirting the stream of ammonia at the cashier; he screamed as it went all over his face. He was holding his eyes and dancing about in the street, trying to find his footing. Bob grabbed the bag and Gus had his designated man down. Philip was squirting ammonia at the other two minders; these two backed away without a second thought. They didn't want a fight, which is what we had anticipated. They took one look at the carnage we had created and decided they didn't want any part of that.

Philip leapt back into the van and was shouting, "Come on come on!"

We all piled in the back of the van. Bob had the bag of readies in one hand and the bottle of ammonia in the other. Some of the ammonia came out and the potent fumes hit us in the back of the throat and eyes.

"For fuck's sake, throw the bottle away!" I shouted.

Bob tossed the bottle out of the window and laughed. "Sorry, chaps."

We pulled to a stop behind the getaway car, which was a Ford Consul. We removed our balaclavas and gloves, then we jumped straight into the car, making our way back to Blackfriars Bridge. We drove over the bridge back into South London. The traffic wasn't too bad and, as far as I could see, we weren't being followed. Gus dumped the Consul in a quiet street in Elephant and Castle, and we made our way to the nearest council estate, where Gus lived. The estate was made of red brick and went up about six floors on each building. As soon as we reached the block, I knew we were home and dry. Gus made us all a cup of tea, whilst the money was being counted and then equally shared out. Not bad at all; a grand each. In the fifties, that was a healthy amount of money and could get me further than any drumming money ever could. It was a quick job and was over in what seemed like a blink of an eye. I was more than happy with the outcome, and we pulled it off like professionals.

The boys suggested going for a drink; they knew a place called the Stork Club in the West End. We felt like celebrating; I was in a great mood, elated that I had managed to acquire so much money with such ease. Where we were going, was full of talent. The firm said there were plenty of girls up there and I was up for letting off some steam after pulling off the robbery.

And that's how our firm started. As a result, we went on to do plenty of successful robberies together, spanning the next few years. It's a common misconception that, after a robbery, thieves are always looking over their shoulders, waiting for a firm grip on their arm, followed by the words, 'You're nicked.' I personally never gave it much thought. It became quite normal for me, pulling off a robbery and living a normal life. The two worlds never collided, and I got on well, living a double life.

Provided you never left any fingerprints behind, and your face was concealed, you never had too much to worry about. The police might suspect you, but there wasn't much they could do without any evidence. However, it was common practice for the police to stitch you up. If they could place you at a scene, they would and, in the 50s, the judges always believed the word of the police as gospel. Even though they were as corrupt as hell, they were always believed. The police's sticky and underhand behaviour would not be revealed until years later. In the early days, it was a robber's dream; there were hardly any cameras, DNA evidence was rare, and informers were few and far between. If the police fancied you, they would raid your house, take you down the cells, slap you around and try to frighten you into confessing. But if you kept your mouth shut, you would eventually be released with a few lumps and bumps and a wounded ego. I was always dipping in and out of the four manors, North, South, East and West. I would frequent all the pubs that thieves would go to, and I got to know everyone on the scene. Being in the mix allowed me to find out what jobs were about and I kept my ear firmly to the ground.

Planning a robbery is a relatively simple affair; the hardest part is finding the right people to work

with, as some can work better than others. It's just a matter of persistence and dedication. I would pick an area and then drive and walk about, looking for suitable targets. For example, if I spotted a security van delivering money, I would follow it to see how many drops it had done, how big the bag was and how easy the robbery would be. If there were any henchmen to consider and if there could be any complications. You must weigh up all the possibilities or obstacles and any problems or factors that could come into play. Making sure you can pull the robbery off and that it is worth your while. My favourite places to rob were trading estates and post offices. I discovered I

enjoyed looking for work; I got a thrill out of it, it was interesting and could potentially be rewarding, depending on what you might stumble upon. If it could be done without too much risk, then there was a high chance of us pulling off the job. I always preferred banks on corners; they had less traffic and were easily accessible, and in general made for a better getaway. I got to know what worked and what didn't. In reality, robbing was a piece of piss back in the 50s. It was an open market, and we were taking whatever job was lucrative, with no thought to anyone else. We were all about making as much money as we could.

CHAPTER 9

FILL UP YOUR PETROL TANK

I met my first wife at a skating rink in Derby. We were both young and full of life and, when I first laid eyes on her, I thought she looked like a young Jackie Kennedy. I was blown away by her good looks and her skill on skates. She had thick brown hair that bounced above her shoulders, a wide flashing smile and enchanting green eyes, which caught my eye straight away. We had instant chemistry and courted for some time before we decided to tie the knot. Pat and I were married on a gorgeous sunny day in 1956, and it wasn't long until we had our son, Steven, in 1957. We were an instant family in just over a year; my wife gave birth before we had even settled in to married life. Our lives were moving at a fast pace; there didn't seem much time for my feet to touch the ground. For me, it was a whirlwind romance; I got caught up in the idea of a traditional life, marriage and family, and thought it was what I wanted.

In the 50s, it was expected of you to get married and have a family, normally when you were in your late teens or early twenties. It would be deemed odd if you didn't get married in the early years of your life, and it was frowned upon to have too many suitors and to have any children out of wedlock, especially if you were a woman. However, a lot of men and women were not cut out for the traditional life and only went along with it because society told them so. Not everyone fitted the mould or could maintain the standard and expectations of living. I was one of these people. To my dismay, we ended up living with my in-laws, which was not my cup of tea at all. Being around so many people with conflicting ideologies did my head in and I was always looking for an excuse to go out. We were critiqued constantly, ridiculed and treated like inferiors. For me, it was suffocating; I was my own man with my own ideas and I never liked being told what to do. Being married so young, I felt like my wings had been clipped and, at times, felt like I couldn't breathe. Looking back, I was not ready to settle down; the big wide world was calling me and staying in one place for too long didn't suit me one bit.

I would describe myself as a rolling stone of the criminal variety. I kept moving, finding the next opportunity, something bigger, something better. I enjoyed travelling up and down the country, making my way in the world, learning about life and meeting new people. I was turning out robberies across England, travelling to Manchester, Birmingham, Sheffield, any town or city. If there was an opportunity to go on a robbery, I was there. The key to being a successful armed robber is to keep on the move, not to linger in one place for too long. I wouldn't normally rob on my own doorstep either, and keeping a low profile is a must in this profession. I only worked with the firm at the time; after meeting them, we only worked together. Pulling of bigger jobs with four of us meant more money and more muscle; no one was going to come up against the four of us and we knew it. At this point in my life, I felt on top of the world. All the jobs we were pulling off were successful, and the amount of money passing through our hands was unimaginable. But at that age, you do not think of the future; you live in the moment and spend it as fast as it comes in, without a care in the world. We were living in the moment. Living the life I always dreamed of, the firm and I were on top of the world and intended to stay there.

My wife and I had a son, Steven; he was young when I was bouncing from one job to another. I'd finish up many a job and decide I was not ready to go home back to my wife. I would sometimes stay away for days or even weeks, with no explanation or care for my wife's needs or wants. I wasn't interested in the mundane life of being a husband, coming home and being responsible, planting myself in front of a television every night. I was all about chasing the thrill of the job and the thrill of the night.

We pulled a job, up near Brighton, which is situated on the coast, about an hour or so from London. A great coastal town, with donkey rides on the beach, some of the best greasy fish and chips and Punch and Judy shows, drawing crowds along the promenade. During the war, Brighton had been hit quite badly; according to wartime records, Brighton was hit fifty-six times during the Blitz. After a while, the South Coast was dangerously exposed. Defence measures were put in place along the beach, including mines, barricades, barbed wire and sandbags. They demolished the centre of the two piers, for fear of the Germans using them as a landing strip. They also suffered low-level air attacks by German fighter bombers, known as hit-and-run raiders. Due to the precautions taken during the war, Brighton was still getting back on its feet. Like many other towns and cities, they were repairing the damage that had been caused and rebuilding structures; for example, the pier was being rebuilt. However, this didn't deter the holiday-makers or stop people from having a good time. In the summer, the beaches were filled to the brim with holiday-goers, without an inch to spare on the smooth pebbles. Children would be building sandcastles near the sea front and the mums and dads would be planted in the direct sunlight on the stripy deckchairs, enjoying the peace. The quaint, cobbled streets, known as 'the lanes', were full of shoppers and there was even a large clear blue paddling pool to frolic in. It was an ideal destination for anyone wanting to have a good time.

After our job, I needed to let my hair down, and the only place that attracted me to go out in was Brighton. Instead of going home, like I should have, I sent a thousand pounds to my wife and son and joined the firm to go and party down on the sea front of Brighton. Brighton was full of life at the time, with lots of people experimenting; it was an up-and-coming scene. We fancied a different atmosphere than West London; this was the place to be. I rented a little flat down in Brunswick Square and decided to stay down there for a while, as I had lived in Hove when I was a kid and knew the area like the back of my hand. We had pulled off another bank robbery and had quite a good touch. With my share of the money from the robbery, I bought a green Jaguar and was showing off my new purchase, whizzing around the sea front. Drawing attention to myself, trying to catch the ladies' curiosity and gaze. The draw of the coast, sea and beach, was a hard one to resist, especially in the height of summer. Clubbing, drinking and gambling were just some of the extra-curricular activities that we would enjoy immensely. One night, we went out as usual, suited and booted; me and my pals went to a nightclub in the heart of Brighton. Someone we knew owned it, so we were well-looked-after and treated like VIPs at the venue.

The night was going well. My wandering eye was checking out the talent in the club, we were enjoying the music, drinks were flowing and all was going smoothly. The music scene was blowing up and clubbing was something we loved, particularly to let off steam. Some of us were at the bar when suddenly one of the bouncers came rushing over in a panic.

"Is that your mate upstairs?" He sounded alarmed; his face had a look of panic. He had obviously seen something horrific, as he was as white as a ghost. We looked at each other with concern; it was more than likely it was someone we knew, as he had seen us all arrive together.

We stormed upstairs, went up onto the front porch and outside of the club to see what all the commotion was. Morris was standing there, his eyebrow hanging off his face, drenched in blood; you could barely see his face. Just his wide eyes popping out of his head and a pulsating gash with an eyebrow halfway down his face. He looked like a mutilated potato head, misshapen and distorted. He looked like something out of a gruesome horror movie. His face was a sight to behold. There was frantic shouting and men crowding round him, trying to help; it was chaos. Morris was holding his face, disorientated and not making much sense, as we were trying to get him to explain what had happened.

We finally got to the root of the problem; a guy called Bob Wetherby was the man who had inflicted such damage. He hit Morris with such force, he had split his eye open. He was well-known on the circuit and not well-liked. Alcohol coursing through our veins, we were ready to put it on him. None of us liked Wetherby, and he had finally overstepped the mark. Now, it was a great excuse for us to take our loathing of him to the next level. I opened up the boot and pulled out my weapon of choice, a mighty chopper. I was ready for confrontation, raring to go. Of course, alcohol was spurring me on as much as my rage. I was trying to find him but he had already left the scene; he was lucky he had scarpered, because I was in the mood to battle. The coward that he was, he had scuttled back to his flat, in Oriental Place.

In our drunken state, we thought it would be a good idea to take him on at his home, so we went there and banged down the door. He opened the front door; you could see the terror flash across his eyes. Five men standing there with weapons in hand would be enough to put the fear of God into anyone. We stumbled inside and the mayhem was in full swing. There was a struggle and, with my chopper, I tried to chop his arm off. I was out of my head with rage, and with too much alcohol in my system. I just went for him, with no thought of the aftermath. I went to slice his arm clean off, but thankfully, the arm stayed attached, and somehow, he managed to get us off his premises. If we had been sober, we would have got him; Lady Luck was on his side that day, as we were in no state to fulfil any of our intentions. Still steaming drunk, we all decided to pile back in the car and venture back to the club.

We were driving erratically when the car ran out of petrol on the A23. We were then stuck at a roundabout, all of us off our tits. We had been there for some time, all of us giving different ideas of what to do and how to get back. Everyone was talking over each other and getting nowhere fast; my patience was wearing thin. The drink was wearing off and the adrenaline of the attempted confrontation was now dwindling; I really just wanted to get home. It had been an hour or so since the incident, and I wanted to get out of this situation quickly, as we were drawing a lot of attention to ourselves. So, I decided I would try and pull over a white van that happened to be passing us. Take out the passenger, nick the car and get back to mine with all of us piling in the van, with the idea of abandoning the car at the roundabout. We were now creating a scene and causing a nuisance for oncoming traffic. But as bad luck would have it, a police car was one car behind the van, so I waved the white van man on, acting as if I was with the police behind it. The police flashed their lights and pulled over; stepping out of the car, they came and approached our vehicle. Morris had run and hid in a bush, to avoid questioning over his bloodied face. Which I found hilarious at the time, watching him run off and dive into the nearest shrubbery, with no grace whatsoever. It was now time to act sober and pull myself together.

"Officer, we have run into a bit of trouble," I said, trying not to slur my words, pointing at the empty petrol tank. He looked at me as if he felt sorry for our predicament and shook his head, as if to say that our predicament was unfortunate. He seemed like he was happy to help.

He kindly led us to the petrol station; as far as we were concerned, the story we told him was bought hook, line and sinker, and we would be on our merry way soon enough. I even gave the officer some money for his trouble, thinking I had managed to act my way out of this one with ease. I was even patting myself on the back for my amazing acting skills. Little did we know that we were being looked for; a call had been put out, in search of five men, regarding an assault and who were heavily armed. The police officers with me were too shaken to arrest us; instead, they let us go as if we were home and dry, leading us into a false sense of security. Next thing, half a dozen panda cars pulled in on us from all directions. Lights beaming, full glare, on us from all angles and sirens wailing, as if some major terrorist attack had just taken place. They were looking for five dangerous men, and we fitted the description perfectly. With nowhere to run or hide, we were arrested for grievous bodily harm.

I was taken down the local station and was steaming at the ears with anger, that I had been caught for this trivial shite. For a while, I had been wanted for a string of burglaries and a couple of other offences, and the law had eventually caught up with me. I just didn't think it would be for something as stupid and careless as this. I was firmly on the police's radar and, in hindsight, I thought that our drunken escapade was in poor judgement and could have been avoided. But there was nothing I could do; what was done was done. I ended up getting a five-year sentence, firstly serving eighteen months in grubby Wandsworth, with poor sanitation and overcrowding. They then transferred me to Dartmoor, which was one of the gloomiest and most depressing prisons in the country, due to its terrible conditions. It was damp, cold and had crumbling walls; it wasn't fit for animals to reside there, let alone humans.

But there was one plus side to being in Dartmoor; breaking rocks with an eighteen-pound sledgehammer was thoroughly rewarding. I enjoyed every minute of it because it was hard, intense labour and I loved putting my body through extreme exercise. I would enjoy waking up each day, knowing I was pushing myself to the limits and would sleep like a baby when it was lights-out time. When I looked out from the top of the prison, I could see a mountain called Yes Tor, the second-highest point in Dartmoor. On a clear day, you could see all of the surroundings area's natural beauty. On sunny days, it held a tranquil, magical quality, and if I were a rambler, I would have enjoyed the many windy-pathed walks sprouting off in different directions, taking you to unknown and untravelled parts of the moors. As you looked out from the top of the prison, you could also see there were lots of pony trails going off in multiple directions. I thought, if I ever get sent back here, there's a hundred ways of escaping, which put me in good spirits, knowing I could get lost in the wilderness.

I was always thinking ahead, and wherever I was, I looked for the weaknesses in the structure of the building, and if there was a way out, I would find it. I was resourceful and didn't take no for an answer. My motto was and still is, 'If there's a will, there's a way.' And I always found a way; I was notorious for that. I served the rest of my sentence in Dartmoor and came out pumped after all the rock smashing, feeling as fit as a fiddle. I knew exactly where my first stop would be on my first day of freedom.

I went straight to Waterloo station to meet the firm, who were eagerly awaiting my arrival. The first thing I said to them was, "Let's go for a drink," as I was gasping and ready to celebrate finally being out. The second thing I asked was, "Is there any work on at the minute?" The reply was that they had a big job on that coming Tuesday. Like clockwork, the job went ahead and I finally had a bit of decent money in my pocket. Straight back to work, without a moment's thought of the repercussions. Prison was never going to reform me; locking me up was only putting a delay on my next move. I got four grand, my start-up money, and decided to set up shop back in London, renting a flat on Ainslie Rise and buying myself a new car to get around in. This time round, my wife and son came to join me in the flat; she could now spend more time with me and I could be around my son, whilst I got myself back on my feet. Of course, like a boomerang, I was back robbing again, every fortnight robbing a bank or an establishment that had an abundance of money on site. I was cashing in, making up for the long five years I had missed on the scene. Back stacking the readies and enjoying the wind blowing through my hair, in an open-top car, filled to the top with petrol!

CHAPTER 10

SITES AND SHOOTERS

Before any robbery, I would walk through the getaway route, as many times as I felt necessary. I was always meticulous about getting the getaway route ironed out to the very last detail. There was no room for error or sloppiness, and jobs were never done on a whim. I would walk and drive around, planning the route in detail. I would firstly work out exactly where the changeover car would be situated. I would find another quiet street not too far away and have a second change-over car waiting in the perfect place for a clean and efficient getaway. When the work went down, we would tear away in the first car and then jump in the second. We would then drive back normally, at average speed, taking the back roads for as long as we could, before coming back onto the main road. We had the whole of London mapped out. When you live in the areas of London, you get to know all the back ways and, in those days, London didn't have any no-entry signs or one-way traffic systems in place. Getting around town was a breeze. By the time the police arrived at the scene to get our descriptions, we were long gone. Plus our faces were always covered with balaclavas and our hands covered with gloves. There was never enough information for the police to go on. Having a second getaway car made it almost impossible to catch us. If our timing was right and there were not any hiccups along the way, we were home free.

A successful robbery was all about timing and good planning, getting the route sorted beforehand and overcoming any resistance through threats or fear. For me, I can't say bank robberies were particularly nerve-wracking; it was over so quickly and, at the end of the day, it was just a way of earning a living. It was all we knew and the money was better than any normal job would have provided. I have been on a robbery at eleven am - a struggle had taken place, shots were fired or someone got beat over the head, that would be a typical morning for me - and then, by four pm, I would be picking my son up from school. There were some surreal moments. I sometimes would laugh to myself and shake my head in disbelief, when in normal day-to-day situations. I would be sitting having a picnic with my son and be thinking, I was just holding someone up at gunpoint this morning. It would make me see how extreme my life was; I was living a double life. I was this hardened criminal, a fearless and some would say violent, dangerous man and, in contrast, I was doing things like the school run or picking up groceries from the shop with my kid in tow. My wife never knew the extent of what was going on; she had an idea, but the less information she knew the better. She didn't ask any questions; if she didn't ask, then I didn't have to tell her any lies. It was an unspoken agreement between us and we were happy with our dynamic; most robbers' wives knew nothing of their escapades. Then, if anything came on top, she couldn't be incriminated in any way. She was happy with the money rolling in, no questions asked. But that was just how the game worked. The more jobs I did, the easier the job was and it became second nature, almost a normal way of life. You don't think you are different to anyone else, your path in life seems as normal as the next. As far as I was concerned, I was earning a crust; however dishonest it was, I was still supporting my family and providing them with a lifestyle they would not have had in other circumstances.

It was the late fifties when our firm switched to using guns. This happened organically; we never thought of guns in the beginning because we never needed them. It was only when we ran into some trouble that it seemed the best way of progression and tight-proofing our game.

It was one cloudy afternoon; we had planned this work for a

while and had the intention of a quick grab-and-run. We pulled up to a building site to nick the wages over in Paddington, North London. Building sites would always have a large amount of cash stashed on site. It was common knowledge they got paid a nice whack of money. If the building site was a big one, you knew there would be a fair bit of cash on the site, due to the numbers of staff needed on a project of that scale. The builders were paid weekly; like clockwork, they would get their wad of cash on a Friday afternoon. We arrived, arrogant, bold as brass; we thought it would be a piece of piss and considered it the same calibre as all the other jobs we had done. We steamed into the minders, thinking they would be our only problem; they were the only threat we had considered during our planning. We had, however, not envisaged all the builders attacking us. They could see their wages being nicked and the whole load of them charged into us; like football hooligans fighting their rivals, they came for our blood. There were twenty-odd men kicking our heads in; it was absolute carnage and a fierce pitched battle ensued. If it had been on camera, it would have gone viral within minutes. The fight was intense and I genuinely thought we were going to die that day. There were far too many of them to take on; being outnumbered and unable to leave the site, I thought we were goners.

The workers were everywhere. We were totally outnumbered and fearful we would be killed, so we kept trying to edge to the exit, where we had so boldly come in. The bag of wages was forgotten amidst the fight. Instead, the four of us were left fighting for survival, trying to navigate our way out of there in the midst of the chaos. All we could do was try to escape the building site. Somehow, we managed to make it back to the car but, for a time, I thought we were really not going to make it out of there. We were visibly shaken and had not expected the robbery to turn out like that at all. We got into the car, absolutely battered, and we were in complete shock as we sped off, never to return to that part of town again, or not for a while anyway. We could have ended up being buried under the rubble, or landed under some fresh cement on the sprawling building site. But we managed to get away by the skin of our teeth. We got back to my flat in Tottenham, standing in my kitchen, bathing our wounds and feeling sorry for ourselves. We were in disbelief at what had just happened and it made us rethink our whole strategy.

I remember saying, "We were lucky today. We all were lucky to come out of there alive."

Bob was nodding, eyes wide as saucers.

He replied, in an earnest voice, "We should have carried a shotgun. That would stop any punch-ups. Plus, we could have got nicked. Much quicker and easier with a shotgun, in and out. Plus, nobody wants to get shot."

I had to agree that Bob was right; why had the idea of a shotgun not occurred to us before? But Bob pointed out that, if it all went wrong, we would be looking at bigger sentences for armed robbery. We all looked at each other and agreed we would have to make sure we carried out our robberies with as much planning as possible, to ensure we didn't get nicked. We would now be stepping up our game with a lot to lose, but we had no choice. We couldn't face another building site saga. Nothing like that could happen again. Guns were going to get us in and out of a job in a flash, giving us plenty of time to take what we wanted, not get into a fight and get away before anyone had a chance to call the police. The sentence for carrying or using a gun was a lengthy one, but we felt we would be able to avoid arrest, as long as the planning was up to scratch.

"I'll tell you what," I said. "I know a mate of mine who might be able to get me a tool. I'll go and see him."

In the early 1950s, when criminals in the UK first started carrying guns, it was difficult to get handguns. But shotguns were plentiful, so everyone used shotguns for that reason. You could buy boxes of ammunition quite easily from gun shops. It was a lot easier than you might think; as long as you knew the right people, anything was attainable. Getting the bullets was easy enough. All you had to do was take some form of false ID into the shops and they gave you what you wanted. Nowadays, you can't just buy ammunition, you need proper permits. Shotguns were difficult to carry, so they were cut down for easier concealment. I liked shotguns because everyone knew not only what they looked like, but the damage they could inflict. They looked extremely threatening, especially when one was being pointed at you. It was only in later years that shotguns started to be used less often, mainly because of their size. The gangsters and robbers began dabbling in handguns, as they were much easier to carry, conceal, and get rid of.

The next day, I went over to Acre Lane in Brixton and saw my pal. I explained I wanted to buy a shotgun and asked if could help me.

I remember he smiled from ear to ear and said, "John Boy, it's your lucky day. I've got two tools I want to get rid of." Music to my ears, I took his offer up in a shot.

Without hesitation, I said, "I'll take them off your hands."

And I bought them right there and then, on the spot. I wrapped them in a blanket, put them in the boot and drove to Gus' slowly, abiding with all the laws of the road, to prevent being pulled over by a panda.

The last thing I needed was to get pulled over by the Old Bill, especially with the guns in the car. Me and Gus cut the guns down in his kitchen, and we were ready to do our first armed robbery. We were not particularly nervous or apprehensive taking this new career path. We didn't think about the victims or their feelings. We only had one focus, getting the job done with ease and efficiency. It was our only concern; we had no care for anyone but ourselves and all the cash we could accumulate.

After the botched building site robbery, there was some time for reflection and realising how lucky we were made me appreciate life just a tad more than usual. When you have near-death experiences or altercations that scare you, you seem to grow as a person and realise what is valuable to you.

A few days had passed. I'd been for a drink in the Coach and Horses, a local pub in Tottenham High Road. The pub was used by the local residents and quite a few of the local thieves frequented it too. Someone had mentioned there had been increased police presence in the area. My ears pricked up; this was useful information, but was unnerving. I didn't respond, but it made me pause for thought and I wondered if it had anything to do with the work me and the boys had attempted and failed, over in Paddington. That attempted robbery would have created a lot of attention and I am sure the builders were looking for blood. It was probably the biggest news all over town. Anyway, I exchanged small talk, whilst I processed the information that I had just received, finished my drink swiftly and then decided to leave. I made my way to Northumberland Park Road, where I was living at the time, and I noticed an unmarked police car parked opposite my flat. My first thought was that it was on me; the paranoia kicked in, and I thought, am I being followed and watched?

In the fifties and early sixties, an unmarked car was instantly recognisable because they were all Hillman Imps or Hillman Hunters, with two distinctive rear-view mirrors. They also all had the same number plates, CXA or BLU. As I walked past, I could see two plain-clothes officers looking at me with interest. That's it, I thought, it's time to leave the manor. That night, I needed to speak to someone about the situation. So, I ventured to Elephant and Castle to see Gus and explained how I felt, that I fancied moving out of North London. I was feeling the heat and maybe had done too much work too close to home. Gus agreed it was a sensible thing to do and said he would help me find a suitable flat. It took about a week for me to find a large two-bedroom flat in Knolling Road, Streatham. During the time I was trying to find the flat, I kept a low profile and I never saw any police cars, but I didn't feel safe. The area just wasn't for me anymore; when you get that gut feeling, it's best to follow it. I thought if I stayed where I was, eventually, I would have been raided and pulled in for questioning. When the flat was ready, I packed my bags and drove over to Streatham, South London. I sold my car and bought a new Ford Consul, just to be extra cautious. My flat was a stone's throw away from Streatham skating rink, and near the rink was a drinking and gambling club called Bali Hai. The Bali Hai was adjacent to the right of the skating rink. You would climb a set of stairs to the building above the rink to enter.

The atmosphere was electric. It had two small dance floors and artificial palm trees dotted about in different parts of the club, giving it an exotic feel. They played Motown and Northern Soul; the city was finding its rhythm and we were a big part of the scene. I started to use it regularly; lots of the South London thieves used to use it. There was always something going on; shoplifters would come in and sell upmarket shirts and suits, perfume or household items. Sometimes, they brought meat and fish and various groceries, practically giving away the stolen goods. They were picking up quality gear; the prices were always a bargain so I was inevitably buying something off the hoisters on many occasions. I rarely came out of there empty-handed and was always satisfied with my purchases. You could have a good drink, a game of cards, or some entertainment was put on at the club too. An eclectic mix of people made the club a colourful, vibrant and interesting place to frequent. There was never any aggro. It was the sort of club that suited me to the T. When you find a good place to drink and let your hair down as a robber, you tend to stick to it as your regular. I maintained a low profile for a while, meaning I didn't do any jobs. I felt like we had a target on our backs and I didn't need to make any instant cash, so I stayed under the radar after the failed building site work. I was still licking my wounds and thanking my lucky stars that we were not dead and buried.

Sometimes, there were lulls in work. We could go a few weeks without anything happening, nothing lined up and no idea where our next job would be. The majority of the time, that was no problem, as we earnt more than enough to tide us over for months on end. I liked keeping my head down and disappearing on occasion. There was something calming about being at home and not socialising with anyone. I needed the down-time to gather my thoughts and compose myself, as a big job can take a lot out of you, both physically and mentally.

One morning, I was having a late breakfast, when my doorbell rang. I opened it to find Gus standing there with a big smile on his face. I could see by his expression he had something to tell me and was eager to get it off his chest.

I beckoned him through the door. "Come in, do you fancy a cup of tea? I'm just having some breakfast." I was making a scrumptious bacon sandwich. Gus followed me into the kitchen, whilst I poured a big mug of tea for him and myself.

"What are you up to?" I asked him. I was now curious and intrigued about his news, as he looked like he had found the pot of gold at the end of the rainbow.

"I think I've found a good bit of work for us." Gus was beaming by this point.

I said, "I hope it's not another building site." With a smile and smirk. I loved a bit of sarcasm.

He laughed. "No, nothing like that. I was over in North London, and I decided to follow this van. It led to a small industrial estate over in Edmonton, right in your old manor."

"Tell me more," I pressed him. He liked to build up the suspense before reaching the climax.

"Well, it's some sort of large manufacturing works. It's on a long cul-de-sac and this factory is the last one on the left-hand-side. The only trouble is, it's right near where you used to live in Tottenham."

It didn't bother me too much; I didn't mind as I was in a different area now, and the Old Bill wouldn't come looking for me in Streatham.

"How much do you think it will come to?" I inquired.

He pursed his lips before saying, "It could be up to about twenty grand."

Without an ounce of hesitation, I said, "For twenty grand, I'm in!"

CHAPTER 11

CABLE FACTORY ROBBERY

Like I've said before, we only used the ammonia bottles in the beginning of our firm's robbing days. It worked well and we never had any problems, up until the building site disaster when we changed direction. We had our strategy down to a fine art but now the guns were in full play. We used them for every robbery, no matter how big or small; the shot gun was our go-to weapon. And oh, how robbing was so much easier! No one put up a fight; every single person who happened to be in the establishment we were robbing, cowered down in fear of their lives, which made it simple to get in and out quickly and efficiently. No fuss and zero drama. We were robbing all sorts; banks, jewellers, firms, anywhere that had a good amount of money and was nearly risk-free, we done over. In those days, most places only dealt with cash or paid wages in cash, so for us robbers, the world was our paradise and was ripe for the picking.

Back in our local boozer, we were casually eyeing up some birds, as we normally did when we were out on the razz. But the conversation would always end up leading back to our next move. Our next money-making scheme. Gus mentioned the bit of work he had told me about at my flat, to the rest of the firm. He went into more detail when we were all together to avoid confusion and crossed wires. It was easier than talking to us all individually, as no information could be lost in translation.

"I saw a security van turning into a quiet road and, on an impulse, I followed them, and saw the van turned into Edmonton. I stopped outside a cable firm; as far as I could see, the driver took a big bag inside."

"How big was the bag?" Bob's eyes lit up a little.

"Was a nice size," replied Gus. You could see he was excited about this job. "It looks like a doddle. I'll tell you what, I'll take you over there and you can see for yourself. Pick me up by midday and you can have a look at it with a fresh pair of eyes."

The lads were good at finding promising work. They had a shrewd eye and could sniff out potential. Once we finished talking about our next possible move and the different ways we could execute the robbery, including possibly get-away routes, we called the girls over and ended up having a good night.

Like clockwork, twelve came and Gus was at the door, not a minute too late or early. Dressed and ready to go, to take me to see this location. The cable factory was located at the end of a cul-de-sac, meaning the road was blocked at the far end. This also meant there would be light traffic, if there was any at all passing through the road. The only people using the road would be the ones who worked or lived there. Which was handy, as we wouldn't have to worry about other vehicles passing and blocking our exit. There were about eight other firms running down both sides and, best of all, there was a large Victorian-style pub at the entrance of the cul-de-sac, which had a small garden with wooden tables and chairs. It was perfectly positioned to watch passersby; you could sit and have a drink and observe the vans arriving, as well as oncoming traffic and people. You had a clear view of the vans entering and exiting the factories' grounds; already the job was looking good. I went for a stroll down the lane to work out the angles. There were no pedestrians or traffic; it was nice and quiet, just how I liked it. I returned to Gus and said it was looking profitable and full of potential.

"What time do the vans arrive?" I asked.

Gus replied, "Two pm, the factory gates are always left open. The van drives into the yard, then passes a wooden box, like a hut, where a guard is situated." Gus had obviously done his homework and I was thoroughly impressed.

"It's looking good," I said. "We'll show the other two tomorrow and see what they think."

Gus returned to his car and drove us home. Over the next couple of days, Bob and Philip had a look too, scoped out the area and decided it was an easy touch. We were all in agreement that this would be our next job. As I had previously lived in the manor, I volunteered to sort out the get-away route, as I knew the area like the back of my hand. I spent a couple of hours walking around the immediate area and sorted an easy and simple route for us to take. I decided to leave the changeover car in a quiet side street about two minutes' drive away from the factory. Once we had the bag of cash, we would drive to the quiet street, swap cars and shoot through a few back streets, since there were few road restrictions in the 50s, so driving in London was a simpler affair. But it was made even simpler by knowing the area. We always made sure we agreed on the plan before we went ahead, to avoid confusion or any mistakes. We went over the plan a few times, etching it deep into our memory banks. It was paramount there was zero confusion, because if there was, we could all end up getting nicked and going away for a long time.

We had to steal two cars first. They had to be inconspicuous, nothing out of the ordinary, no motors that stood out, and we would have to re-plate them. Then we would stash them in some rented garages. We decided we would watch from the pub garden. Once the van arrived and the money was safely delivered, Bob would drive into the yard and wait in the car. Gus would hold the guard up and make sure no one interfered. Then Bob and I would steam into the office and do our regular routine. I would hold up the staff and Philip would grab the bag containing the wages. We would leave the cable factory the same way we got in. Then we would drive directly to the second car, driving straight back to South London. Home and dry, wasting no time in the process.

The day of the robbery was a dull and drizzly day, which wasn't a bad thing, as your vision is slightly impaired when the rain is pouring down. Rain creates a lot of confusion, and we now had the advantage of more time and the element of surprise on our side. We arrived at the pub at one-forty-five on the dot. We drove over in the two stolen cars, and we parked the changeover car nearby on the quiet street and made our way swiftly to the pub.

As planned, Bob stayed in the car, whilst Gus, Philip and I lingered in the pub garden. We couldn't sit down due to the bad weather. "I hope they're on time," said Gus. "I don't fancy standing here for too long."

"Don't worry, no one is looking at us," I said, but my gut feeling was we did look odd standing in the pub garden when it was pissing down with rain.

If the landlord got suspicious, he could phone the Old Bill. It would look more bizarre the longer we were standing out in the pouring rain in the empty pub garden, and if the van was longer than anticipated, we would be overstaying our welcome in the pub. We wanted it to be as inconspicuous as possible. I didn't too much like drawing any attention to us whatsoever and it was beginning to look like that might just happen. I understood Gus' anxiety; the lead-up to a robbery can take over your nerves. All sorts of shit runs through your head. If the van was late, we could either pull out or hang around and we would have to make that judgement call when the time came. But the time was going slowly and every minute the van was late, felt like an hour. I hated the waiting part; I was impatient and was always desperate to get the job over and done with.

Gus and I had a sawn-off shotgun, heavy pieces of metal hanging down under our arm, held by a loop of string under our raincoats. By this point in our career, we had mastered the art of concealing weapons and carrying them without anyone noticing.

I glanced over at Bob in the car and raise my eyebrows, signalling this could all fall apart if the van was late. He shrugged, and I knew time was now against us. I could feel the tension in the air getting a little thicker and I was almost ready to pull out and say,

"Let's go home."

Then suddenly, to my relief, the van pulled in, making its way to the factory gates, a little late but the main thing was it had arrived.

"Thank fuck for that," Gus muttered.

We waited until the van disappeared into the factory yard before getting into the car. Bob drove towards the factory slowly; timing was everything. We had all our robbing gear on and were ready to pull the balaclavas over our faces. As we drew nearer to the factory, the same van drove back past us and it never gave us a second glance. Bob sped up and swung into the yard outside the offices. The guard had left his post; instead of manning the entrance he had wandered off to see what was going on in the office, rather than doing his guard duties. I remember he saw our balaclava'd heads appear and a look of pure panic swept over his chubby face; he seemed to freeze in time. But before he could think or move, Gus was out of the car shouting, "On the ground! On the fucking ground!"

The guard took one look at the menacing barrel of the shotgun and dived to the floor without a second thought. Philip and I burst into the office; their startled faces wore a look of complete shock and horror. They were petrified, quivering with their hands rigid in the air.

I pointed the gun and shouted, "Stay where you are, anyone move a muscle and I will shoot!"

A woman let out a scream, but they remained motionless on the spot. Philip ran to the counter, scooping up the bag with grace. We ran outside and jumped in the car. Bob stepped on the accelerator, full throttle, and we sped away, leaving dust whirling in the air behind us. I turned and looked out of the back window and caught a glimpse of white faces, peeping out of the office window and the guard stumbling to his feet. Bob slowed down as we neared the main road, and we took our balaclavas off with a sigh of relief. There were a couple of women behind our car, carrying shopping bags full of groceries. They were chatting away, which kept us waiting a few minutes, but they didn't notice us at all. They were fully immersed in their own world. People miss a lot of what goes on around them, too concerned about themselves. We got into the second car and now we could relax a little more. My body became more relaxed and my mind less tense. The pressure of pulling off a successful robbery was now over. We drove back to South London at normal speed.

Philip said, "That was fucking easy, that guard shit himself when Gus put the gun on him."

"How did it go in the office?" Gus asked. I knew he wanted to know if we had secured the bag or not.

"No problem, I pointed the gun at everyone and, whilst they were all looking at me, Philip grabbed the bag without a problem."

"It was less stressful without all the coshes and the ammonia," said Gus.

"No doubt about it. Shooters are the best use for our line of work." I was confident shooters were the way forward.

We all nodded and that is how my career as an armed robber took off. The whole process was easier because no one wants to get shot, no one is going to struggle with you or try to disarm you. They would be really fucking stupid if they tried.

Bob drove to Elephant and Castle to Gus's flat. We trudged into the kitchen and Gus made us all a nice cuppa. We counted the money, and it came to about four grand each. They were slightly disappointed as they expected more. I looked around at the firm in disbelief; they were getting greedy and expecting too much.

"I don't know what you're moaning at, it's better than working for a living."

It felt like, sometimes, we forgot what real hard graft was. Four grand in an hour; some people would work months for that and have nothing to show for it.

After their initial disappointment faded, we planned a night out, as we normally did after a robbery. We all had a good night up the West End.

"I fancy a good drink after a solid, hard day's work," I laughed.

Once a robbery had been executed, there was always this wave of relief. Firstly that it had gone well and we had secured the cash and, secondly, that we had managed to get away without any problems.

We became a tight firm; we worked well together and partied just as good. We soon came to realise how easy armed robbery was, so we robbed anything worth robbing; jewellery stores, banks post offices, you name it, and any town or place possible. It gave us a lavish lifestyle. I would buy expensive suits at Fred Terry's shop opposite Old Street Station and at Stanley's in Shepherd's Bush, where a lot of film and TV stars used to shop and hang out. It was the place to be and be seen at the time, and we were rubbing shoulders with many well-connected people. I even bought many a different style of car, which used to give me a great buzz when I drove around. I felt invincible and free. I became a regular up the West End, cruising around the nightclubs, having a blast. I would try and pull as many birds as possible, but I never flashed my money around. Some people would show off and be eccentric; I, on the other hand, preferred to keep a low profile.

Philip moved around a lot. At this point, he lived with his wife and daughter in a nice flat at the top of Stanford Hill and used to gamble his money on the horses. He had a terrible addiction to gambling; he could never get enough of a good bet and, when you start to lose, it becomes a vicious cycle, that you can't seem to get out of. Because of this, he was always short of money and always relied on me to find the work. His gambling addiction became out of control. The more money he made, the more he gambled. It was like a drug addiction for him, and I could see it became a burden for him towards the end. Like a weight getting heavier and heavier, but I suppose any addiction will do that to you over time. To be honest, I didn't mind finding the work. It was good for me, as it kept my mind active, and I always got a buzz off finding a new venture. I loved a challenge; as long as we were thorough in our planning, there was no way of us getting caught. A watertight plan made me content with going ahead with any job.

We carried on for over a year; we would go, five of us in one car. We loved doing bank jobs.

I would run in with a shotgun and scream, "Everyone down or I will shoot!"

This got their attention, and the staff and customers would all look at each other with pure panic and confusion. The firm would go behind the counter and empty the tills; in and out, as quick as you can. If I didn't feel like the bank staff or customers were abiding by my every word, I would let off a shot into the ceiling as a warning not to try anything stupid. Because the ceilings were made cheap polystyrene, the shot would rain down the white stuff like snow; it was fantastic to watch. I was warning them, there was no point in being a hero in these situations. Just let us get on with the job in hand. Once we had secured the bag of money, we would run out together and go down the side street, jump in the car and make a swift exit to the next get-away vehicle. We became pros; it was like breathing air to us, we knew how to execute a robbery to the finest detail. The only thing we made sure of, that was paramount and was an iron-fisted rule, was not to shoot anybody. Only if you had to, if there was no choice; then in extreme circumstances do it in the leg, and avoid the main artery at all costs. We were never looking to kill anyone. We set out with guns to be only a deterrent, and a scare tactic. Unfortunately, sometimes things don't go to plan...

CHAPTER 12

MITCHAM DAIRY FACTORY ROBBERY

We used to have regular meet-ups in a small drinking club in Ladbroke Grove, Notting Hill. It was an ambient club with soft lighting, which gave it an intimate atmosphere, making you feel more relaxed and at ease in people's company. They must have made it that way on purpose, as I always felt chilled and in the zone when I sat down. The club knew how to create an inviting atmosphere, with pockets of dark and light, to set the tone for the evening. It was normally a cosmopolitan crowd, which meant there was never any trouble, only punters looking for a good night to let their hair down. A mixture of small-time actors, models, musicians and local villains, who never wanted to draw attention to themselves. You never got any trouble and was an ideal place for a quiet meet.

One night when I entered the club, I spotted the firm sitting around a table in a quiet corner, deep in conversation. I bought myself a large drink and went over and joined them.

"What's up?" I said. "I hope you haven't dragged me here for nothing."

I was in a bit of a bad mood and wasn't up for socialising. Tonight, I was tired, and my wife was wanting to spend some quality time with me. It was just one of those nights where I was not in the mood for partying.

But I could see something was afoot.

Bob grinned and said, "I've fallen on a good bit of work. I was driving through Mitcham, and I spotted a van turning into a small lane leading into this dairy. So, I stopped the motor, got out and hung about for a while. After about ten minutes, it came back up the lane and drove away. So, I went down and gave my eyes a good chance. At the end of the lane was a large factory. It was the head office of the Royal Arsenal Co-operative Society Dairy. The dairy itself is huge. It must take plenty of money for their wages, even without all the milkmen's takings-in, and I think it's worth looking at."

"How much do you think it comes to, Bob?" asked Gus.

Bob hesitated, pursed his lips in and had a good think before saying, "It could come to roughly forty grand, give or take."

Bob now had our full attention. This was a big job and I got excited at the prospect of that much cash.

"What time was it when you saw the van?" asked Gus.

"About six o'clock," Bob replied. "If we could get in position as the van arrives, then as the van leaves, we can steam in and nick the money without too much trouble."

We all looked at each other. It sounded like a good bit of work.

"Let's all go over there tomorrow and look for ourselves," I said with some excitement in my voice.

Gus agreed and said, "Let's make our own way over to Mitcham Green and meet at midday."

"Sounds good to me," I replied. The deal was sealed, we had a few drinks, and began eyeing up the talent.

"There's a couple of birds over at the bar. Let's ask them over for a drink." Gus nodded towards their direction.

"No, not for me, not tonight, I'm going home. I promised Pat I wouldn't be too long, I'll see you tomorrow." I left promptly to go home. I wasn't in the mood, which was probably a good thing, as my wife was waiting for me.

The next day, we all arrived at Gus' flat, and made our way to Mitcham Green. We walked around the outside of the dairy to study the layout. Mitcham is classed as London; even though it is technically part of the city, it's more of a leafy part of town, a lot quieter, not much hustle and bustle and less noise. The factory was situated at the end of a narrow approach road on the right-hand-side by the factory gates. There were wide open, and there was a small hut, occupied by an elderly uniformed guard. He obviously checked visitors, along with all the lorries and cars going in and out of the dairy.

"Is this the only entrance?" I asked Bob.

"Yes," he replied. "You have a school running along one side and that's it. "

"Are the gates always open?" Philip inquired.

"As far as I know, the gate is always open," Bob responded with confidence.

"But you're not one hundred percent sure?" Philip pressed.

"The best thing to do," I said, "is come here regularly and check what happens, there's no rush."

We all agreed this was the best course of action to take; taking our time with this job should pay off. We then went our separate ways.

Over the next few days, me and Bob studied the routine with immense precision. As far as we could see, all the gates were always left open and, when any vehicles arrived, the guard always waved them in, without checking them, which included the wages van. We could tick the gates off as a guarantee of always being open.

We couldn't see where the wages office was because it was obscured behind a long brick building. I suggested it was time for the firm to have a meeting to discuss some important details that needed to be sorted out. We met at my flat and sat in the kitchen, drinking tea. I began to explain that someone would have to go right inside the factory and find out exactly where the cashier office was situated. Once we knew the location, we could steam in once the van left. We all agreed this was the best thing to do. Not only did we have to find out where the office was, we also had to find out how many office staff worked there. We also needed to make sure there weren't any reinforced doors or obstacles in our way.

Once this was done, there was no reason why the raid shouldn't take place. So, I said I would sort out a get-away route, after which they could all come and see if they thought the route was viable. Everyone agreed and we went about our business. Working out the route was one of my strong points and I always enjoyed finding the shortest and most discreet route back.

Over the next few days, I strolled around, giving my eyes a chance to see if there was something I had missed. Going back to your targeted robbery a few times before you pull it off, gives you a chance to spot something you could have missed and potentially be detrimental to the job. I discovered that running alongside the factory was a quiet dimly-lit residential lane, which had a school. As far as I could see, the playground backed directly onto the factory's yard. Things were looking promising, as an idea began to form, and a plan of action was starting to take shape. That evening, I returned to the school with Bob. He kept watch while I clambered over the iron fence and ran across the playground. I discovered the school toilets also backed onto the factory's yard. I decided to climb onto the roof of the toilets and found I had a clear view of the cashier's office. I couldn't believe our luck; the only obstacle was a low brick wall. Only five feet high, which divided the school from the factory. All we had to do was cross the playground and lie on the toilet roof, where we would wait for the arrival of the van and the cash to be delivered.

Once the cash had been delivered, we could jump over the wall, cross the yard, steam into the office, take the money and return the same way. That way, we wouldn't have to drive past the guard. He wouldn't know what had happened until it was too late. It seemed like a perfect plan. I retraced my steps, climbed over the railings, and Bob and I walked down the lane, back and forth to get a good feel of the place. All was quiet; the residential houses had their curtains pulled firmly across the windows, blocking the view. At the end of the lane, there was a row of garages on the left-hand-side. We could park the get-away car there. I noticed there was a railway line running along the lane, which had a small footbridge for pedestrians to cross over to the other side. Once over the bridge, you came out to a completely different road. We crossed the bridge and turned left into the main road. After a ten-minute walk, we saw a small crescent on the left-hand-side, leading off the main road. In the crescent, we could see there was a space to park the second get-away car and it could not be seen from the main road at all. Better still, there was a narrow passage-way leading directly into a pub car park, where we could park the third car, the last car ready to drive away. It was one of the best get-away routes I had ever found. I was over the moon with it; such a clean and easy escape, it felt impossible for anything to go wrong. I was quietly confident this would be one of our most successful robberies to date.

Bob drove me home and I asked him to tell the firm to come round to mine and sort the final information out before we went ahead. When he left, I had a good drink. I was celebrating the plan and was rather pleased about going ahead with the dairy job. I relaxed with Pat and my son, with the comfort that a large amount of money was coming our way. As far as I was concerned, it seemed like a lucrative opportunity and a good day's work.

A couple of days later, we all met up at my flat to discuss the layout of the office. One of us had to gain access to the cashier's office. To make sure we could get in easily and with no fuss, I suggested I should go in and say I was looking for a job as a lorry driver and pretend to enter the cashier's office by mistake. All I needed was a couple of minutes to have a look around and remember the layout. So, one morning, I decided to do just that. I dressed in some smart clothes and walked slowly down the road leading to the factory gates. As I walked by the gate lodge, I caught a glimpse of the guard, drinking a large mug of tea. He gave me a peculiar look; maybe they didn't get many visitors walking past on foot. But he didn't seem to care about me being there and he carried on drinking his tea, minding his business. He must have thought I was an employee. I walked through the factory gates, turned left past the brick building, then right and walked the short distance to the cashier's office. A short flight of steps led to a wooden door and I examined the locks. That was no problem; give it a good boot and they would fly open.

The security of this place is awful, I thought to myself, how has this place not been robbed yet? I don't know!

I passed through the wooden door and found myself in a small passage. To my right was another set of wooden doors, which led into the office. The locks and doors were flimsy; even if they were locked, we could still crash through them on the night. Anyway, I pushed the door open and entered the cashier's office. The first thing I saw was a long wooden counter, topped with a four-foot metal grill. It could easily be climbed over. On the right-hand-side, there was another door that gave entry to the staff. Once again, it was secured by an ordinary Yale lock. If needed, we could smash through it, no trouble. As you know, my expertise with Yales comes from my stint as a drummer and, as always, knowing about locks came in handy. Directly behind the wire grill was a long wooden table running down the office and, standing against the left-hand wall, there were three medium-sized safes.

A woman approached me and said, "Can I help you, sir?" A helpful look swept over her red, round face.

With a smile, I responded, "Yes, can you direct me to the personal manager's office, please? I have a job interview today."

She smiled and, with an animated expression, she said, "You're in the wrong office. If you turn left and walk across the yard, you'll see a green door. That's the office you want." I thanked her and left.

As I walked towards the gate, I looked across the yard. Directly opposite were the school toilets, just behind the dividing wall of the school and the factory yard. We would have a clear line of sight into the cashier's office. It was looking better and better. I left the way I came and drove myself back to my flat with a big grin on my face. The route was perfect, the floor plan was immaculate; it felt like a dream robbery.

Once again, the firm and I got back together to discuss the final details. With a robbery like this, every detail needed to be ironed out and everyone needed to know the step-by-step plan. Otherwise, things could go wrong and this one was going to be big money, so I was keen to get it right. Once again, we were back in my kitchen, finalising the details.

We all agreed that using three cars for the robbery made sense. We would have to steal them and then replace them. On the night of the robbery, we would put two of them into position and we would be ready to go to work. Robbers of our calibre didn't much like stealing cars. However, this was paramount for the job in hand. We agreed three of us would steal the cars; Bob, Gus and I volunteered to find and provide the cars. Philip would go and replace them afterwards. We then turned to the question of who would do what on the night. Bob said he would go into the office. It was a funny thing, as there was a slight hesitation in the conversation; it was in my mind to say I'd stay by the car. I must have had a fleeting premonition that the minder would be important. But then I changed my mind and said I would go with Bob, and Philip said he would go into the office too. This would leave Gus, who was the biggest, to frighten off any workers who wanted to play the hero. Once everyone knew their job, all we needed was three cars; one for the four of us to use to get over to Mitcham, one car to leave on the other side of the foot bridge and one to be left in the pub's car park. Once we got to the car park, we would be home and dry. Old Bill wouldn't have a clue where we were.

"I'll drive you home," I said. They all agreed. "I will nick one car, Bob another and Gus will do the third. Philip can replace them and stash them away in the garages. Now, don't fuck about; get the motors quickly," I told them in a bossy tone.

I've always been the type to want to get a task over and done with, as quickly as possible. I never liked leaving anything to the last minute. If things were not done on time, I was likely to pull out. If we are not organised and everything was slapdash, I didn't want any part of it.

The next morning, I went over and nicked a Ford Cortina from a car park in West London. I drove it to one of our four garages and told Philip to replace it straight away. He assured me he would.

Bob stole a big Rover, so now we had two cars. One more to go! A couple of days passed, and we still hadn't got the third car. We all knew Gus could be lazy at times, and it was bugging me that he hadn't got off his arse to get one. I felt like going out and getting the car myself.

But I thought, fuck it, it's his responsibility. Let him do it.

I waited till Thursday and then went to see him, albeit in a salty mood. "The firm are waiting on you to get the third car. If you fail to deliver, we can't go to work. Saturday's nearly here and, if that happens because you're too lazy to nick a car, you'll be off the firm." I was in no mood to pussy-foot around my annoyance with him. "We're friends, but this is business, don't fuck about. Get a motor."

Gus could see I was seriously pissed off and promised he wouldn't let me down. Looking back, I should have nicked the car myself, but it's easy to think those kinds of things in hindsight.

He finally, after much pushing, managed to get a motor, an Austin Westminster.

"Well done," I said. "Where did you nick it from?" I wanted to get an idea of how he acquired such a car.

"I didn't nick it," Gus replied. "It belonged to another firm. They nicked and replaced it, but the work fell through, so I took it off their hands."

I wasn't too pleased at what he had done; normally, I would say dump it and get your own car. This was sloppy work, and I could feel my impatience running at an all-time high. But the work was going down the next day. So, I shrugged in exasperation.

"Alright, take it to the garage and wipe it down for other people's prints and we will have to use it."

This decision, although at the time I had no idea, would cost me dearly and haunts me to this day...

CHAPTER 13

THE AUSTIN WESTMINSTER AND THE LUGER

We arranged to pick up the cars and guns at five-thirty on Saturday night. I took my wife and son out shopping on the Saturday afternoon. We came home, had a light lunch and relaxed for the rest of the day. At six, I changed into dark clothing and put my shoulder holster on. I was meant to be armed that night, as it was my job to carry the money. I checked my forty-five automatic gun to see if it was in full working order. I stuffed a pair of leather gloves and a balaclava into my pockets. I had decided to carry a gun just in case it would be needed. Although I didn't have to, as Gus would be carrying a Second World War Luger and Bob had had a thirty-eight revolver. So, we had plenty of fire power. We had no intention of using it, but it was there, ready, if needs must.

When it was time to go, I kissed my wife and son goodbye.

"What time will you be home?" asked Pat. She always worried about my nightly escapades.

"Around eight," I replied.

"What would you like for dinner?" She was always attentive to my needs.

"I wouldn't mind a nice beef curry for dinner," I replied with a cheeky wink. I could see she had a look of anguish on her face.

"Take care of yourself," Pat said. I knew she was concerned, as she always worried about me.

I nodded and grinned and said, "Don't worry, I will be alright," and hurried downstairs.

Bob was waiting for me in the Cortina, ready to drive us to

Mitcham, both now in the zone and preparing ourselves for the night ahead.

"It's a good night for it," Bob said.

A light rain had started to fall, typical for a November night. This weather suited me fine; the rain and cold normally had people cooped up indoors, which was great for us. He drove me to the garage where the Westminster was stored. Bob would drive home and I would follow him to his flat, where the other two would be waiting. The Rover was parked round the corner from Bob's flat. We went inside, where Gus and Philip were waiting for us.

As we went in Bob's wife said, "Do you want a cup of tea?"

"No thanks, I'm alright," I replied.

I wasn't in the mood for idle chit-chat. I was in the zone, preparing myself for the robbery. I didn't want any distractions and small talk just before the robbery would cloud my thoughts.

"Right," Bob said, "let's go."

We left his flat and walked round the corner, where the cars were waiting. Bob and Gus got into the Cortina and Philip drove the Westminster. I would follow behind in the Rover. We were all fully prepared and ready to roll.

It was a dark and chilly November evening. The fine rain kept falling, but we could see clearly on the drive. Once we all had the cars nicely in their position, we all got into the Cortina and drove the short distance to the school. When we arrived, we parked outside the school gates. The rain-swept lane was deserted. I noticed all the windows had their curtains drawn to keep out the draft of the chilly wind and cold air. Most likely, the residents were at home with their heating on, settling in for the night. Most likely, they were watching the television after a hard week earning an honest crust. We got out of the car and had final one look around, then quickly clambered over the black iron railings and ran across the school playground to the toilets. We climbed onto the roof and lay quietly. By this time, it was seven in the evening. From our vantage point, we could see clearly into the office windows. The door of the safe was open, waiting for the arrival of the money.

We could see three clerks sitting around, also waiting patiently, stuck in their normal monotonous routine. I remember the rain soaking into the back of my jacket and I started to feel cold, damp and uncomfortable.

For fuck's sake, hurry up and get here, I thought.

I was carrying an empty mail bag to put the money in. This made me chuckle, as I had sewn enough of these in my time. Bob joked about the bag, that it could possibly be one that any one of us had sewn in prison, which gave the situation an ironic twist. We saw the glow of headlights and the van swung slowly round the corner of the long brick building and came to a stop outside the office.

One of the guards got out and banged on the side of the van and, a few seconds later, two bags of cash were handed to him. The guard walked quickly through the doors into the office and one of the clerks took the bags and signed for them. The bags then went out of sight and the driver got back into the van and drove slowly away. We waited for a short time for the van to leave, as we readied ourselves to jump into the yard. Two workers came out of the office building, one with a billy can of tea. They sat down, poured their tea out, lit cigarettes and began to chat amongst themselves. We exchanged looks of dismay. I couldn't believe it; of all the times for them to take a break, it was now. We slid down the roof onto the ground.

"What shall we do?" Philip asked.

I wasn't quite sure; we were all so prepared, but we hadn't planned for this. All I knew was I was soaking wet and had extreme bollock-ache. I fancied pulling out and coming back next Saturday. I had this nagging feeling that would be the right thing to do.

"What do you reckon?" I asked Bob.

He said, "Well, we're here, so we may as well carry on."

Philip nodded and Gus said, "We may as well drive straight in and do the business."

Three against one, so I didn't voice my doubts, but I could see the boys were keen and, if they all thought it was a good idea to go ahead, then I would follow suit.

"What about the guard?" I questioned.

"Fuck the guard," said Gus. "By the time he gets his act together, we will be on our way out."

"Come on then, we might as well do it, now we're here." I wanted to get out of the wet, get it done and dusted. I was starting to feel mind-numbingly cold.

We ran across the playground, over the railing and piled into the Cortina. Gus was staying outside as he was behind the wheel. He drove to the top of the lane, then right again as we sped towards the factory gates. As we pulled our balaclavas down over our faces, we passed the guard; he looked up in surprise and came to the door of his hut. Gus turned right, drove past the brick building and jerked to a halt. Philip, Bob and I leapt from the car and rushed into the office. While Philip and Bob threatened the clerks, I seized the top of the grill to pull myself over and the entire frame came away. I slung it to one side. The clerks behind the counter stared at us with a mixture of fear and astonishment.

"Get down on the floor and no one will get hurt!" I thundered.

They all complied and threw themselves mercilessly at the floor. Things were going well; the civilians were being compliant, which always made the job easier.

"Where's the money?"

"It's in the back," one clerk bawled. She was half crying, so her voice was distorted.

I thought she said, 'It's in the bag', so I raced over to the table, where a bag was sitting, but there was only a few quid in it. I stared at it for a split-second in shock, thinking, what the fuck is going on? I didn't have the chance to ask the clerk where the actual money was, as next thing I knew, I heard a shot from outside. I looked up and Gus came bursting in, all flustered.

"Everybody out, everybody out!" he shouted. "I've just shot someone in the yard."

Philip and Bob immediately ran outside, and I grabbed the

bag and started making my way to where the rest of the money was.

But Gus screamed, "Leave it, let's go!"

I had no choice but to follow him. When I got outside, I could see the shape of a man. As I drew nearer, I could see him lying face up on the tarmac. He wasn't moving. I remember the rain falling on his upturned face and a large pool of blood spreading in all directions from the back of his head, diluting on the rain-soaked tarmac. It was a sight to behold, and fear spread thought my body; I literally had chills travel along my spine. I turned towards our car.

What the fuck has Gus done? I thought.

I heard an engine and saw a lorry coming towards us. I saw Gus take aim before firing another shot at the driver. The bullet drilled a hole in the lorry's windscreen. The driver threw himself sideways. But I could see he hadn't been shot and the lorry jerked to a halt. We piled into the Cortina and roared out of the factory, past the guard's box. Gus skidded to the left and left again to the garages. He then brought the car to a quiet stop. We leapt out of the car and ran across the footbridge, pulling our masks off as we rushed to get into the Westminster. I drove quickly to the crescent and coasted to a standstill outside the houses. We got out and closed the doors quietly, then walked at a quick pace through the alley to the third car. We got into the Rover and drove away. None of us had spoken, but one thought was on all our minds. Silent, in disbelief, how had it all gone wrong?

Gus broke the silence. "Did you get the money, John?"

"I never had time, you pulled us out so fast, I just grabbed what I could," I answered, still in shock.

"What about the guy?" Philip asked. "Do you think he's dead?"

"Oh, he's dead alright. You can be sure of that," I replied. The image of his face kept popping into my head, like flashes of light I couldn't turn away from.

I remember Philip's face turning white and he shook his head in disbelief. The atmosphere in the car was awful; you could cut it twenty times over with a knife.

"What makes you think he's dead, John?" Bob asked, his tone telling me he was hoping I was wrong.

"He wasn't moving. If he had been alive, he would have been wriggling around on the floor or screaming out in agony."

No one said a word. If it was possible, our mood was even grimmer and the journey to Bob's flat went by in complete silence. You could have heard a pin drop in the car. As the end of our journey to Bob's flat drew closer, our situation started to sink in. We got to Bob's kitchen to sort out whatever money there was.

Bob had come full circle and the situation was now real; he now had his thinking cap on. "I want all the guns and I'll make sure they disappear."

"I'll take care of the guns, Bob," I said. "That way, I will know they are gone for good." I took a shopping bag and stuffed the guns inside. "Make sure you burn all your clothes and shoes as quickly as you can." I was now only thinking about destroying all the evidence.

"What does the money come to?" Gus asked, doubtful there would be much at all.

Bob pulled a face, before saying, "It comes to about a grand apiece."

I shook my head. "All this aggro for a poxy grand." I couldn't believe it. I was fuming inside but kept myself calm. "Tell me, Gus, why did you shoot him?" I glared at him, waiting intently for a response.

"Well, he came round the corner, I shouted at him to stay where he was, but he kept on walking towards me, so I fired a shot in his direction, and he went down."

I just wanted to scream at Gus for what he had done. He could have fired a warning shot or just got hold of him or shot him in the bloody leg. Why the head? But I realised, what was the point of telling him? There was no point; what was done was done.

"The important thing to do is not get ourselves nicked. The best thing to do for now is split up and keep our heads down and live quietly for a while. And whatever you do, don't tell your wives.

I know it's going to be hard enough without them panicking, with what could come after this. Do you all understand?" They all nodded; it was paramount nobody said a word, not to anyone.

"But there's one last thing. I'm worried about the Westminster. I fancy going back and taking It away," I told them. In my head, that Westminster was a problem, and my gut wasn't sitting right with it at all. "What do reckon?"

Bob said, "Supposing the Old Bill have got the motor under observation, to see if anyone comes to move it away."

Despite this opinion, I still fancied going back for the car. It was the worst decision I ever made, and had a disastrous effect on all of us. Instead of going to get the car, a seed of doubt grew like a rose bush in my mind and I decided to leave the Westminster exactly where it was.

"Who's going to dump the Rover?" I inquired.

"I'll do it," Gus volunteered.

"Ok, make sure it's cleaned out and dumped far away and no one sees it. Don't fuck this up, as we could come unstuck on this. They could hang the lot of us." I couldn't believe I was saying all this; the whole night was becoming a raging nightmare. The looks on their faces showed they understood how serious this was. I said, "If anyone has a problem, phone straight away and we will meet at the Manor House pub in Green Lane in Haringey. I will take the guns and get rid of them now."

And with that, I picked up the bag of guns and my grand and left. With a sigh of exhaustion and distress, I made my way home. I thought to myself, the best thing to do is throw the bag of guns in the Thames. I thought, not now, I will do it tomorrow and I will throw them off one of the bridges. I didn't want to make any hasty decisions; I was still in shock and wasn't thinking properly.

I remember driving home after this disastrous robbery; my mind was racing, mostly hoping and praying that, by some miracle, the shot man wasn't dead. There would be an intensive investigation by the police, but then if he was dead, it would be a different story. They would go flat out to find us, leaving no stone unturned, and it would be a hanging offence, without question. Eventually, I arrived home. I left the guns in the boot of the car, took the chump change out of the glove compartment and went inside. My son was asleep in his bed and Pat was watching the telly.

"Hello," she said, "I've made you a nice curry. I'll go and get it."

She pottered off into the kitchen. Normally, I would be starving hungry after a job; she knew my routine and was always ready to make a fuss of me when I got back. I poured myself a large brandy, slumped into my armchair and tried to compose myself. I didn't want Pat to have any suspicion that something was wrong. Pat came into the lounge with a tray and a healthy-sized plate of beef curry. I must confess, the last thing I wanted was anything to eat. But to keep in theme with my normal routine, I managed to force it down. God knows how I did; I felt sick to my stomach, my throat was throbbing in my mouth. After I finished, I went into my son's bedroom. I remember looking down at his angelic, sleeping face and thinking, I wish I had your worries, I wish I was you right now. I managed to make small talk with Pat until the ten o'clock news came on. The robbery was the main topic, but all they said was a man was shot during an armed raid in Mitcham. It went on to describe what took place. But all it said was a man was shot; it didn't say whether he was dead or alive.

My wife's eyes were burning into the side of my face, and her glare didn't leave me. "Was that you, John?"

I replied as confidently as I could, "No, it's nothing to do with me. Don't worry yourself." I got up and said, "I'm going for a bath." I was trying to act as normally as I possibly could.

I had to have some time on my own and process everything. I was overwhelmed and couldn't manage staying in the room any longer with Pat, pretending I was ok. My stomach was in absolute knots; the reality of what we had done was sinking in thick and fast and I couldn't see the light at the end of the tunnel.

I spent a restless night in bed, tossing and turning, not sleeping at all. I rose early on Sunday morning and walked the short distance to the local newsagents. I was praying that he was alive. I was wishing it with all my heart and soul. But the first thing I saw was the headline in the News of the World, on the front page in bold large writing: "A man was shot dead during a raid on a Dairy." It was to become known as the infamous Mitcham Dairy Murder. I bought a copy but never read all of it. I didn't see the point; he was dead and that was all that mattered. When I arrived home, I put the newspaper in the rubbish bin so Pat wouldn't read it.

The realisation of what had happened swept over me, that I was in terrible trouble and full of dread and worry. For the rest of the day, every time the news came on, I managed to switch it over to another channel. I waited until it got dark and drove to Blackfriars Bridge to go and dump the guns. Before I did, I put some gloves on and cleaned the guns, paying real attention to the murder weapon. I removed the magazine, took the bullets out and put all the guns into a holdall. When I arrived at Blackfriars, I parked the car and waited until there was no traffic, then threw all the guns and bullets as far as I could into the Thames. I stood there and watched them disappear into the murky depths of the river. I would burn the holsters and clothes later. I thought of the future; at the time, I had quite a bit of money. So, I had no worries about finances; my main concern was to keep my wife from learning about what had happened. It wouldn't be easy, but I had no choice. She couldn't know anything.

A few days passed and she noticed things had changed. She asked where the firm was, and I told her we are taking a bit of a break. After that, she kept quiet about them. But I could see her growing suspicion. I had a pal who lived in Tottenham; he was a scrap metal dealer, who travelled around North London with a horse and cart, doing the best he could to get by. I decided to approach him and offered to buy him a lorry and start working with him. He jumped at the chance. With a lorry, you can get a lot more work done. I bought a decent second-hand lorry and I started working in the scrap metal business. Of course, it was all for appearance's sake and to help me keep my mind off things.

A couple of weeks later, Gus phoned me and said he must see me as quickly as possible. I knew without being told that something serious had happened. I phoned back and arranged to meet him in a shady pub on the Walworth Road at two o'clock. I arrived early and bought a drink, making it a double and waited patiently for him.

When he appeared, I could see he was worried. "What's up?" I asked.

"Philip has been nicked." Gus had been to see Philip's wife and she confirmed that he had been arrested over a stolen car.

That fucking car, I thought, I knew I should have taken it away.

Gus told her to tell him to say nothing and, if he wanted, we would spring him from Brixton Prison, where he was being held on remand.

I pondered for a while and asked Gus, "What are you going to do?"

He thought for a moment and replied, "I am going to sit tight and carry on."

I nodded and said, "I will keep in touch. Take it easy."

As I drove home, I sat there thinking about the car Gus had got for the robbery. But I thought Philip would hold out, for his own good. The Old Bill wouldn't break him, and he knew the rest of us wouldn't let him down. I arrived home to find my wife in tears. The television news had been on.

"I knew something was wrong with you that night," she said.

More information had come to light, and she had finally put the missing pieces of the puzzle together.

I comforted her the best I could. "Don't worry," I assured her. "No one knows I was involved and, if the police do come, you must not say anything. Do you understand?"

She nodded; I kissed her, and we left the conversation there. I had another uneasy night, worrying about how Philip was holding up. The next morning, I drove to work, but I didn't feel right. So, I phoned around the firm and arranged a meeting at the Manor House pub in Green Lane for nine that evening. It was a miracle the meeting ever took place...

CHAPTER 14

A SAILOR'S PROMISE

At seven-thirty that night, I was sitting in my lounge watching the television, when suddenly a terrible premonition swept over me. I felt like I was in great danger.

Without thinking, I grabbed a set of car keys and said to Pat, "I'm going out. I won't be long."

I hurried down the stairs, swept into the street and took a lungful of fresh air. Panic, dread and fear infiltrated every cell of my body.

I had two cars; a Jaguar and a Ford Zodiac convertible. I looked at what set of keys I'd grabbed; I had the keys to the Ford. I got into the Ford and, as I put the keys in the ignition, a wave of policemen appeared from nowhere and rushed right past my car, carrying torches and truncheons. Some of them headed towards the rear of my flat and others surrounded the Jaguar. I didn't panic, but I couldn't believe they had missed me. I started the engine normally and looked at all the activity around me. Swarms of police were passing me, trying to enter my flat, and I sat in astonishment for a moment, staring out of the window at the scene before me. I jumped as a plain-clothes policeman rapped his knuckles on the bonnet of my car.

"Move on, move on," he barked.

They obviously didn't know I had two cars, so I drove carefully away and swung left past my flat. I could see three burly police-men standing outside my front door. This could only mean Philip had broken down and grassed everyone up. I couldn't believe he would do that; the pressure must have really broken him. All I could do was warn the others and we would all have to go on the run. I drove as fast as I could to Green Lane and parked my car down a quiet side street. I practically jogged to the Manor House pub, eager to see the firm and let them know what was happening. I'd managed to call them from a phone booth not too far from the meeting point. I made my way to the pub, thoughts buzzing through my head, trying to work out what the police knew, if they knew anything at all. There was still some time to kill before the others arrived, so I bought a drink and sat in a quiet corner facing the door, waiting patiently for Bob and Gus. They came in individually; each one could see by my face I had bad news for them. When they were all seated, I dropped my bombshell, that the heavy mob had just come and raided my flat, looking for me and I had missed them by seconds.

"It's obvious that Philip has gone and grassed. You must assume you're in the parcel as well."

"It was that fucking motor," said Gus, shaking his head with deep concern stretched across his weary face.

My eyes rested on him for a moment; he looked like a person who was tormented, not really living, just existing. I wondered, had this whole ordeal affected him more than everyone else?

"It was," I agreed. "But it's no good ranting and raving about it, it's too late for that. The best thing to do now is not go home. We can't return to our houses."

"What are you going to do?" Bob asked.

"Well, after this meeting, I'm dumping my car. I've got a pal that will put me up for the night. In the morning, I'll go and rent a flat and stay out of the way. If my face doesn't go on the telly, then I should be alright. I've got some money to collect; I'll give Pat half and, with the rest, I fancy leaving the country, never to return." I had already thought about what I was going to do on the way here, and all I could think was this was the easiest option and the only way to maintain my freedom.

I looked at the two of them; I could see they were in serious shock, as things were now looking sticky. They knew their time was up and now some big decisions needed to be made. Bob thought for a moment and spoke first.

"Well, John, I will be going on the missing list. I know someone in Southampton who I can stay with until I sort things out. I fancy going back to Ireland, out of the way there."

"Good Idea," I said. Leaving the country was probably the only option we had, and I liked that he was on the same page as me.

"I'm not sure what to do," Gus said. "I'll sit tight for a while before making any moves."

"Gus," I said, with a stern look on my face, "you're wanted for murder. If they find you, they will have you for sure. Whatever you do, don't go home."

He nodded, as if he agreed, but it felt like he was going through the motions. I had some misgivings, as he seemed like his head wasn't right. I think he was in denial about his fate. Maybe it was a coping mechanism, over dealing with committing murder. He needed to get a hold of himself; if he didn't, he was going to lose his own life and could take all of us down with him. But at the end of the day, it was his choice. Hopefully, he would make the right decision once he had processed the magnitude of our situation. There wasn't much more to talk about, so we finished our drinks. We had come to the end of the road and now it was all about survival. We left the pub, shook hands and went our separate ways. Knowing I would probably never see them again, for a moment I felt a little nostalgic, as it was an end of an era.

I drove to King's Cross and dumped my car at a block of council flats. Maybe the police would think I had left London if they found the car, by way of King's Cross railway station. Anyway, I caught the tube to Old Street station and walked the short distance to Singer Buildings, where my pal answered with a warm greeting. When he answered the door, I told him I'd had a row with my wife and that she'd slung me out.

"Can I stay the night?" I was praying he would be fine with me sleeping at his and that I hadn't caught him at a bad time. "I'll go and sweeten her up in the morning."

He started laughing. "Come on, I've got a spare bed. You'll sort it out with her, mate, not to worry."

We sat in front of the television, catching up over missed time and chatting casually. We were having a drink and a laugh until the twelve o'clock news came on. The first segment of the news was about the police raiding a flat in London. It said the man they were seeking was wanted for questioning about the Dairy Mitcham Murder. He was believed to be armed and dangerous. They continued to warn the public no to approach him.

My pal nodded towards the television. "He's in terrible trouble. If they catch him, they'll top him, that's for sure."

"What do you think will happen to them?" I said, trying to be as nonchalant as possible.

"They will all hang for this, for sure." He shook his head in dismay.

My stomach gave a lurch when he said that. I asked him for another stiff drink and made my excuses that I was tired. After that conversation, I needed to be on my own, so I bade him good-night and went to bed, and to my surprise, I went straight to sleep.

I rose early in the morning, had a quick cup of tea, thanked my pal and left with haste. I decided to rent a flat in Earl's Court; at the time, it was an area full of students and always had plenty of bedsits available. A stranger wouldn't be noticed. I checked my money; I had about eight hundred on me, enough to get me started, until I could arrange to get some more. I could make It last. I would have to.

I took the tube to Earl's Court and bought a local newspaper. I flicked through it and found an advertisement for a basement flat in Philbeach Gardens, just around the corner from Warwick Road Tube station. Philbeach was a picturesque, tree-lined crescent, and I quite fancied myself living in this area. After arranging the viewing, I walked slowly along, looking for the number of the flat I was going to view. I rang the bell; the landlord answered the door and showed me the small basement flat. I noticed the kitchen windows looked straight out onto the railway lines that ran through West London. If I needed, I would have a ready-made escape route, which was handy. I paid three months' rent in advance and then went straight out and bought myself some pots and pans and rented a television to keep me company. What I intended to do was to stay indoors during daylight hours and only go out under the cover of darkness. It was the terrible winter of 1962, which helped me cover up and float about London in disguise. I used to wear a duffle coat with a scarf wrapped around my neck and a cap pulled down over my face. I felt I was reasonably safe from recognition. But it was a lonely and isolating existence; I felt like I was living in purgatory and found myself feeling depressed and with no real purpose. The Sunday papers published articles about me; I was said to be desperate, and I was believed to be armed and, according to them, I had no money.

Thankfully as of yet, no pictures of me appeared, which meant I was only known by the police and not the public, which gave me more of a chance of staying undetected. I decided to start growing a beard in case photos of me were released. I looked scruffy and downtrodden by this point; it was hard work being incognito. Money was dwindling away fast, and I now needed to access more funds. I had money at a pal's house, but I dared not go and collect it, so I recruited my brother-in-law, who lived in Streatham, to go and collect it for me. I felt like I could trust him; after all, he was family. I got in touch with him and explained the situation. I asked him to collect the money from my pal, then take half to Pat and give the other half to me. A simple request, which he happily agreed to. I told him I would give him a nice drink for his trouble. I thought the best thing to do would be to get the money delivered, so I gave him my address to deliver the money and that was one less problem I needed to worry about. At least, that's what I thought at the time.

Back in the flat, the time passed slowly. The flat next door was full of Australian students, and they used to hold late-night parties. I could hear the music as they partied the night away; they didn't know how lucky they were. I wished I had their worries. I used to think about my family, my wife and son. How they were holding up, if they were missing me. But I realised that part of my life was over. There was no point dwelling on them, as I knew I would never be able to return home again. I was thinking of ways to leave the country, the different routes and ways of leaving. The sooner the better, as far as I was concerned.

It was coming up to Christmas 1962, and I was returning to the basement flat after being out and buying some groceries from Church Street market. I turned a corner and noticed a newspaper placard, with bold writing scrawled across it. A man had been arrested in connection with the Mitcham Dairy Murder. A shock of apprehension ran through me; I bought a newspaper and, sure enough, Gus had been nicked. I knew he would keep his mouth shut for his own protection. But it was a serious blow, and I couldn't help but feel uneasy. Our luck had started to unravel, thick and fast. I had to get out of the country as quickly as I could. I had a friend named Chris, who I thought could get me out of the country; I just had to pay him a bit of money. He had been a good thief in his day but was now in poor health. I decided to phone him and arranged to meet him, in a quiet West End pub. When we met, I explained my situation.

Afterwards, he smiled and said, "You know, it's a funny thing, but I fancied you for the Mitcham turnout. Anyway, I've got a man in Liverpool who can get you away, no problem. He's a seaman, so you can't go wrong with him."

"How much will it cost me?" I was thinking I was going to have to raise a fair bit.

"Five hundred pounds," Chris said.

"No problem," I replied. For me, this was a bargain. "When do you want the money?"

"When he comes to collect you, you can give it to him yourself."

"What about you?" I asked, expecting him to take at least a drink for his trouble.

"Nothing, I'm just pleased to be able to help you." Which was kind of him, but I don't like taking favours.

"No, mate, you have to have something for your trouble." I gave him two hundred pounds, despite his protests.

After all, he now knew my predicament, so I wanted to keep him sweet. I arranged to phone him every day to check if the ship was ready and he would sort out the rest of the details. I returned to the flat a much happier man. There was now a glimmer of hope in sight, and I finally had something to look forward to.

Then it came to Christmas Eve; it was the one day I didn't bother to phone him, as I assumed everybody would be busy celebrating the Christmas festivities. I never realised that ships sailed no matter what time of the year it was. I waited until New Year before phoning again. I called Chris just after the new year, and he was excitable on the phone.

"Why didn't you phone on Christmas Eve? The sailor was with me, ready to take you to Liverpool. The ship was sailing Christmas morning for New Jersey."

I couldn't believe my bad luck; all I could do was apologise and ask him to set it up again. I had been so close to leaving the country.

I was still in touch with Bob on the odd occasion. We met outside Madam Tussaud's, and we exchanged news. I told him that I was waiting to go to America and was counting the days to start a fresh life. I had a nice few quid to get me started and I knew I would be alright. Bob said he had to leave Southampton as his pal was on bail, on a charge of receiving stolen property. Therefore, the house he was staying in was no longer a safe hideout. He was looking for somewhere to stay.

I told him, "That's no problem. You can stay at my place for now and, when I leave, you can have it." Secretly, I was pleased to finally have some company.

Bob was well pleased. "When can I move in?" he asked, eager as finding alternative shelter was a matter of urgency for him.

"Whenever you like," I responded with a smile.

"I'll come tonight," he stated without hesitation, and I gave him my address.

I could see he was over the moon and some relief swept over him; he seemed to walk a little lighter on his feet. We shook hands and went our separate ways. I was just as pleased as him that he was coming to live with me, as it had been terribly lonely, hiding out on my own. At this moment in time, everything seemed to be going well. We were as inconspicuous as we could be and I thought, in no time, I would be out of the country and a free man. Little did I know, my brother-in-law was driving about in a stolen car with false plates and, shortly, the police would arrest him. They would scare the shit out of him and, to save himself from being charged, he would make a deal and give up my address.

In the meantime, Bob arrived and made himself at home. I continued to phone Chris every day and the words I wanted to hear finally came through.

Chris said, "You're on for Thursday morning."

I was well pleased I'd finally cracked it; two more days and I'd be gone forever. I could start my new life. Full of excitement, anticipation and hope, I got myself prepared for my departure. On Wednesday evening, I was watching the telly and, to celebrate, Bob had gone out to get some fish and chips for our supper. I heard a knock at the door and got up to answer without thinking, as I thought it was Bob with our food. I rose to my feet, casually walked to the door and slowly opened it.

It crashed open with a bang, and I was forced back into my room by a rush of bodies. The flying squad came hurtling in like a hurricane, and chaos circled my calm existence. All I could hear was shouting and screaming.

"Get on the ground!"

I was given a few kicks and blows, then hauled to my feet and searched. The raid happened so quickly, I didn't have a chance to do anything. I was completely blind-sided.

One of the police looked at Bob's suitcases. "You've got a lot of luggage here," he said. "Is anyone staying with you?"

"No," I replied.

I was praying Bob would notice the carnage unfolding as he

returned with our dinner. I was then handcuffed and bundled out to a waiting police car and driven to Tooting police station. I sat in the car thinking, I am in major shit here.

At the police station, I was searched and placed into an empty room, but the door was left unlocked, and there was a uniformed policeman on guard outside. I just sat quietly and waited. After about twenty minutes, the CID officers came in and sat down.

"You know why you're here?" the officer prompted.

I made no reply.

"Who did the shooting, John?"

Again, I made no reply. This went on for about ten minutes or so, and they could see I wasn't going to talk. Then they left the room. After this, I was moved to a cell. They were obviously rethinking their approach on how to question me.

About an hour later, they returned and were now trying to coax information out of me.

"We know you're a sensible man, John. We also know you didn't do the shooting. So, you won't hang. If you help us, we'll put a good word in for you, when the time comes."

They were trying now to get me on-side, butter me up. All these games have been played before and they could see I wasn't going to bite. Their transparent tactics were a classic way of manipulating you; this could only work if you were new to the game.

"I don't know what you're talking about," I retorted.

The officer nodded and smiled. "Well, at least make a short statement, telling us the part you played in the robbery. Then afterwards you can have a hot meal and get your head down."

"I've got nothing to say until I see my solicitor," I responded, and I felt like saying, "You can stick your hot meal up your fucking arse."

At this, they gave up and left. The cell door was slammed shut and I was left alone. I guessed my brother-in-law had done the business on me. Yet, I had no idea how they'd found out; I was more worried about Bob walking into a trap. I could only hope he would smell the Old Bill. Really, it was a forlorn hope, as a couple of hours later, I could hear the sound of footsteps walking past my cell. I knew it must have been Bob and, sure enough, a short time later, my door was opened.

A plain-clothes officer informed me, "I thought you'd like to know we have nicked your mate."

He looked delighted with himself and then proceeded to slam the door shut. I was gutted that Bob had been nicked, though I realised it couldn't be helped; it was a case of bad luck. But I still felt guilty over Bob's capture. There was nothing I could say or do, to change what had happened. So, I just lay on the bed and stared at the ceiling, spending an uncomfortable night, tossing and turning, worrying what was in store for my future. My door was unlocked in the early hours of the morning. I hadn't slept well at all, as I knew my future was now well and truly hanging by a thread. I was given a mug of tea and two slices of dry toast. It was eight am by the time I had finished my breakfast, and it was a struggle to get it down me, as I felt sick with anguish. I then lay back on the bed and was deep in thought, wondering what my chances were of getting out of this mess and, after much deliberation, I knew I was royally fucked.

CHAPTER 15

"HUNG BY THE NECK"

By ten am, my door was unlocked and I was escorted by two scrawny policemen to the desk sergeant and was charged with armed robbery and being connected in the murder of a factory employee. After a brief appearance in court, I was remanded in custody, in dismal Brixton prison, to await my trial. All men charged with murder were kept in the hospital wing under constant supervision, as they were deemed vulnerable prisoners. We were watched constantly, thinking that we would end our own lives, instead of letting the penal system do it for us.

Gus was kept apart from all of us, as he was charged with the capital offence of murder and was watched even more closely, in case of any suicide attempt. He was being watched twenty-four hours a day. I could only imagine a fraction of the pain and anguish he was going through. Philip was also kept on his own for his own protection. Being a grass didn't bode well in prison and I wasn't going to be happy to see him, that was for sure. There was talk that he was taken up to the attic in Tooting police station and his head was repeatedly submerged in a water tank, until he was ready to give up the names of his accomplices. I could well believe the police were capable of such torture. But I still felt Philip should have held out. There were much worse things they could do. Bob and I were together. I apologised to him for what had happened to him, but he understood; it's just the way the game goes. He said not to worry about it, which was a relief.

After a short time of feeling sorry for myself and drowning in self-pity, I decided to pick myself up, dust off my shoulders and put up a good fight. They weren't going to take me down without me at least attempting to get a good defence together. My solicitor was busy on that. I strongly felt we were flogging a dead horse, but if I didn't try, I would always wonder, what if? The trouble about going to a trial firm-handed was that we would be dragged down by each other. But we had no other course of action we could take. This was the only way to do it. The time lagged on until the date of the trial and then the anxiety and anticipation grew stronger and stronger. All I could think about was the trial and how it would play out. It consumed my every waking moment. I wanted to get it over and done with, so I could then accept whatever was thrown at me and play out my fate. Being back in prison felt like a huge anti-climax in comparison to my getting away to another country. The new life I was yearning for was now a distant memory. I had almost had my dream getaway in my grasp, but instead, I was living my worst nightmare. All I could do was hope, but hope can be a dangerous thing. Especially when the odds are stacked against you.

One afternoon, my cell door swung open, and standing there were four hospital staff, dressed in white coats.

"Come with us, Hilton," one of them instructed. "The doctor wants to see you straight away."

Escorted from my cell to the doctor's office, bewildered and fascinated at the immediate importance of being seen by the medics, I entered. The doctor looked straight through me.

"Sit down, Hilton," he said, which I found to be strange, as normally you are not invited to sit down with any official within the prison. That would be a nod at being an equal to them.

"Would you like a cup of tea?" I found this even more odd.

"No, thanks," I answered with curiosity in my tone. I sat there, waiting for him to get to the point.

The doctor went on to say, "Are you sleeping alright?"

In my head, I thought, why do you care how I am sleeping?

"Yes," I replied. I was getting a little pissed off now and finding the charade of caring about me or any prisoners a little tedious.

He carried on with his questions of concern. "Are you eating alright?"

"Yes," I replied. I started shuffling in my seat, growing impatient.

"What about your bowel movements?" he asked. This was getting weird now.

"Quite normal," I replied. Not that it was any of the fucker's business, what my shitting habits were like.

"Right then, I want to see how much you weigh." He gestured me over to the weighing scales.

So, I got up and stepped up on the scales. I still couldn't understand what these apparent health concerns were about. The scales went to fourteen stone and one pound. He told the screw standing by the bookcase, who proceeded to write my weight down.

"Right, one last thing, just stand under the measuring ruler and let's see how tall you are."

Finding this all bizarre, I took myself to the ruler, obeying his command. I was wracking my brain furiously, trying to fathom the doctor's real intention. As I knew there was no care of the community going on here. Suddenly, the penny dropped. I was being weighed and measured in case I was sentenced to death!

I had a sudden rush of blood to the head and I couldn't control the words that came shooting out of my mouth. "You dirty bastards!" I cried out. "I haven't even been to trial yet and you're getting ready to top me!"

"Calm down, calm down," the doctor tried to reassure me. "It's only routine. We take all these details in all cases of murder. Anyway, you can go back to your cell now; we are finished here."

I was speedily escorted back to my cell and the door was banged shut behind me. I sat on my bed and tried to compose myself. I thought, fuck me, that was some serious shit. The reality that I could be sentenced to death now was looming closer and I was scared my fate was well and truly sealed. It's a funny thing but that incident really changed my perspective of trouble. I always thought, you don't know what trouble is, you mug. I suppose you could call this a defining moment in my life.

Time passed slowly in the prison. The build-up to the trial was at times unbearable; it was on my mind from morning to night and I even dreamed about it. March the 13th 1963 was our day in court. Gus, Bob and I were standing in the felon's dock at the Old Bailey. Philip had pleaded guilty so he remained in the cells below. The prosecution began to outline the case against us. I could see we had no chance of acquittal; however, our barristers had done the best they could, under the circumstances. When the judge completed his summing-up of the case, he mentioned there was no proof that I was ever in Mitcham on the night in question. Except for my own verbal admission that I was there but did not do the shooting.

According to police reports, I was supposed to have admitted to being at the robbery, whilst I was struggling with four of the flying squad at the time of my arrest. Which was absolute bollocks. Like I have said before, in those days, they allowed verbal admissions to be part of evidence in court. That's why three-quarters of armed robbers were found guilty. The courts took the view that policeman would not lie on oath. That they were honest and good men, but this couldn't be further from the truth. If anything, they were a gang in themselves, just a legal one. The policemen would always lie to get a conviction, so you had no chance up against this corrupt system.

I can still remember waiting at the bottom of the stairs that led to the dock, like it was yesterday. Waiting with fear and worry for the jury to return with their verdict.

Bob looked at me saying, "What do you think, John?"

"I reckon we will all be found guilty," I replied. Bob's face turned ashen; you could see everyone looked sick with worry. He slumped down onto the wooden bench. "Pull yourself together, Bob," I snapped. "We are going up soon." I was adamant we needed to look like we were not worried or guilty. We had to show no emotion and no guilt; what was done was done.

A short time later, the bell rang to let us know the jury was returning.

The screw told us, "Right, up you go."

We climbed the short flight of stairs leading to the court. When we entered, I was flabbergasted, as suddenly the court was crowded. Every spare inch of space was taken up by an official or a civilian, and the magnitude of this case began to set in. All eyes were on us. I scanned the sea of people and spotted a few family members and well-wishers. Everyone had come to see the show. It was a spectacle, due to the high publicity of the case, so I should have guessed it would be a theatrical ending. Everyone was watching us to see our faces; any signs of weakness to gauge our reactions. I kept my face impassive; they were not going to psychoanalyse me.

All the evidence was given, not that there was much to give. It turned out the Winchester was a big piece of the case, as we had got it off another firm, and it was already a dodgy car. Someone from the other firm had said we had used it when they were arrested, thinking that this other firm was part of the robbery. So, they were quick to give us up. I knew that car was a problem from the get-go. Never use other criminals' cars; it's a solid rule that should have been kept to. After a long and agonising wait, my anxiety was at an all-time high, and we finally got a verdict.

The clerk of the court rose to his feet. "Have you come to a verdict?" he asked the jury.

They replied, "Yes, we have." A lump rose to my throat and I felt physically sick.

"What is your verdict?"

"Guilty as charged."

I gulped; this was it, we were royally fucked.

I glanced at the firm's faces; they were all impassive, which pleased me, as they were all holding up. Stiff upper lip and all that. I looked towards the judge; his face was as impassive as the boys'. Behind him stood several officials; one was holding a bible and they were dressed in black tunics with white cravats. The judge's secretary was standing on the left-hand-side of the judge and he began unrolling a black square cloth and placed it on the judge's head.

The judge ordered Gus to step forward. He looked at him for a moment and studied his jaded face, before saying, "You have been found guilty of capital murder and quite rightly so." He went on to add, "When the jury found you guilty, they did not know of your previous convictions."

He then proceeded to read them out. It was a lengthy list of all of Gus's previous crimes. I was taken aback by this; it was unusual to read out previous convictions. It was almost as if he was justifying Gus's sentence to himself and to the audience he had before him. After all, there were many who opposed the death sentence, so maybe the judge's conscience came into play and he wanted to be able to sleep soundly at night.

"Do you have anything to say?" he inquired. "Before I pass sentence."

Gus shook his head. "I have nothing to say."

I thought, well done, Gus.

The judge continued speaking. "The sentence of the court is that you will be taken from here to a place of execution and be hung by the neck until you are dead. And may God have mercy on your soul."

I think it was Gus's wife, but I heard a quavering scream of pure agony that ran through the court like a piercing knife to the ear. The scream was shrill and blood-curdling and I felt the vibrations of it run through my body, I shuddered at her cries. It was the most harrowing sound I had heard in a long while. That scream stayed in my head for months to come. Even to this day, it pops up now and then unexpectedly, at random parts of the day.

"You may remove the prisoner," the judge ordered.

As Gus turned, I could see his face was pale, but he kept himself composed. He was escorted down the stairs to the cells. It was my turn next, and I thought, this is it, my life is now officially over.

"John Hilton, you have been found guilty of a particularly brutal murder. During this trial, I have seen that you have shown no remorse whatsoever. The sentence of this court is that you will go to prison for the remainder of your life, and if there ever comes a time for you to be considered for release, I hope the Home Secretary of the day takes into account your character and the nature of your offence."

I stood impassive as the sentence was passed; the thrill-seekers wouldn't get a change or rise out of me. I darted a quick glance to my right and saw my wife's tear-filled eyes and the sadness etched into her loving face. I felt tremendous guilt over her and how this case had affected her and my son. I had effectively changed their lives forever. The Dairy Murder seemed to have an uncontrollable ripple effect, hurting far more people than we could have imagined.

Then I was escorted down the stairs to the cells and along a dimly-lit passage to a holding cell. All the cells beneath the court room were all the same style. The bottom half was painted dark green, and the top part had whitewashed walls, etched with names and sentences of previous occupants. As the cell door clanged shut behind me, I remember staring up at the small, heavily-barred window, set high in the grubby whitewashed wall. My eyes then moved to the walls, scarred with old graffiti and the names of all the past convicts before me. As I recall, my main emotion was anger, that I was in this mess. Anger that the robbery had got so out of hand, questioning how the robbery had escalated to a man losing his life and now my friend would lose his life too. I started pacing up and down the narrow confines of the cell, until eventually I sat down on the small wooden chair and let the time pass. I wanted to escape my own mind and I just couldn't.

I sat there, thinking about my sentence; a whole life sentence. I was fucked; I would die in prison, it was as simple as that. I thought to myself, this is going to take some getting used to. But I decided I wouldn't allow this sentence to crush my spirit; I was stronger than that. I would fight back and, no matter what happened, I would survive, and that made me feel slightly better. For the remaining time in the holding cell, I sat there quietly reflecting on my life choices. Deep in thought, I travelled back in time and thought about the different paths I had taken and all the what-ifs crossed my mind. I didn't allow these thoughts to sit with me for long. If I had, I would have driven myself insane. I can't remember how long I was in the holding cell; time seemed to merge into one moment. All I remember was the door opening and I was taken outside, handcuffed once more, to await transport to one of the most depressing and grimy prisons in London; Wandsworth Prison.

CHAPTER 16

THE APPEAL

I joined the other newly-convicted prisoners bound for Wandsworth nick. Some of the other convicts of the court had already got wind of my sentence and nodded in sympathy.

"Hard luck, John boy," someone remarked.

I just shrugged and managed to squeeze out a smile. I was drained and tired and too wound up to talk. As I lingered in the corridor, I saw Bob waiting for me.

"What happened with you?" I asked. I was happy to see him.

"Same as you mate, life." We stood in silence; what a surreal moment it was.

There was nothing we could say to each other; we were both in a hopeless place. It was a dismal situation to be in. I almost wondered whether a death sentence would have been easier. I could not fathom being in prison until I died. The thought of never seeing daylight again made me shudder.

Then my thoughts turned to Gus. His sentence must have sent chills down his spine. He must have been in turmoil; a death sentence, being hung by the neck. To hear these words and have no control over your destiny must have broken him. The way I saw it, he was in purgatory. Waiting to die, knowing his life would be ending sooner rather than later must have been torturous. I really felt for him; he crossed my mind most nights when I was just left with my thoughts. In the darkness of the cell, I would replay the sentence and that dreadful scream would make me flinch.

After waiting and waiting, we were finally taken to our resting place. We were handcuffed in pairs and led to a waiting coach in the courtyard of the Old Bailey. We boarded the coach and our handcuffs were checked again. The doors of the coach were secured; it had been raining heavily as we lurched off. I could see all the shop lights reflecting in the puddles, making colourful, blurry pictures in the rain. I looked at all the cars, buses and the free people going about their business and thought to myself, well, John boy, it's going to be a fucking long time before you hit the streets again.

All too soon, we were driving along Heathfield Road and the grey, dreary walls of Wandsworth prison loomed into full view. My memories of the building were all too familiar. The huge metal studded doors waited for us, as if they were smirking as we drove in. The driver hooted his horn and we drove through, to be greeted by more steel gates, which only opened when the outer doors were closed and locked behind us. We turned left along the wall to the reception wing entrance. The coach doors were unlocked.

"Right, everybody out!" the screw bellowed.

We filed down the coach and went into the reception wing. We stood in line while our handcuffs were removed. Then we sat on a long wooden bench, waiting to be processed. The reception screw walked along the row of seated convicts, eyeing us up one by one.

"Which one of you is Hilton?"

I stood up. "That's me, Gov."

"Come with me." He beckoned me to follow him to the reception desk.

"Name?" another screw asked.

"Hilton," I answered.

"Sentence?"

"Life," I replied.

The screw wrote my details down and said, "I know you escaped from Borstal, didn't you?" He looked at me for confirmation.

I said, "Yes, Gov," and nodded. I couldn't lie about this one. I knew what was coming.

"I'm putting you on the escape list."

I thought, fuck me, any other screw and I would have slipped through the net, but he knew of me. If I wanted to make a move to escape, I was well and truly fucked. It would be almost impossible now for me to escape prison. Which, if possible, dampened my spirits even more.

"Go behind the screw and strip off," he barked.

I did as he asked. After which it was the normal routine of bend and spread your legs and search. Which is still something you never get used to, no matter how many times you must go through it. When he was finished, he handed me a distinctive yellow-striped uniform. This was partly to humiliate me and so I stood out like a sore thumb amongst all the other convicts. From now on, I would be always watched, sticking out like a beacon in the night.

As I changed into my glowing prison outfit, I could hear the screws shouting at the other convicts, "Come on, come on."

I thought, nothing changes, welcome to my new home, for God knows how many years, Wandsworth. Hell on earth, with some fire sprinkled on top for good measure.

A short time later, two screws beckoned me over and escorted me to D wing. I was taken to cell D2. I had to undress and place my yellow, florescent eyesore of a uniform in a cardboard box with my shoes. They also wanted me to put my cutlery in there too, which consisted of a knife and spoon. Forks again were prohibited and my knife was as blunt as a bag of mice. This was to become my routine every night. They didn't trust me or my intentions. I was one of the most high-risk prisoners and was watched constantly, which was exasperating, to say the least. To make matters worse, they put a red light on me on all night. This light was used for the purpose of seeing that I was in my bed at night, rather than climbing over the prison wall. The thing with the light was, it made it near on impossible to sleep; the brightness was irritating and the flickering of it would send my mind into overdrive. It was only after months of this torturous beam that I learnt how to not let it bother me and, in turn, get a good night's kip.

The night of my sentence, when the door slammed shut, I sat on the wooden chair plonked in the corner of my cell, looked round the claustrophobic four walls and shook my head. I couldn't believe I had ended up back in here. Not for a short time, either; it was now to serve a life sentence. Trying to digest the magnitude of my circumstances, I covered my face to block out the glare of the red light and contemplated my gloomy future, stuck in prison. Eventually, I drifted off into a deep sleep. That night, I thought to myself, it wouldn't be a big deal if I didn't wake in the morning. At least death meant I would escape my living nightmare.

The next day, they put me straight to work, typical. All I wanted to do was lie in my bed and process my sentence. I followed the screw down the landing to the mailbag shop at the end of D wing and stopped in front of the towering steel gate, whilst the screw took his time to unlock it. He ushered me through and I entered the mailbag shop. As I did, a gust of dusty stale air hit me straight in the face. I walked across the room; the smell was overwhelming and I had to catch my breath a couple of times to acclimatise to this awful room. The discipline screw was sitting in a high wooden box, overlooking the rows of convicts. Many of the convicts looked up at me, smiled and gave a look of sympathy. The screw looked at my striped uniform with the luminous lines.

"You can sit over there." He indicated a seat in the front row, so I was right in his line of vison.

Each seat was bolted to the cold concrete floor. I thought this might be so the chairs could not be used as weapons. I sat like the rest of them, with a mailbag over my knees, stitching the rough canvas together, listening to the multiple conversations around me. All I could do was keep thinking of Gus, in the condemned cell, under constant watch, waiting for the noose and thinking of all the years I had to serve before I was free again. I still couldn't get my head around his sentence of death; it felt so surreal. We were all in this dire situation and I wondered if there was any way of appealing the verdicts. My mind ticked over for days and, eventually, we all decided an appeal was the best course of action.

If anything, we would kick ourselves if we didn't try to get our sentences reduced.

Six weeks after our conviction, the three of us went to the appeal court with the hope our sentences would be reduced. All we had was hope and this was our last shot at gaining some freedom or, if anything, a less harsh sentence for the whole firm. On the day of our appeal, we were taken to the reception block in Wandsworth, handcuffed and piled into a van, on our way to the Strand where the Royal Courts of Justice are situated. The van was directed to the dropping-off point and we were led along an eerie, dimly-lit tunnel. We were deep underground, under the main court, back to the holding cells. We had to wait in our individual cells until the court was ready for us. I waited patiently until they called me into the appeal court.

The court itself was a huge, high, domed roomed that seemed to hold a thousand law books, on stacked shelving that ran seamlessly from wall to wall. I noticed there were a number of young men dressed in dark blue uniforms; they were called plaintiffs. Their job was to deliver any particular law books that might be required by any of the defence or prosecution counsels. The room was filled with low murmured conversation; as all three of us appeared in full view, they looked up at us as if we were aliens from another planet. We were worlds apart from these people. They glared for a moment, then returned to study their books. The court room felt like a theatre, as if they were actors reading their scripts, not really attached to the situation, just doing their job. Making sure they knew all of their lines; the system was a joke and we were just puppets in the production.

We were all lined up, waiting on the three judges to make their appearance. There was an atmosphere of anticipation and tension that swept through the court room, like a sea breeze you cannot quite catch. After all, this was a capital murder appeal, so a man's life was at stake. The judges entered the appeal room from behind heavy blood-red curtains and took their seats, not too far from the dock. They stared at us for a while, I'm guessing as a form of intimidation, and then the senior judge started proceedings. Gus's Counsel was a man called Humphreys, who at the time was a leader of a Buddhist movement. Due to his religious beliefs, he did not condone Judicial hangings; he had a real passion for hanging to be abolished. He rose to his feet, adjusted his robes and proceeded to put his case for the defence forward. I could see he was struggling to articulate himself, and his point was not being put across as well as he had hoped. He was getting himself in a muddle, which the senior judge also noticed and halted proceedings. Eventually, Humphreys got his point across and Gus's appeal went through.

Next up was Bob; the case for his appeal was that the previous judge had not taken Bob's alibi into consideration. Bob had put forward that he was waiting for a ferry to Ireland the night of the robbery and had someone to vouch for that. My appeal was that I was at home the night of the robbery, with my family. The judges put the appeals forward and we waited for the verdict.

Philip couldn't appeal because he had pleaded guilty, so it was Bob, Gus and myself looking to raise any doubts in the verdicts. Being in court always reminded me of being in a library, with its book-lined walls and its hushed, stifled atmosphere. Emotions were running high; you could feel the tension in the air throughout the proceedings, as we had everything riding on the appeal. If this didn't work, we were royally screwed. We had a good case for appeal, due to lack of evidence and failure of the police to conduct a thorough investigation. Just maybe, we would manage to throw some doubt against the previous verdicts and somehow make our sentences a little lighter.

The appeal lasted five, long, drawn-out days. Five weary days seated in uncomfortable chairs was exhausting and nerve-wracking. Listening and watching these total strangers determining our future. Our future was hanging on a knife edge; we were so aware of this that you could hear a pin drop in the court room.

Eventually, the verdicts were handed down; Gus had his death sentence squashed and a life sentence substituted instead. This was on the grounds that the prosecution had failed to prove who fired the final shot. This was a great relief for all of us, especially for Gus; you could see the weight of the world literally drop off his shoulders. He couldn't help but curl up a small smile and glance in our direction. I was over the moon; the thought of him being hung was mind-boggling. Thankfully, the last death sentence carried out in Britain was to be the year of 1964, which must have come as great relief to all the villains that were awaiting trial for anything of this nature. Bob also had his life sentence squashed, on the grounds that the trial judge had failed to instruct the jury regarding his alibi. A big mistake by the Judicial system, as this threw his case completely into disarray. He was returned to Brixton prison on remand on an armed robbery charge instead, which was a massive win for him. He would be out in no time and I was over the moon for both of them.

Unfortunately, my appeal was dismissed, and I was returned to Wandsworth prison, to continue my life sentence. My long-running history with the police and courts, being in and out of the system, probably didn't help my appeal. They all had it in for me and my lack of remorse or empathy for the victim probably didn't help my appeal either. As far as they were concerned, I was a dangerous, violent man and it was safer for me to be locked away than walk the streets with the public. I could see their point, but I didn't fire the shot, I didn't kill anyone, so why should I do life in prison? I was angry with the verdict, but being mad and moody would not change the outcome. I accepted my fate. Of course, the appeal had been worth a shot; at least I had tried, otherwise I would have always of wondered what if.

You must be wondering, what of my marriage? My wife and son came to visit me twice, shortly after my conviction. They visited me, but there was no pleasure in it. We sat each side of the table with a wooden divider running across the middle. I felt like there wasn't much to say. I could see the disappointment in her eyes; they were sad and tired and she seemed to have aged a lot in the last few months, wrinkles sitting heavier around her eyes and forehead. The stress had taken its toll; she looked like she had lost everything and then some.

We couldn't even hold hands because of the screen between us. Nothing about the visit felt natural or comfortable and we couldn't behave normally, as we were being watched. In fact, it felt more like an interrogation room or some sort of hazardous hospital room. There were two prison officers in the room; one was watching us and the other was writing a summary of our conversation. It was intrusive and inhibiting for Pat and me, as we couldn't really have a normal conversation.

After the second visit, my son asked me, "Daddy, when are you coming home?"

He was only five at the time. I will never forget the look of longing for me to be with him on his face. It broke my heart into tiny pieces. I felt such heartache, that I was unable to cope with seeing them anymore. I told Pat not to come and visit me, which I could see was a great relief to her as well. Prison was no place for a woman and child. My son could not understand why I couldn't play with or cuddle him. I would be doing him a favour and saving him from the hurt of not being with his dad. I couldn't go through that with my son on every visit; it was too emotional and painful for all of us. He didn't understand why he couldn't be with me and I felt maybe they could have a normal life if they just forgot about me and moved on. Why should they suffer for my wrongdoing; it wasn't fair on either of them.

I didn't break down, but I will never know how I didn't. I just mumbled something and left. That feeling of your child missing you, being sad and confused and, as a father, being totally helpless to do anything, is an excruciating tug on the heartstrings. I couldn't handle seeing his sweet, innocent face like that again.

The next day, I wrote to my wife and said not to come for a while, as it was too painful for both of us. I, for one, couldn't face the emotional strain. If I were going to survive the next however many years, I would have to grow strong and severe any emotional ties. At least then my family could get on with their own lives and

I would no longer be a burden to them. My son's memory of me would eventually fade and he would go on to have a happy, loving childhood with his mum. I had to be at peace with this decision, as it was the only way for all of us to cope. I've seen too many convicts pacing up and down their cells, driving themselves mad with paranoia, wondering what their wives were up to. Years later, when I was in Durham security wing, my divorce papers came through. I felt a sense of relief as that part of my life was over and now it was finalised. I hoped that my wife would re-marry and make a fresh start for herself, she deserved some happiness and normality after what I had put her through. Eventually, she did re-marry and I was genuinely happy for her. We didn't both need to serve a life sentence because of my actions; one of us had to be free.

I got back to the mundane and gruelling regime of Wandsworth nick and tried my best to forget about my family.

CHAPTER 17

"GOUGE THEIR FUCKING EYES OUT"

After the appeal, I was taken back to Wandsworth prison, but taken to a different part of the prison, A Wing. They came promptly to the reception block and escorted me to the main prison. I picked up my fresh bundle of bedding and followed the screw out of the reception, across the yard into A Wing. As I entered the wing, I heard the familiar sounds of convicts shouting and hollering.

Then I heard someone shout, "John Boy!" I looked up to the landing and, sure enough, I saw a couple of pals of mine grinning at me.

"I knew you would end up back here, we have been waiting for you."

It always amazed me how quickly news spread round the prison. I wondered how such an isolated place with no access to the free world knew so much.

The screw leading me to the wing said, "You are in room twenty-one on the twos landing."

I climbed the stairs and made my way to the cell. It was clean, which was a pleasant surprise. I dumped my stuff on the bed and thought, there is no rush to unpack, it wasn't like I was going anywhere in a hurry. Instead, I went upstairs to see my pals. We shook hands and were overjoyed to see each other; it was always pleasant seeing old faces and catching up. One of my pals looked disgruntled.

"We heard what sentence you got, John, and we are gutted for you."

"Don't worry," I said. "I'm ok. I didn't expect anything different, to be honest."

I was clutching at straws, trying to get my life sentence reduced, but it had been worth a try. The outcome for Bob and Gus was a good one. I was especially happy for Gus; at least he wasn't going to be hung by the neck and killed. He now had a fighting chance of some sort of life.

"Come on, we will go to my cell and have a cup of tea," one of them said.

Trying to cheer me up with a cup of tea wouldn't work, but it was the thought that counted. It seems like a cup of tea is England's answer to everything. I was sitting in their cell, and they were marking my card about the wing's routine. It seemed to be a relaxed one, but I wasn't really listening; I was too caught up in the realisation I was doing life.

Another one of my pals walked in.

"I know what you need," he said and he pulled a nice lump of hash out of his pocket. He said, "This is for you."

I started laughing. I said, "Come on, skin up and the music was turned on."

Everyone was relaxed and there was a good vibe in the cell. Just what I needed; a bit of escapism. At the time, the government droned on about the health implications of hash, but as far as I was concerned, it never did me any harm. In fact, it made me feel good and relaxed me. I found knocking back too many spirits was far more detrimental to the body. With hash, there were never any hangovers, and I could quite easily get on with my day. Thousands of convicts smoked it to help counteract prison life, to take the edge off the mind-numbing boredom and monotonous prison routine. A bell rang, which was a warning call, letting you know it was nearly time to get off your arse and get your dinner. So, I made my way to my cell and, while I was waiting, I unpacked my gear. Due to me being a category A convict, I was told to collect my prison food and eat alone. Cat A prisoners are people who pose the most threat to the public and their inmates, as well as being the highest risk potential escapees. When you get your prison grub, you get it down you as quickly as possible, you try not to hold it in your mouth too long and endure the taste. Because if you did, you wouldn't be able to stomach the food. All it does is serve a purpose, to keep you alive and that's about it.

After they finished checking and feeding everyone, you could go to association with the rest of the cons for a little play time. I went upstairs to see the boys again, only to find lots of other cons who I knew were waiting to see me. Naturally, I was asked how I felt about my sentence. I told the truth; I had two choices, I could get on with it and accept my fate was sealed or I could top myself. I'm not the type to have suicidal thoughts, so I would do my best with the cards I had been dealt. I didn't see the world as if it was against me or have 'woe is me' moments. I took most of the crap thrown at me on the chin.

The lads got the puff out and we spent time chatting, until another pal of mine came by, who worked on the outside stores. He entered the cell carrying a plastic bag containing two bottles of vodka and blackcurrant glasses and it was drinks all round. I asked him how he got the drink in.

"No problem, John boy, I've got the store boy straightened up. I give him the money and he brings in the booze. Anyway, in the morning, I have something I want to talk to you about. Maybe things are not as bad as you think they are. You have plenty of help and they are all good people. Anyway, we will speak tomorrow."

His words got my mind in a frenzy; my thoughts were racing a hundred miles per hour. I knew he was talking about escaping and this lit me up like a halogen light bulb. Suddenly, there was hope and I felt a little more alive than when I had entered. The booze flowed, an abundance of weed was smoked, good times were had by all. By the time it came to lock up, I was half drunk and extremely stoned. When the door was locked, and the screws had gone off-duty, I sat on my bed and shook my head. I'd had an amazing day, and now there was a slither of hope. Here I was, drunk and stoned after receiving a whole life sentence and all that was left was to go to bed and have a good kip. Which is exactly what I did.

Over the next few days, I just settled in and got into the routine of prison life. A few weeks in, I was studying the layout of the prison, and I looked out of the recess window onto the yard and saw something that caught my eye. The yard was outside, and was not used by the inmates; it was used as a builder's yard for the prison maintenance workers. I could see it was filled with ladders, metal poles for scaffolding and piles of large wooden boxes, ideal for a makeshift climbing frame over the wall. I was always looking for a way out and this yard had potential to execute an escape. If I could find my way into the yard, I could easily scale the wall. The metal bars over the window of the recess could be cut during association time. If I could do this, then I could be free again; I could potentially have luck on my side this time round. I approached my pal about what I had seen. He had obviously already cottoned on to this idea and was not surprised at my findings.

He said, "Don't worry, the storeman is willing to bring in a small jack for five hundred. Once we get it, all you must do is sit down and relax. I've got a couple of guys who are willing to jack the bars apart, so you can squeeze through and drop into the yard. We will also make a rope out of some sheets and, when you get into the yard, the rope will get slung out. Then all you must do is tie one end to something heavy and, once you're on the wall, pull the rope up, let it down to the other side and slide down, then you will be home free." My pal had it all worked out; he seemed to be sure we could pull this off. I admired his confidence and determination; he was almost a mirror of myself.

"What about the money?" I enquired. Getting hold of that sort of money in prison was going to be a bit tricky and needed some time.

"Don't worry, we will all put something in for the jack. All you must do is simply nothing and we will do it all for you."

It all sounded too good to be true, but my mind ran away with the idea. Like a steam train, I went full steam ahead with how the plan would unfold, imagining all the possibilities. I must confess my heart skipped a beat at the thought of being free. The Home Office would have a fit if I were to escape and the police wouldn't be too pleased either. The establishment hate being made a fool of and I would be making a mockery of the prison system once again. Either way, it would be a joyous and triumphant occasion for me, just not for anyone running the system.

The days crept by; we were all waiting patiently for the jack to be brought in. As time went on, I began to have some doubts about the jack and its potential delivery. It was taking too long and there was no progression and zero updates on the delivery date. In my experience, if something takes too long, it's not going to happen. That's exactly how our plan unfolded. The storeman's bottle went; he didn't mind bringing in the booze, but he knew the jack would be used for an escape and he did not want an inquiry leading back to him. To be fair, I didn't blame him. He would get into as much trouble as the escapees. The plan and dream of escape faded away and I had to grapple with the idea of being a prisoner for a long time to come. I still had a drink and a puff, which the storeman smuggled in, but the hope of leaving this dire place dwindled away and the reality of prison life was now embedded into my bones.

I woke up one glorious day, to receive a slip telling me that I was being transferred, which was a shock. Usually, you got an idea you were being transferred, but this came out of the blue. Winchester was to be my next destination; I had no idea why they decided to move me there, as it was a local prison. It wasn't too bad there; the routine wasn't too bad and I settled in quite quickly.

At the time, Winchester was more relaxed than a lot of the other prisons and the screws were more chilled; maybe they were smoking what the inmates were. Like with every prison, I looked for the possible ways of escaping, but I was being watched intently. There was no way I was getting out of Winchester, so I could only hope I would be transferred and get an opportunity to escape in the next prison. One sunny day with some light wind flying around me, I was outside on exercise, doing my usual walking up and down the yard. Pacing up and down, I was enjoying the sun on my face and the fresh air in my lungs, when suddenly the screw in charge of the yard yelled, "That's it, exercise time is finished, it's time to go back to the mailbag room!"

I was not happy; how dare he shorten exercise time? It was the one pleasure we looked forward to. I thought, that's a bit premature, cutting our exercise time down is a real kick in the teeth and I was not in the mood to be messed about with, not today.

"We still have another fifteen minutes."

The screw's face turned red; none of them liked being challenged. "Don't argue with me, get into the workshop and keep your mouth shut."

When he spoke to me in this diabolical fashion, something inside me snapped. I must have had so much pent-up anger, it was time for it to be released. I flew into a fit of rage and stepped forward to give him a right-hander. But before I could do anything, another convict stopped me and shouted, "It isn't worth it, John," and hustled me inside the mail bag shop.

To be honest, I wish he'd just let me give him a right-hander, as I was past the point of giving a shit and this screw was the person I wanted to take my frustration out on. He guided me into the mail bag room; I went inside reluctantly and tried to calm myself down. Because of my outburst, I was told to go to the office to collect some mailbag canvas, to walk off my anger.

Suddenly, four screws came and in, and informed me, "You are going to be taken to the punishment block."

In the sixties, every prison had red metal buckets filled with water, in case of a fire. Just in front of the work office, there were about six beaten-up fire buckets, and as the screws came towards me, my temper flared up again. They were testing how far they could push me and their behaviour was rubbing me up the wrong way completely. One screw stepped up in front of me.

"Come on," he demanded.

I thought, fuck you! I bent down and seized a bucket, threw

the water over him, then struck him over his shoulders with a sharp blow. He staggered back, clutching his shoulder in agony. Meanwhile, other screws started streaming into the workshop. I stood there with no fucks given, waiting for them to do their worst. One screw drew his truncheon and struck me across my arm, knocking the bucket from my hand, and the others rushed on top of me. There was a short, intense violent struggle before I was subdued and rushed out of the workshop onto the wing, dragging me by my legs to the chokey. I was then thrust into an empty cell. There was a bunch of screws waiting at the door and I knew they were there waiting to give me a good kicking. This was normal practice when a con stepped out of line, especially when there was an assault on an officer. I invited them to come and do their worst.

I said to them, "But if you do, in the morning, I can promise you the first screw I see, I'll gouge their fucking eyes out. So, give me a kicking, but remember what I just said."

They hesitated for a moment, then slammed the door shut, leaving me with rage and adrenaline pumping through my veins. I hadn't been this wrathful and indignant in some time. I had no idea what had come over me, but it felt good to feel alive again.

I thought I had a good result there; I had somehow gained a bit of power over the screws. The fuckers didn't want to mess with me, and I liked that. They knew they had pushed me too far and I felt ready to go to war with the lot of them. The next morning, I went before the Governor, charged with assaulting a prison officer and refusing to obey an order.

"How do you plead?" he asked.

"Guilty," I replied. I mean, what else could I say? Stupid fucking question, to be frank.

"Very well, I am remanding you for the visiting committee."

Which meant three local magistrates would hear my case and then be able to award me all sorts of wonderful, sadistic punishments. I was taken back to my cell until such time as the arrival of the visiting committee. Whilst I waited for my fate to be sealed,

I spent my time reading and working out. I worked out twice a day; it gave me a great buzz keeping fit, all the endorphins would make me stay positive and feel powerful under this oppressive regime. It took days for them to arrive, and I was waiting with some anxiety as to what punishments they would enforce. Then one morning without warning, they appeared, and I listened to my charges being read out. Evidence was given, after which I was asked If I had anything to say on my behalf. I looked at the three magistrates for a moment. I felt like saying, "Fuck the lot of you."

But instead, I held my tongue and stated, "I have nothing to say."

They had a brief consultation, whispering in the corner, before they came to their decision for my punishment. They decided to give me fifteen days of bread and water, plus forty-two days of a number two diet and that I would be confined to my cell to serve my punishment.

Great, I thought, another bread and water diet. This punishment is always hard to do, as you get terrible indigestion and constipation. But like everything else within this horrific prison system, you make the best of the situation. I had done bread and water before, so I knew what was in store for me. Eventually, after a gruelling punishment, I finished a few pounds lighter. Weak and disorientated, I went back to my normal diet as if nothing had happened. That first mug of hot sweet tea was indescribable; it was a real cup of heaven and made me truly grateful for the small pleasures in life. A fleeting moment of bliss. In prison, you hold on to such luxuries for as long as you can.

CHAPTER 18

PARKHURST TO DARTMOOR

A week later, I was informed that I was being transferred to Parkhurst prison, which suited me fine. In the sixties, Parkhurst was well-known as a decent prison. You were allowed plenty of fresh air and had daily access to the gym, which I was looking forward to. The journey to Parkhurst was quite pleasant; I was being transferred there in style, travelling by taxi, so I had a decent view of the free world. Which merely reinforced my determination to escape, the first chance that came my way. The journey to the Isle of Wight was by ferry; normally, the sea is choppy and unforgivable but this time it was smooth and easy. I took great pleasure in looking out at the never-ending sea and thinking how beautiful the world was, and then realising I was missing all the beauty it had to offer. I took every opportunity to suck up as much fresh air as I could. I looked out at the glorious waves and listened to the birds overhead and promised myself I would see the sea again, by any means necessary. I didn't want the ferry ride to end.

Once we were off the ferry, we drove a short distance to the prison and halted sharply outside the front gates. The driver sounded his horn, then the doors slowly opened and in we drove, once again leaving the beautiful, big wide world behind me. My first impression was favourable. Large flower beds greeted me; you could almost mistake the prison for a fancy hotel. A variety of flowers in bloom, the place was decorated with bursts of colour and the flowers danced gracefully in the wind. The outside brickwork was a dusky pink; it gave off a pleasant vibe, unlike your usual gloomy, grey and sinister-looking prison structure. The normal routine in the prison reception commenced. There was one other prisoner in reception, a stark contrast to the busy and chaotic reception welcome I was used to. Once they had checked every crevice of my body, I was taken to B Wing and left alone. Fully aware of the routine, the screws knew I didn't need any guidance. I unpacked my belongings and went to have a look around my new hotel, her majesty's finest. Straight away, I bumped into some old friends of mine.

We shook hands and exchanged war stories.

"What's it like in here?" I asked.

"Not a bad nick, we have a good Governor, which helps. Hariot's his name, you can always talk to him when he does his rounds. The screws are not too bad; you have a few arseholes here, but best thing to do is stay out of their way and you'll get by here, no trouble."

Later that day, I was called to the wing office by the principal officer. He invited me to sit down, which was unusual in those days. Treating prisoners as your equal was unheard of and I was hesitant to take up his request, feeling something was amiss. He proceeded to give me the low-down on Pankhurst.

"I see you are serving a life sentence, plus you have already assaulted an officer in Winchester and you are on the escape list. Not a good start, is it?"

"No, Gov, "I replied. I wasn't sure where he was going with this conversation.

"Well, we will have to see how things go. In the meantime, you'll be working in the laundry room. You'll start in the morning. That's all for now. Off you go."

And with that, I left his office. Of course, this was a warning; step out of line and you're out. So, I took his little speech onboard and thought I would do alright here, as long as I kept my head down. After all, it was one of the most favourable prisons I had the pleasure of residing in.

I was quite pleased to be in the laundry. It wasn't a bad job, and the perk was you could wash your own clothes whenever you wanted. I could be in clean clothes every day, which cheered me up no end. Nothing like fresh bedding whenever you wanted, either, especially when you were hot and sticky in the summer. Prisons didn't offer the luxury of air conditioning or heating; when it was a blazing summer's day, you really felt the heat and, when it was winter, you would pray for those months to pass.

In the morning, I reported to the officer in charge of laundry. He wasn't a bad screw; everyone called him OMO, after the washing powder, which was a brand around in the 50s. A bit like Lenor or Ariel today. I was given the job of packing all the clean clothes into large baskets, which was easy as pie and quite therapeutic. It was somewhat relaxing and calming, folding the clothes neatly away. I had my job sorted out, I had good use of the gym facilities and I had plenty of friends to mix with. I felt quite settled; this prison was better than most and I was left to my own devices, which is just how I liked it. No one breathing down my neck or making my life miserable. The weeks drifted by and I was in a nice routine. I got into a habit of taking a small glass jar of coffee with me for my break-time. I had been doing it for months without any problems and no objection from any screw on shift. It was one luxury I had and looked forward to when break-time came around. Just like every other day, I walked into the laundry room and a screw spotted the jar poking out of my pocket.

"What's that?" he asked, nodding towards my bulge.

"It's some coffee, Gov, it's for my break," I replied.

"You can't have it. You're not allowed glass jars at work. Give it to me, I'm confiscating it."

"Can I take the coffee out and you can keep the jar?" I thought this was quite a reasonable request.

"No, I want the jar and the coffee," he barked.

He was exercising his power to the best of his ability. I could see he was one of those arseholes. He wasn't going to compromise or back down. So, I got the jar out of my pocket, unscrewed the lid and emptied the coffee out onto the floor. I watched the coffee spread itself far and wide, making a mess everywhere. I thought, fuck you, I will make my point now, you awkward bastard.

"Here's your glass jar, you can have it." I gave it to him with a snigger. I thought, you won't fuck with me.

His face filled with blood; his features were contorted, and he looked like he was ready to explode. You could see the other cons were watching to see how this confrontation was going to play out.

"Right, Hilton, I'm nicking you for refusing to follow a direct order."

"You fucking arsehole, you can do what you like."

I flew into a rage, stepped forward and hit him as hard as I could in the jaw. He staggered back, turned to the alarm bell and pressed it. The alarm was to be used for emergencies only. It was there to call all the spare staff on the wing, so they all ran to the laundry room, thinking they were to be facing a real emergency. Maybe even something life-threatening. Instead, they saw a wimpy screw, whining about a punch to the jaw. As they entered, the screw was slumped into a chair, holding his face, and I could see a lump rising from his jaw. I started laughing at him.

"How's your jaw?" I quizzed him with a huge smile on my face.

Then I was rushed by about twelve screws, who rugby-tackled me to the ground, whilst he was screaming at the top of his lungs, "He attacked me!"

Putting on some extra drama for his colleagues' benefit. I was immediately pounded on and frog-marched to the chokey. On my way, I received a few punches to the body and face, but I didn't care. It was no big deal to me; for me, it was a small victory. I found it laughable they needed so many screws to drag me away. Who did they think I was? I entered the chokey block, they searched me before they left and my shoes were removed. I was thrust into a cell, and left there, for God knows how long. To my surprise, they didn't come back for a bonus kicking. I half hoped they would, as I was up for a fight.

The next day, I was in front of the Governor, and the screw gave his evidence. A pathetic excuse for a man, he had caused all the drama and now he wanted everyone to feel sorry for him.

Then the Governor asked me how I pleaded. I said 'guilty' and he wanted to know If I had anything to say in my defence. I said no. I knew I was going to be doing a long stint in the chokey, so I thought, fuck it, there was no point in explaining myself. They were never going to take a prisoner's side in these situations. He started spouting some shit about my previous behaviour.

"What I can see from your previous, assaulting an officer before back in Winchester, is that you're going to be a nuisance in my prison, so I am giving you fourteen days confined to a cell and, after that time, you will be transferred to another prison."

Great, I thought. I was quite happy in this nick and knew I would be doomed, being transferred anywhere else. This was the one place I didn't mind being in; for a prison, it was half decent. I just knew they were going to transfer me to a shit-hole. I had a funny feeling I would be transferred to Dartmoor. After my long and tedious fourteen-day punishment, they came early the first morning, swung my door open and I was escorted across the yard to the reception block. They couldn't get me out of there prison quick enough. The normal routine went underway and I was taken outside, where a prison van was waiting for me. I entered the van, along with two screws, who were there in case I decided to cause any trouble. The driver started the engine and we were on our way. I didn't ask where we were going. I thought it best for it to be a surprise. I looked out the window, staring at the never-ending fields that spread like a patchwork quilt over the ground. All the colours were so inviting; I could see the farmers took great pride in their land. I felt like I was a part of society once more as we scooted onto the motorway and dashed past the hundreds of cars. The journey was endless, tedious and dull. We drove through bustling Bristol and made our way to, you guessed it, Dartmoor.

My instincts were almost always right. My stomach flipped a couple of times at the thought of Dartmoor's crumbling prison walls and their dark atmosphere. By this point, the sun was going down and all light was fading outside. The journey was becoming uncomfortable; it felt like I had been in the car for hours and my arse was getting numb from sitting on the hard plastic seat. Before the dark set in, I could occasionally catch glimpses of the ponies and sheep scattered across the cold moors, but the light was dimming and I could barely make out anything as the journey progressed. Then it fell pitch-black and I knew we were deep into the Moors, getting lost in the wilderness.

Dropping off, my head rested against the side of the van, while I was sitting upright in the back. I could barely keep my eyes open. I must have dropped off, as the van jerked and I opened my eyes to glaring lights, blinding my vision, and I knew we had arrived. The prison was lit up like a Christmas tree and all I could think about was a hot sweet cup of tea. I was dog-tired and bursting to use the toilet. We turned left and drove through a granite arch. The gates were wide open and we drove down the path, parking outside Dartmoor's punishment wing. It was an intimidating building, with a grey and black floor, a cold and hostile atmosphere, and I was not looking forward to being here at all.

Dartmoor's set-up was a strict one. I was aware I would have to tread carefully with these screws in this establishment. The chokey screws all wore steel-studded army boots, with their caps pulled low over their eyes. Trying to intimidate the prisoners at every given opportunity, they were in no way there to be your friend or be nice to you. You could see straight away they were thirsty for a fight. The first chance they got, they would kick the fuck out of you. No hesitation, I thought, they were the type to fuck you up for the fun of it. I didn't fancy being stamped on with those army boots either, as they would do more than a cheeky mischief.

Normal formalities took place at the reception block. I stripped naked and was searched, then the screw beckoned me in for my name and number: Hilton, 605204.

He said, "The doctor will see you soon."

When I walked into the room, the doctor was sitting in front of a roaring fire. The warmth coming off it made me realise how cold I actually was.

"Are you in good health?" he inquired.

"As far as I know, Doctor," I replied. I was growing weary and couldn't be bothered with this crap.

I had a towel wrapped round me; he asked me to drop it, bend over, and placed his rubber-gloved hand under my balls and asked me to cough. Which I did.

He said, "Right, you're ok, you're fit for work."

This was a new procedure for me. I had not had a doctor's examination of this kind before, and thought it to be peculiar, but I didn't ask any questions. I was too tired. Each prison seems to have its own set of rules and half of them never made much sense.

I replaced the towel back around me, dressed as quickly as I could and was taken to the damp and chilly wing. After which I was handed a large corn-beef sandwich and a large mug of tea, which I was so grateful for. I was freezing, my bones felt like ice blocks and all I could think of was to get under some covers and get myself warm. I was taken to a cell and locked in; my bedding this time was waiting for me. I looked around and thought, nothing has changed, same shit-hole it has always been. Welcome to Dartmoor. I ate my sandwich, drank my tea and made my bed. The cell was so cold, I could see my breath making patterns in the air. I was shivering, partly because of the cold seeping into my bones and partly because I was exhausted. My body was shutting down. I kept my socks and shirt on for extra layers. I didn't fancy stripping off in this cell. I lay on the damp and lumpy mattress, which had mould around the corners and smelt like stagnant pond water. I wrapped all my blankets as tightly as I could around me. Shattered from such a long and mentally draining day, I fell into an exhausted sleep in my mould-encrusted bed. I could have slept anywhere that night, I was that tired.

I was rudely awoken by someone kicking my door, telling me to wake up. I kicked the blankets off and quicky dressed. The cell was absolutely freezing; I'd really fucked up, being transferred here. I looked up at the window and I could see a thin film of ice on the back wall. How could this prison be fit for anyone to sleep and live in? I thought to myself, what a piss-hole I am in, and made a promise to myself that I had to get out of here, the first chance I got. The door clunked open and I was told to go and get my breakfast, which was a small bowl of porridge and a cob of bread with a small pinch of margarine. The food was nothing to rave about and I was still hungry after breakfast.

As I returned to my cell, the screw said, "You're going over to D Wing in a bit."

I thought, thank fuck for that, as this wing was not fit for anyone to sleep in, and spending another night in there would end up making me sick. I also told myself to do my best to avoid the chokey whilst I was there, as I didn't fancy dying in prison. This was not the place to fuck about!

CHAPTER 19

DREADED DURHAM

In early 1966, I was still in Dartmoor. I had done about two years of my life sentence and I was still classified as an escape risk. We were known as E-men and had to wear a special uniform. The trousers had a bright yellow stripe running down the trouser leg and the jacket had a yellow square sewn on. This seemed to be the same for every prison I had the pleasure of being transferred to. Every night, I had to put all my clothes and shoes outside my cell, and I had a red light shining in my face whilst I was asleep, the same as the light shining in on me at Wandsworth prison. Every fifteen minutes, a screw would look through my spy-hole to check I was still there. They watched me like a hawk, far more so than they did in Wandsworth. The constant checks were a real pain in the arse and would often wake me up, leaving me to rarely have a good night's kip. I also didn't like them treating me like a petulant child, as if I was a toddler that needed looking after. It was exasperating and would often leave me frustrated as I craved time to myself to gather my thoughts.

They made me move cell every two weeks, so I could not contrive an escape route or use my cell as a means to store contraband and so forth. They tried their best to make me unsettled and irritable and, to be fair, it was working. But I refused to react to their fucked-up mind games. I merely got on with it, thinking at some point this stupidity would end. Their ideology was to make sure I was never comfortable and never establish roots or solid friendships in any prison for too long. Always disrupting my routine, so as to fuck with my head as and when they pleased.

Despite all these precautions and mind games, I felt all I had to do was be patient. Keep a low profile and eventually there would be a weakness in the system for me to be able to escape. It was all about the right timing. There were a lot of rumours flying about that three of the wings in Durham, Parkhurst and Leicester were being turned into escape-proof wings. These units were intended to house the train robbers and all the other high-profile armed robbers, and I knew I would be high up on the short list. Time was against me, and I was hoping I could make my move before it was too late. If I were to be transferred to a high-security, escape-proof wing, I would be stuck in a unit with no way out and that would be the end of any chance of escaping prison.

In Dartmoor, I was back sewing mailbags. I was sick of the sight of them; the work was repetitive and mundane, and I yearned for a different challenge than sewing the same thing repeatedly, day in, day out. Bored out of my mind, I was challenging the system's decision to put me on the escape list. Over the two long-winded years, I had made various applications to be removed from the escape list, using various reasons, none of which had worked. On my last application, the Governor had told me he regarded me as untrustworthy and, if I escaped because he took me off the E-list, he would lose his job. The hope of coming off the escape list had now come to an end; there was no way it was going to happen, at least whilst we had this particular Governor. At this time, the rumours were spreading and growing stronger about the special security wings. Especially after the Great Train Robbery. I was in awe of the Great Train Robbery; they had managed to pull off such a successful robbery. Though they got caught, to this day, the bulk of the money was never recovered. The Great Train Robbery was the robbery of over two million pounds from a Royal Mail train, heading from Glasgow to London, which took place in 1963. All eleven of them were convicted, and their large-scale robbery had spurred on the construction of such wings. I could feel this pressing niggle that my luck was running out and time was no longer on my side.

So, I started making plans to put an escape together. I got a pal of mine, who worked in the blacksmith shop, to make me some six-inch strips out of thin iron with two holes drilled in each end. My intention was to bolt the strips together, making an iron hook, eighteen inches across and two feet long, rather like a Meccano set. I would keep the strips inside my mattress until needed. The rope was to be made from torn strips of sheets when needed at the last minute. All I was waiting for were some hacksaw blades to be smuggled in to cut through the bars and window frame. I fancied a chance of getting away in fine style. All I could do was hope and pray the new security wings would not be ready before the blades came in. For now, it was a race against time, as I had a strong gut feeling they would move me to a high-security prison sooner rather than later.

Alas, I lost the race, as I thought I might. One morning, I heard loud footsteps coming towards my cell. It was about five-thirty am when my door was unlocked. I could see about six burly screws crowding in the doorway.

"Right, Hilton you're on the move," one of them bellowed.

I had this deep sinking feeling in my stomach. They liked to keep me on my toes; it was frustrating as hell, especially being woken up so early. I got out of bed, got dressed and grabbed my few worldly possessions. I was taken from the wing across the yard to the reception block. I was handcuffed to a screw, put into a police car and driven off at high speed across the Moors. The joke of the journey was that police sirens were wailing from behind and in front, as if I was some high-profile mass murderer or a celebrity. It was highly embarrassing and unnecessary, but this also gave me an indication that I was going to a high-security wing. I looked through the window; I could see sheep grazing and the odd wild pony cantering in the fields and all the wildflowers sprouting in random patches through the long, green grass. It looked like it was going to be a fine, sunny day. Not one cloud in the sky. I was fucking gutted how things had turned out, but all I could do was sit quietly and work out where I was heading. Even though, deep down, I knew where we were going, I held onto a sliver of hope, that it would be an ordinary prison.

As we reached the edge of Dartmoor, another police escort came into view, another one at the front and one behind, with lights blazing and wailing sirens. I thought, what a scene to make. The noise was giving me a headache, such a shit-show. We drove at high speed towards the motorway. I could see people's faces turning towards our convoy as we flashed past them, trying to get a glimpse of who was in the car. They most likely expected some high-profile celebrity or the Prime Minster, but alas, it was just a mere armed robber. I watched as the traffic was forced to one side; nothing, it seemed, was allowed to impact our progress of getting to our destination. The further north we travelled, I knew I was bound for Durham, which at the time, was one of the worst prisons in the country and, to top it off, they hated Londoners with a passion.

I knew I was on my way to E Wing, which before it was changed into a high-security wing, was a punishment wing. If you tried to escape or were considered a nuisance, you would be sent to E Wing for three months, as a punishment. If you were a Londoner, you had to watch your step and I knew I was in for a rough time. Northerners didn't like us at the best of times, and in prison, tensions were even higher than they would be on the streets. As we approached the outskirts of Durham, it started to rain, which merely reflected how I felt. How miserable the day became matched my dampened spirit, the nearer we reached dreaded Durham.

When we arrived at the main gate, it was already open to receive us. I thought, after such a scene on the road, they might have rolled out the red carpet for me too. Give me a royal welcome. We swept through the gate and came to a stop outside the entrance to E wing. I was taken through a small steel gate into the wing. There were about ten screws hanging around, giving me daggers, weighing me up and seeing how I would react to my new set-up. Their attempts at being intimidating were pathetic; did they think I hadn't done this rodeo a hundred times before?

I was taken into a small office, where I was uncuffed and the Dartmoor screws left me to sit in the reception block and fucked off back to the car we came in. A principal officer was seated behind an old, battered, wooden desk.

He pointed to a blanket in front of him. "Stand on the blanket and strip off," he ordered.

As I did, some screws drifted in and stood staring at me. This was obviously an attempt to intimidate me when I was in my most vulnerable state, naked and unfamiliar with my new surroundings. The principal officer pointed to a pile of clothes on the floor.

"Put them on," he barked.

As I dressed, I could see they were old garments and second-hand. Which pissed me off greatly; had they even washed these hand-me-downs? I doubted it very much. When I was dressed, my possessions were dumped onto the table. The principal officer pawed through my belongings like they were his own. With no regard at all, he dumped them on the table with a loud thud. I had managed to grab half a box of chocolate biscuits as I left my cell In Dartmoor, and I was looking forward to eating them after the long drive to Durham with a nice cup of sweet tea.

He picked up the biscuits and said, "You can't have these."

And he tossed them into the dustbin with force. My pen was taken away and all I was allowed was a couple of photos and some old letters. I could see some of the screws smiling, and I knew they wanted a reaction. They wanted me to get upset, throw a strop and shout at the top of my lungs about the injustice of it all. But they would never get a rise out of me. A bundle of bedding was thrust into my hands, and I was led upstairs to my cell. I was now entering the new high-security wing, a prison within a prison. How much more tragic could this moment be?

As I walked into the cell, the door was immediately slammed behind me. I dumped my bedding on the floor and looked around. The cell was brand new, with freshly painted walls. I could still smell the paint. It had a grey plastic tiled floor and, outside the normal barred window, was a set of alarm bell bars. These were hollow bars with a thin wire inside; if you did manage to cut into the bars, you would set the alarms off. The furniture was the usual prison bog-standard attire. I looked at the grey-painted door; it looked insanely strong. It was solid iron and looked impossible to break. I thought to myself, they must be electrically managed, like the alarms. I remember shaking my head thinking, how am I going to get out of this place? They have fucking buried me. I made my bed and lay down, staring at the ceiling. My mind was buzzing with all sorts of thoughts and emotions. This was a far cry from the plan I'd had. I didn't envisage these high-security wings would be ready so soon and I was thoroughly pissed off that I had not tried to escape sooner.

Suddenly, I heard someone knocking on the wall.

"Come to the window," someone shouted. I went to the window and a voice called out, "Who's that? Where are you from?"

"John Hilton from Dartmoor," I replied. I really wasn't in the mood for small-talk, as I was in a terrible mood and felt completely deflated and miserable.

Someone laughed. "I thought you'd come here, John." It was a friend of mine from Parkhurst. I was pleased to hear a familiar voice, as knowing people when arriving in a new prison has some great advantages.

"What's it like here?" I asked, dreading the answer I was to going to receive.

"It's a fucking piss-hole. All the screws do is try and wind you up. It's a different vibe altogether. They want to get a rise out of you at any given moment."

That's about right, I thought, these set-ups are designed to cause you a constant level of anxiety and unease. I thought to myself, we must be a part of their sick and twisted experiment. I was not looking forward to being a part of it one bit. I didn't like being a part of a test trial and I had a feeling this would be exactly that.

"Anyway, John, I will see you later. If the screws hear you talking at the window, they come round and cause problems," he said, I could tell he was living in constant fear by the tone of his voice.

What arseholes, I thought to myself.

"I'll see you later." I left the window and returned to my bed.

I felt a little better now; at least I wasn't on my own. I was going to go through this nightmare with a pal and that put me in a slightly better mood and more at ease. At least I wasn't going to go through this on my own.

A short time later, my door was opened by three screws.

"The wing governor wants to see you," one of them said.

I was led along the landing to the wing office. The governor was sitting behind the desk, examining my record. He looked up. "I see you have assaulted officers in Winchester and Parkhurst. Well, Hilton, this is a tough wing for tough convicts and sometimes people walk into doors or fall downstairs."

I thought, what a fucking threat, I've only just got here.

He paused to see my reaction. This was obviously the 'Welcome to Durham' speech. I was in no mood to listen to his patronising, condescending speech that had been said a thousand times before to every Tom, Dick and Harry that had entered these dreary walls. I had serious bollock-ache and this lot were getting on my last nerve.

"I'm doing life, so I haven't got much to lose and, if I fall down the stairs or walk into a door, I will put one of you down, no matter what happens to me afterwards."

Judging by the expression on his face, I don't think this was the answer he was looking for. I'm pretty sure no one had responded like that before to a Governor and he was genuinely taken aback. I think he was speechless, as his mouth fell open ever so slightly. I could see the screws on guard edging closer and preparing themselves for a ruckus of some sort. I'd make sure I'd do one of them before I went down. I wasn't going to be taken down without a fight. I didn't give a fuck about the rules anymore; this place was a death sentence, and I had nothing to lose.

But all the Governor said was, "Take him back to his cell."

Which intrigued me greatly, as that was not the reaction I expected at all. I was hustled down the landing to my cell and the door smashed shut behind me. Strange to say, I felt better, as I felt like I had won a mini battle and I started laughing to myself. I was pleased I had managed to wipe his smarmy smirk off his face. Welcome to Durham, I thought, what a fucking joke.

CHAPTER 20

DURHAM RIOT

I soon learnt that my cell had a new type of steel door with alarm studs set deep into the hinges, so if I did manage to open it, the bells would go off. It was a new design, that only these high-security wings had and I was curious as to how it worked. I studied it in detail but never managed to figure out how to disarm it. Alarm bells were also fitted to the bars that covered the window and I guessed they had the same type of design. It was far too technical for me and I was frustrated I could not get my head around the mechanics of it. There was a wooden table, a chair and a wash stand. I had my usual bog-standard bed, a wash stick, a bucket to piss in, a mug for tea and just a spoon to eat with, not even a blunt knife this time. I looked around and thought, why me? Why had I ended up in this dire, hopeless place? It was so quiet, I wasn't sure if anyone else but my pal was in the wing. I later discovered I was the seventh prisoner to be transferred to E wing, as it was infamously known.

At the time, only ten cells were in use. The atmosphere of the wing was hostile; it was no use complaining, as our complaints were largely ignored every day. I was to learn that I was on the wing with some of the train robbers. Four of them were on the high-security wing in the mid-60s and, in later years, I think around 1974, I was with another two of the firm in a different prison. I found them to be a decent bunch of men. I always respected their principles; when they got nicked, they all stood firm, nobody crumbled and not one of them tried to do a deal for a lighter sentence at the expense of their friends. Unlike some of the modern-day thieves, who would throw you under the bus the first chance they got. All honour, pride and the code of conduct between villains seems to have dwindled away. The train robbers never complained and did their sentence the right way, with no fuss.

We were treated with zero respect and had little in the way of rights. I expected an explosion of violence to come sooner rather than later. At times, you could almost taste the tension, like a bitter lemon dripping into your mouth; there was no release or escape from it. Strangely enough, it was accepted by both sides, that the pressure cooker was heating up every day and it was only a matter of time before things blew up. We were locked in our cells twenty-three hours a day. You could only exercise for half an hour, and only three people could go to recreation at a time. Bath time was a horrid affair. The screws would stand there and watch us bathing through a glass screen. All of them standing there and staring at us, their eyes fixed on us. We had five minutes to bathe, once a week, which is not healthy or hygienic at all. For an added bonus, the hot tap was removed, so we couldn't even warm up our bones. When the cold sets in, all you need is a hot bath. These types of conditions could potentially make you sick, and they knew what they were doing. We would wash in freezing conditions; it was impossible to clean yourself properly, especially in the time we were given. Then the screws would rap their knuckles on the window to warn us we had a minute left. There was zero privacy and we constantly felt anxious. Any joy was sucked out of us.

There were no recreational facilities provided and, all the time, there was the constant unspoken threat of violence by the wing staff. In today's more enlightened and sensible penal system, steps would have been taken to defuse the situation, but things were different in the 1960s. The media didn't help, as they created a culture of fear and mistrust. Stories were constantly being spun; the media would invent weird and wonderful horror stories of how prisoners could escape, even from this wing. Due to the type of prisoners that had been selected for E wing, the prison decided to step up the security to another level. The authorities decided to move a small army detachment to Durham, to guard against any escape attempts from within E wing and to repel any assault on the prison by outside sources.

One Thursday evening, about 7:30pm, I was standing at my window getting some fresh air, when I heard the screech of a van outside. We all assumed it was a new prisoner arriving. On the road below me, a red transit van stopped. The doors flew open and out jumped a soldier, who stood in a crouched position, pointing his rifle at our cell windows. By this time, every window was occupied by a con with an astonished face, looking in amazement and bewilderment at the scene below. About eight soldiers tumbled out from the van, head to toe in fully-clad combat uniforms. To make things even more bizarre, they carried rifles and fixed bayonets.

A Sergeant got them in line. "Load weapons," he ordered. There was a series of metallic clicks as bullets went into the rifle breaches. "Carry on," he ordered, and the soldiers fell out and began to patrol the grounds around E wing.

We couldn't believe what we were seeing. Was this some sort of distorted alternative reality, or were we dreaming? Why were there soldiers with guns patrolling the prison? As far as I knew, this type of behaviour had never been seen before and I was completely baffled. Why would the prison need extra security of this level? Weren't the alarmed and steel doors and window bars enough of a deterrent? We stood watching for about an hour.

Someone shouted, "What are you doing here?" But we got no reply.

The soldiers obviously had orders not to speak to us. They acted like we were invisible, so all we could do was watch them, dumbfounded and mesmerised at the show unfolding before us.

In the morning, we woke and were eager to continue watching the outside entertainment. We could see that, during the night, the soldiers had built a sand-bag wall and placed it in the middle of the yard around an extraordinarily large machine gun, manned by two soldiers. They would aim the gun at us as we walked around the yard, and we knew they would have happily of shot us, if anyone stepped out of line.

This sorry saga carried on for a couple of weeks and we got used to their presence. One morning, I had an agonising toothache, from a severe infection. The screws got me an appointment with the dentist. A normal procedure; however, I was escorted by four army officials with bayonets, just to see the dentist! It was ridiculous; one man with a gun is extreme, but four army officials was insane. The poor dentist was shaking when he was examining my mouth. I felt for him; he must have thought I was a complete loon, with all this security around me. I wasn't as dangerous as these idiots liked to make out.

This went on for about three months, with the soldiers patrolling around, as if preparing for battle. We had no idea why the prison felt they needed to add a bonus threat of violence for good measure. After all, we couldn't go anywhere and we were locked up for twenty-three hours a day. Thankfully, the soldiers left the prison as quickly as they had arrived and I wondered if it was linked to three of the train robbers, who were removed from our wing and transferred to other high-security wings. The harsh regime ground on nevertheless. In today's more modern dispersal prisons, with their more relaxed regime, it is hard to appreciate what Durham's E wing was like when it was first opened. Today, you're allowed your own clothes, radio, CD players and access to telephones. For those who need it, there are doctors and psychologists to talk endlessly to, but in the 1960s, we had nothing. We were literally left to rot, and if your mind was not strong, your mental health would deteriorate at a rapid pace. You could lose yourself and never return if you allowed them to seep into your mind.

Overnight, the Home Office and police had created a special class of prisoner. We were in a league of our own, because if you had committed a serious crime, usually an armed robbery, you found yourself dumped in the waste pile of the category A system.

The regime in Durham was designed to break the spirits of prisoners, crush all hope and strip away any remaining piece of good within you. Once this new classification had been introduced, the governors used it to get rid of any undesirable prisoners and we were exactly that.

As time went on, E wing's population had grown to twenty. While the residents of the wing were increasing, we had quite a few protests over the conditions. Something had to change, as this simmering resentment was bursting at the seams. We were all waiting for a catalyst to spark something. For the last pin in the cushion. There were rumours that the new prison governor was going to introduce a new code of practice. New rules, more work, fewer privileges. This was the last straw.

We all decided enough was enough; we had to make a stand. After some days of intense discussion, we decided to storm into the wing offices and barricade ourselves inside them. And in so doing, we would bring our plight to the attention of the Home Office. In those days, we weren't allowed to have personal radios, for security reasons. Instead, there was a radio in the wing governor's office, which would pipe music or news to speakers in our cells.

On the evening we decided to take action, there was a football match being broadcast. I went to the officer in charge and asked if he would tune the radio into the match, so we could listen to it after we were locked away. He agreed and unlocked the gate leading to the office to go and follow my request. Once he was inside the room, me and another con hid in the doorway of a nearby cell. As he came out, we leapt onto the screw and I tore the key chain from his belt. As I did so, the rest of the nineteen cons charged down the landing and into the offices. The alarm bell went off and reinforcements arrived, but it was too late. I ran to the upper gate and we barricaded the entrance with anything we could lay our hands on. A couple of cons went to the telephone and took the opportunity to contact solicitors and newspapers; others followed, talking to their families. I was standing by the phone waiting my turn, when I heard this con talking to his young son and wife.

I heard the son say, "Dad, I'm going on a school outing tomorrow." I had to laugh. Amid all this pandemonium, a small voice of sanity telling his dad about his school outing.

I was looking around the office, trying to find items to use to keep the screws out. There was a metal filing cabinet standing in the corner, so I went over to use it for the barricades. But first, I ripped the door open and out fell all our records. We were elated; we could finally get to see all our information, which had been kept a secret from us, from the first day we entered the prison system. It's not every day a con gets the chance to read what the prison and police have written about them. It made interesting reading. Some of the reports were quite funny and way off the mark, while others were spot on. We shredded all of it during the night, mixing all the pieces together like spaghetti. A sense of freedom flooded over me when I tore mine into tiny shreds. It was an extremely liberating experience; the riot was worth going ahead with, just for that moment.

Throughout the night, we could see policemen and screws laying out hosepipes, in case we set fire to the offices. The screws were milling about, waving their three-foot riot batons in a threatening manner. Not quite knowing what to do, because we had caught them completely by surprise. All they could do was wave their pathetic sticks at us, as if to say, "We will get you when you come out." I can't say we were particularly worried. We were nineteen-handed and, if it came to a battle, they wouldn't have it all their own way. We were going to put up one hell of a fight and they knew it. During the night, the heating and electricity were turned off and the telephones disconnected, but it didn't bother us. We were used to living with fuck-all.

We sailed through the night; it was completely uneventful, and we enjoyed chatting and the camaraderie of sticking it to the man. In the morning, the wing governor approached the barricades and asked if we would consider coming out and returning to our cells.

We refused point blank; instead, we handed the governor a list of our grievances, which he promised would be carefully read by the number one governor and a Home Office official. With that, he left and we settled down to wait and see what response we would get.

At about nine pm, the wing governor again approached the gate and spoke to us. If we came out peacefully, our list of complaints would be looked at. And those complaints that could be put right would be done. We discussed what would be the best thing to do and agreed to end our protest. As far as we were concerned, we had won a bloodless victory. Which was all we wanted; a fair and just system. We agreed to come out two at a time, waving the white flag of surrender. If there was any violence, the rest would remain where they were, but we only had the intention of leaving peacefully. Me and another con agreed to go first, which was a brave step to take, considering how pissed off these screws were. I remember walking down the landing and all the screws were glaring at me; burning hatred penetrated my body. If looks could kill, I would have been dead on the spot. In their defence, they did do a decent turn; they let us have a shower, fresh clothes and a hot meal. The meal was a surprise; there was a big spread, with a roast dinner and custard for dessert. It was the best meal I ever had in there, which was much needed. And that was the end of the E wing protest. The final curtain.

The next day, we were told we would remain in solitary confinement, pending charges. Eventually, each man received a brown envelope, containing the charges. They read: damaging government property, taking over parts of a prison and mutiny. At that time, I believed we were the first convicts to be charged with mutiny since the Dartmoor mutiny in 1932. It all sounded grim and there was talk of us being tried in open court, which would have suited us fine, as we could expose the prison for what it was, if they did that. The riot had highlighted the conditions of the prison to the world. Now the high-security regime was fully exposed; their reign of terror didn't last and the wing was shut down in 1971, after a series of reports that the conditions were inhumane and the treatment of prisoners was unjust. The day in court never came, most likely because it would expose the true darkness of the system. It turned out, all that happened was that each man received forty-two days of solitary confinement.

I'd served about four weeks of my punishment, when once again, I was awoken by the sounds of four screws entering my cell, accompanied by a PO.

He snapped, "Get your personal belongings together, you're being moved."

I assumed I would go to Leicester or back to Pankhurst, to one of their high-security wings. Wherever I was going, I was elated to be moved, as now there was a small chance of escape! I grabbed my gear and shouted a quick farewell to the other cons, before being hustled out of the wing. Handcuffed, I was put into the back of a police car and away we went. The car swept down the motorway, through quaint towns, with blaring sirens and flashing lights, and I realised we were headed for Portsmouth. This meant the ferry to the Isle of Wight, back to my favourite place; Parkhurst. I was over moon, as Parkhurst high-security wing had the reputation of being quite liberal, which suited me fine and I had enjoyed the routine whilst I was there. When we arrived, I couldn't believe my luck; everything seemed great from the outset.

We went to the reception for the main prison, which meant I was out of top security classification and back into the main prison population, which was another brilliant bonus. So far, my day was going super well and I literally had a spring in my step. I had spent a few weeks in Parkhurst in 1963 and it was a relaxed regime. But by 1967, Parkhurst had changed drastically. By the time I got through the reception block, I could see I had jumped from the frying pan into the fire...

CHAPTER 21

PARKHURST RIOT OF 1969

I had already been in Pankhurst a few years before and it wasn't a bad prison then; it was relaxed, and the screws left you alone. Only the odd one would cause you bother. I was looking forward to being transferred there. As soon as I arrived, I asked a pal of mine, what the set up was like.

The reply I got was, "John, it's fucking terrible. They're giving out severe beatings down the chokey and nicking you for the most trivial things. They are always intimidating you with the unspoken threat of violence. Everyone is on edge when they are in their cell. Whenever you hear footsteps or the rattle of keys, you instinctively tense up in the fear they are coming for you."

I thought it would be near-on impossible to find a prison worse than Durham. Wasn't I lucky to be slung into hell on earth, only known as Parkhurst? The atmosphere and tension in Parkhurst prison now were far worse than Durham. I couldn't believe it; I had done three years' hard time, living like a caged beast; all I was looking for was some light relief and a break but, alas, it wasn't to be. When I hit the main prison, all my fears were confirmed; you could find yourself on report for the most trivial offences.

One of the main areas of resentment was the way the punishment block was run. It was a regime of continuous aggravation and harassment. There was a grim joke doing the rounds at Parkhurst about the two types of shifts working down the block. There was the kicking shift and the nicking shift, and it was an accurate description. So once again, I found myself in a potentially explosive and volatile situation. Every day was a day of tension, every day was a day of near confrontation, and everyone could see trouble was coming, sooner rather than later. It was only a matter of time and, once again, the Governor and the people in charge did nothing to diffuse the situation. I did not believe that the conditions and treatment of prisoners could be allowed to deteriorate to such a level.

Sometimes, people exaggerate just so the story is more gripping, and your attention is focused on them. But unfortunately, everything I was told was true. The atmosphere was awful; all the convicts lived on tenterhooks, thinking they were going to get it next. There was no rhyme or reason for the attacks on the prisoners; the guards enjoyed taking their anger out on us. You only had to look at them the wrong way and you were in for a rough night. They were drunk with power, and we didn't deserve all the abuse we got. And yes, we were criminals, and some of us deserved to be punished, but wasn't prison punishment enough?

This situation continued for at least two years before it kicked off. There was so much violence, hate and tension, something had to happen. I've found that it always takes a catalyst that occurs and it's always the prison management that kicks things off.

Not one convict says, "I know, tomorrow we will have a riot."

It is always one bad decision after another by the prison governor or the screws, that lights the fuse, igniting the fire in the bellies of the prisoners. In the 1960s, the Parkhurst Governor was a charming man, friendly by nature and outwardly approachable. After meeting him, you'd think he wasn't a bad Governor or person. It was a big mistake to take him at face value as a good guy, though; the Governor allowed the staff to do what they liked. He didn't give a fuck about our well-being. He turned a blind eye to the trivial reports and, more importantly, to the constant violence the screws inflicted on a weekly basis against the cons. One example was on the chokey landing at the bottom of the prison. Directly underneath B Wing, so under your cell, would be some poor soul doing chokey time. Other convicts used to talk to them from above and you could hear everything that went on. It was used as a torture room, for the screws' sick and twisted fantasies.

Everything came to head one gloomy Sunday. One con said he didn't want any dinner. The chokey screw said he must come and collect his food; it was a direct order. The con refused once again and said he didn't want any dinner. The screw left without a word, shut his door and continued unlocking the rest of the cons for their evening meal. When everyone had finished eating, a few screws went back to the con who had refused to eat, opened his door, rushed in and gave him a severe beating. They left his head and face alone, instead concentrating on his body.

The man started screaming, "Help, help!"

A few cons jumped to their windows, shouting, "You dirty, cowardly cunts."

This con was unlucky because he was on the kicking shift, down in the chokey. They wouldn't nick you; they would give you a beating instead. The other shift was the nicking shift, where you were nicked but not beat up; it all depended on what screws were on shift. You were tremendously unlucky if you got the fucked-up shift.

A few days later, this con came back up on the wing and showed us his body, which was red raw and brutally bruised from the intense and horrific kicking he took. He was a mess; his whole body was marked, so he looked like a prisoner of war. Everyone on the wing was outraged; the screws were taking their love of power, control and violence too far.

The prison was becoming a place of constant fear and uncertainty; the winds of change were fast approaching, and I could feel something brewing. The straw that broke the camel's back was that the governor gave the order that all the Cat A prisoners had to move onto the landing. Which happened to have dark, damp and rotten cells. Going from one shitty cell to an even worse one tipped the cons to another level of contempt. Every single one of the Cat A prisoners made an application to complain. They wanted to know why they should be moved from a decent cell, down to the dungeon-like cells. A group of cons gathered round; about twenty to thirty cons were bitching about the proposed move. Then someone said what we should do was what I had done in Durham and put a barricade up in the association areas as a protest. A light bulb moment! This idea was favoured quickly amongst the cons, and this was the beginning of the infamous, so-called Pankhurst riots.

We planned our protest for the Friday evening, October the 25th at seven pm. At that time, no con intended any violence to anyone. The intention was a peaceful protest, to get our point across that we were unhappy, and things needed to change. But instead, the so-called Pankhurst riot of 69 turned into a short, brutal and bloody affair. Over the time I was there, I had watched intently how the mechanics of the prison worked. This was an occupational hazard of mine. I had noticed that the steel gates, which led up some stairs to the recreational areas, opened outwards. As quickly as the cons threw the furniture down the stairs to form a barricade, all the screws needed to do was unblock the gates, pull the barricade out and make a swift entry. I did try to tell a couple of the cons, but my misgivings of the idea were brushed aside. They were already pumped with rage; like bulls to a red flag, they were ready to charge full steam ahead.

Even with the doubts I had, I decided to join them and make my mark with the rest of them, fucking the consequences. What did I have to lose? I was doing a life sentence anyway, so how much more could they punish me? The word spread of our rampage like wildfire through the prison, that a serious protest was going down and it would take place that night. Of course, what wasn't considered was that some arsehole would mark the screws' card, letting them know exactly what was going to happen. There is always one puny grass, who ruins it for the rest. So, the night in question, before the riot started, they were fully prepared with intel and had several three-foot riot sticks stored in the laundry room, near the isolation area. The screws couldn't wait to steam into us; they were like bloodthirsty hounds, on standby to pounce at the slightest opportunity. That night, around a hundred prisoners made their way to the association area. Two screws, upon entry, were looking rather nervous, and I can't say I blamed them. I would be scared for my life if the shoe were on the other foot.

Suddenly, a con threw a table down the stairs and then the ripple effect ensued. It kicked off, big time. Cons were ripping up and throwing anything they could use; all their rage and pent-up aggression was now at full throttle and was a sight to behold. I remember helping to dismantle the snooker table to use as a barricade, thinking to myself that this had got out of hand; the place was wild. They stormed the kitchen and ripped the hot plates off; steam filled the prison like a misty fog, making it difficult to see what was going on. Debris was thrown everywhere, and the stairs were piled high with broken furniture and anything that was not stuck to the walls or floor. There was no way the screws had time to clear the stairs, as the furniture kept coming, thick and fast. Everything the cons could get their hands on, they smashed to smithereens and the whole place was in pandemonium.

We took two screws hostage, but they were not harmed. They were put into an empty room, where they stayed safe and sound throughout the entire affair. They stood by an open window, talking to the screws in the grounds so they could see our captives were in no danger whatsoever. But the two screws in the room freaked out; they were like deer in headlights. One con took a screw's hat from his head and his truncheon from his trouser leg. The screw was frozen in fear; he seemed so traumatised he did not know what to do, and who had done what. The other screw stood by the window, talking to his mates with a look of concern etched on his face. You could see he was trying to style out his fear, but his body language was enough to know he was shaken. I could imagine he was saying to his fellow screws, 'For fuck's sake, get me out of here.'

It took an hour for the first wave of screws to come; they fought their way through the barricade and into the association area. There was a con standing in the recess near the stairs. A screw went in and, before the screw knew it or could do anything, he had his throat cut. Sliced from one side to another, blood flowing down him like a river. The last time I saw him, he was being helped down the stairs, holding a blood-soaked towel, trying to stem the bleeding. That's when I knew the riot had gone too far; protest is one thing, but attempted murder is quite another.

My pal was standing beside me. He said, "Fucking hell, John, there are going to be murders tonight."

A big, fat, gluttonous screw, who was well-known for being a bully, got struck in the head by a billiard ball. I saw him stagger and thought, you deserve that you bastard. He too was helped away. The cons were causing casualties left, right and centre. By now, the war was on, and blood was being spilt on the battle ground. The screws that were left standing were enraged. Their blood was boiling and they beat down and attacked anyone they could get hold of. There were some cons that never took part, but there were mini battles going on all over the prison. The screws forced their way along the corridor, pushing cons backwards until there were about twenty-five of us crammed into a room. We just stood there quietly and hoped for the best. A couple of screws came to the door and if they recognised anyone, they said, "Outside." I was standing behind some cons, hoping no one had seen me. But no such luck.

"Come on, Hilton, you're one of them."

I looked down the landing and I was shocked by the damage and destruction covering the ground. It was littered with broken glass, doors ripped off, debris everywhere. I remember seeing a bloody handprint on the wall; for a moment, I thought, this is what horror films are made of. It was an eerie experience and unnerving as I walked out into the chaos before me.

I saw the passage lined with about thirty screws, foaming at the mouth, carrying truncheons. I took a deep breath and proceeded to walk down the corridor, knowing what was coming my way; a good kicking. I was moving as quickly as I could, but mostly concerned not to lose my footing. Doing my best to avoid the kicks and blows aimed at me. It wasn't easy but eventually I emerged, all limbs still intact, but badly bruised and bloody-faced. I walked down the next landing, turned right to go down the stairs and I had another shock, as more screws stretched in front of me. They were wearing black leather gloves and carrying their personal truncheons, which they probably kissed goodnight, the night before. My mind went blank. Only one thought was in my head; for fuck's sake, keep on your feet and move as quickly as you can. I took a deep breath and plunged into the guards. I had punches and truncheons, blows raining down on me from all angles. As I reached the end, I thought, that was not too bad. I walked past the governor; he only had a three-foot riot stick in his hand and, as I passed him, he struck me across the kidneys.

The force of the blow knocked me to my knees. As I got up, I leaned over and vomited. The pain was excruciating. I staggered down the landing, which led to the chokey. There was a bunch of screws waiting for me. Oh fuck, I thought, I was going to get some more kicks and blows. I was thinking I really couldn't cope with anymore. However, all that happened was I was ordered to remove my shoes, after which I was thrust into a cell and the door slammed shut behind me. I must say, I've never been so happy to get in a cell and out of the way of all the commotion. I just slid down the wall; I couldn't stand up. I crumpled up; my kidneys, they were so painful. I didn't know what to do, so I just sat there for a long time before I could move to go and lie on my bed. I remember getting up in the night for a piss and I was pissing blood, which was so painful. It was one of the worst beatings I have ever had from the screws. That night, I did wonder if I would survive.

After some time in the chokey, I was marched to my own cell and slung inside, sweating and out of breath. I was still in a lot of pain, and I was just about managing to walk. I sat, slumped on the floor, trying to muster up some energy. I took some time to count my bruises and counted the lumps on my head and face. I was completely covered and imagined it would take ages before

I would get better. I would only recover If the screws didn't lay into me again. I was kept in solitary confinement for about five months. Mentally, solitary confinement is hard, even harder when it goes on for months on end. The endless boredom and lack of contact kills your very soul. But I always reminded myself that it wouldn't and couldn't last forever. With that thought firmly at the forefront of my mind, I stayed sane.

For a short while, the screws thought they had delivered a crushing blow to the convicts, but what they did not consider was that, once they brought the charges against convicts for various offences, it created the chance to reveal the true conditions that existed in Parkhurst. Solicitors were allowed in the prisons; convicts were interviewed, and the sorry truth emerged. Parkhurst was plastered all over the press and an investigation was launched. I find it strange that only one question remained unanswered: why weren't steps taken to prevent the onslaught of abuse in the first place? To protect the rights of the prisoners, to protect our human rights.

CHAPTER 22

BLOOD DIAMONDS

Eventually, in the early part of the 1970s, I was nearing the end of my sentence . Time had been a cruel burden on me; it had passed so slowly, full of boredom and uneventful days, but I was now seeing the light at the end of the tunnel. I was transferred to Hull prison. After the years of continual trouble in Durham and Parkhurst, Hull was the relief I needed. It was a relaxed and easy regime, and I could finally lick my wounds and reflect on the misery I had suffered in those God-awful prisons.

I spent four uneventful years there and was taken off the category A status and eventually moved back to sunny Lewes prison, where I was given my discharge date. Lewes was a home from home; I had been in and out of there more times than I'd had hot dinners. I was hoping to spend my last few months in there, but as you know, they liked to transfer me to different prisons for the fun of it. They decided to move me to Coldingley prison for the last six months of my life sentence . Coldingley was a prison situated in Surrey; it was a brand-new nick, opening in 1969. It was set up to be a training prison, designed to support people into work. To learn a new skill or upskill, in preparation for release. Getting prisoners used to hard labour and making an honest living by setting up work schemes, like painting and decorating. They thought somehow this type of prison would rehabilitate me and make me want to become a working member of society. An honest, law-abiding citizen; it was laughable the hoops they made you jump through for your freedom.

It was at Coldingley that I first met and became friends with

Alan Roberts. He, like me, had only a few months left to serve. Like all convicts, we talked about what we do once we were free. We both agreed the only thing to do was to return to crime; after all, who was going to employ a dangerous armed robber? Alan gave me the name of the pub in the East End where he could always be found, so I had his location stored away for a rainy day. I would be released after serving fifteen years; the time had been a long and tough sentence, and the last year dragged, as I anticipated my release. I couldn't wait to be back in society again.

After a lifer has won his release date, he must go through a planned routine. One of the conditions of your release is that you must live and work in a pre-release hostel for the last six months of your sentence. The theory was, it was a slow and gradual release back into society, whereby we would get used to work and the world we once lived in. I arrived in Maidstone hostel in 1977, with about five months to serve before I would be released from a life sentence. You were expected to find work, to be eligible for regular weekend home leave. I hunted around until I found a job at an engineering works in Stroud. I worked regular nights, testing oil pumps for various makes of cars and I hated every minute of it. It was dirty, boring work. Night work turned my body clock upside-down and I always felt tired. But I had no choice; I had to stick it out, for the sake of my freedom.

On my first weekend home, I got in touch with an old friend of mine who, like me, was just out of prison and asked him if he could get a bit of work, which ideally could be done on a Friday or Saturday night, whilst I was on my release. I couldn't wait to go on the rob; it was an itch I had to scratch.

He smiled and said, "You've not changed, have you, John? Even a life sentence doesn't deter you. As a matter of fact, I know a small bag that could go without too much trouble. It's the week's takings from a clothes store in Hackney."

In great detail, he explained; every Saturday night, this guy would bring the week's takings in a leather bag, and put the bag in the boot of his car, which was parked in a nearby car park, which was dark and quiet. We thought that would be the best place for the robbery. My pal would drive the getaway car and I would squirt the guy with ammonia, nick the bag and we would go.

"How much will it come to?" I inquired.

"I reckon about six grand, give or take," he responded.

I shrugged; it wasn't much, but I had no money and it sounded like an easy touch. So, we arranged the robbery for the following Saturday. I was happy with any work that came my way. I couldn't be fussy, as I only had two days out of the week to pull off the job.

I returned to the hostel and carried on working as normal. The week would drag, and the labour was intense. I thought, fuck, imagine doing this line of work forever, for a pittance. On Friday, I made my way to my friend's flat, had a few drinks, wound down and spent a relaxed evening. On Saturday morning, I went out and bought a woolly cap and a bottle of scrubs and household ammonia, which I transferred to an empty bottle of Fairy Liquid. My pal provided me with some appropriate clothing, a pair of gloves and a balaclava. We decided the robbery would take place at seven pm on Saturday night. We drove over to Hackney and parked the car near the store owner's car. I got out of the car with a carrier bag containing the ammonia and stood on the corner, waiting for the man to finish locking up, before making his way back to the car. As he did so, I walked behind him and let him go to his car to open his boot.

"Excuse me," I said.

As he turned, I squirted the ammonia in his face. He had no idea what was coming. He gasped in shock; as he was now confused and vulnerable, it was my opportunity to attack. I punched him as hard as I could on the side of the jaw. He staggered back and fell on the ground; I snatched the bag, ran to the car and we roared away. It was over in seconds; we dumped our car a short distance away and made our way to my pal's flat. When the money was counted and cut up, my share came to just over three grand. Not a lot, but at least I had some moving money, and I was satisfied with how things had gone. Like a duck to water, I was back doing what I know best. It felt good to be robbing again and making some real money.

I returned to the hostel on Saturday evening and carried on as usual. With some of the Hackney robbery money, I bought a new car, a Ford Cortina. We decided that my pal could use it during the week, but at the weekends, it was mine to use, and do with as I wished. I was still working long and tedious nights, but the time started to pass nicely. Then the day of freedom came; my final discharge papers from a life sentence. I was now a free man; I had jumped through every hoop required to be walking the streets again.

I was given a probation officer upon my release. I remember asking him during one of my weekly visits, if I needed help, would he help me out? If he could find me work and get me back on my feet. Of course, this was only a bluff. I never needed any help, but I was curious to see if he could or would and what his reaction would be. I was also trying to throw him off the scent and make him think I was looking for regular employment.

He would just smile. "All I can do is give you advice, if required."

I nodded; fifteen years in prison and all society could offer me was advice. It's just as well I didn't rely on anyone except myself. The system was a joke; there was nothing in place for prisoners once they left prison. They were left to their own devices; no wonder more than half of criminals out of the nick returned to crime. To keep up the pretence that I was on the straight and narrow, I decided to rent a stall in Ridley Road market in Hackney, selling handbags and purses. It was a convenient cover; if anyone asked how I was earning a living and if my probation officer ever decided to check on me and dig a little deeper into my finances, he would see the stall and think all was well in my new line of legal work. Then, hopefully, the law would leave me alone and harass some other poor soul.

Ongoing, I was required to report to a probation officer in Lordship Lane, Tottenham. I was supposed to be living in White

Hart Lane with a friend of mine, dealing in scrap metal for a living. I was using it as a registered address. But instead, I was staying in the West End and that was where I met my pal, Alan Roberts, again.

One glorious Sunday, I thought I would shoot over to the Spread Eagle and have a drink with Alan. The pub was packed with lunchtime drinkers. I pushed my way to the bar and ordered a long, stiff drink, scanning the bar for Alan. And sure enough, there he was, tucked up in the corner, reading a newspaper, looking relaxed and deeply immersed in the daily news. We were pleased to see each other; we exchanged news over drinks and the conversation turned back to our line of work. He told me he was on bail for armed robbery, and he couldn't work with his regular firm, as the police would most likely have them under observation. I knew he was going to offer up some work; I could see that all-too-familiar glint in his eyes that I had seen a thousand times before.

"There's a guy I know, who works in Hatton Garden. I want to stick up this jeweller, who carries a parcel of diamonds home with him. We can do it two-handed once we have strapped him down."

"That's no problem," I replied. My heart was singing; diamonds meant big cash.

"Also, the guy who's sticking the work up wants two of the stones, as well; that will be his drink," Alan remarked.

"How much are we talking about?" I asked, with the hope of dollar signs lighting up in my eyes.

Alan lowered his voice. "Four hundred thousand."

Without sounding too excited, I replied, "Sounds alright to me, but I'd like to meet this guy and look him over and we will need his number as well." I was over the moon with this potential work. This type of money could set me up for a decent amount of time.

Alan agreed to arrange a meeting. They guy seemed alright, nothing special about him. But I was happy enough to sign off the work and go ahead with the job. He also gave us the location of the jeweller's office. So, it would be a simple task to track his routine. The jeweller was an alert and quick driver, but invariably took the same route every night. It was just a case of tracking him in stages, following him so far, then picking him up from where we left off the next night and so on. Until eventually we tracked him to his house in Limes Avenue in Golders Green, North London.

Limes Avenue was a dimly-lit street, lined with beautiful trees. The houses were made of substantial brick, each with its own idyllic front garden. The dim street lighting left dark patches of shadow, ideal for concealment. On my scouting trips to Limes Avenue, I noticed that a fairly large lorry was usually parked, opposite the jeweller's house. My plan was to lie directly under the lorry, hidden by the cast of the shadows, by the rear wheels. From there, I could see the road to the pavement leading to the jeweller's house. Alan would hide in the darkness of some nearby garages.

The night of the robbery was gloomy and overcast, with a fine drizzly rain coating the roads; typical British weather. We drove along Golders Green main road and turned left into Limes Avenue; it stretched out in front of us, cold and deserted, which meant no witnesses. The tarmac gleamed with rain, bouncing shimmers of light across the street. All the houses had their curtains drawn, to protect their thin windows from the chill of the night air.

We drove slowly down towards the jeweller's house and coasted to a halt, a couple of houses before the jeweller's home. If the jeweller took any notice of a strange car, he was likely to assume it was someone visiting a nearby house.

Alan and I got out of the car; we were both dressed in dark clothing, with caps pulled down to hide our faces. We split up without a word; Alan had brought a small truncheon, which I thought was far too small for a robbery of this nature. He would use it to hit the jeweller over the head and snatch the bag, which we believed would contain four hundred thousand pounds of diamonds. I decided to carry my weapon of choice, a sawn-off shotgun, in case things got out of hand.

I watched Alan blend in perfectly in his dark clothes and drift away in the shadows. I walked over to the lorry, glanced around quickly and slid under it to hide behind its rear wheels. The shotgun lay by my side, within easy reach. I hoped the jeweller would be on time; already, the damp was seeping through my trousers, and I was getting rather uncomfortable, squashed under the lorry, lying on the cold, hard ground. Lights suddenly flashed along the avenue, and I heard a car approaching. I reached for the shotgun, but the car drove by and disappeared around the corner.

Silence settled on the Avenue, and I shivered as the damp seeped further into my clothes. Minutes ticked by; I could hear footsteps drawing nearer. Come on, I thought, this is taking too long, and my patience was wearing thin. I heard voices getting louder as they approached, but it was only two pedestrians on their way home, probably from a hard day's graft or drinking. I knew he wouldn't be long now. The next car to the Avenue slowed down and parked just behind the lorry; it was the jeweller's maroon Daimler. I saw his shoes and trouser cuffs as he climbed out from his flashy Daimler, locked it and walked slowly across the Avenue in the direction of his house. As he was walking away from me, I could see he wore an unbuttoned dark overcoat and carried a black bag in his left hand.

Suddenly, the silhouette of Alan came from the shadows of the garages, his cosh in his hand, ready to strike. We had not expected the jeweller to put up a struggle, but he was quick and determined; he wasn't going to let the bag go without putting up a good fight. As Alan struck the jeweller, he raised his bag to deflect the blows and quickly retreated towards the safety of his house. I rolled out from under the lorry and went after them; the jeweller was already outside his house, still struggling with Alan. It felt like we were in danger of losing the prize and I had to make a quick decision. I aimed the shotgun at the jeweller's legs, intending to give him one barrel. That would stop him in his tracks. But, as I fired, Alan twisted around in the struggle and took the shot in his left thigh.

He dropped to one knee but immediately regained his feet. The jeweller turned and fled towards his front door. I could see he was getting away, so I shot him in the back, knocking him off his feet. Like a scene from a thriller film, he seemed to hang in mid-air before crashing face down on the pavement. I grabbed the bag, thrust Alan into the rear seat of the car and tossed the bag after him, landing on his chest. I threw the shotgun onto the front passenger seat and took off at high speed. Spinning right, then right again, up towards the main road, past Limes Avenue, past the cinema, skidding sharp left and away to safety. In the mirror, I could see Alan hunched over, holding his leg in the back seat.

"How are you?" I was hoping the shot was just a flesh wound. Nothing too serious.

"I'm in trouble," Alan replied in anguish, and I could hear the pain in his voice.

"Try and stop the bleeding, we have a fair way to go."

He nodded. "I will do what I can. Did you get the bag, John?" Robbers always have one thing on our mind; no matter the situation, money came first.

"Yeah, I got it." Was the bag of diamonds worth all this fucking aggro? I started to wonder. This must be what it means when they say blood diamonds.

CHAPTER 23

ALAN

The original plan was to go to where Alan lived, but that was now out of the question. I was in a terrible predicament; if I took Alan to the hospital, there was no way I could get him out of the car without my face being seen. If I dumped the car outside a hospital with Alan in it, it would be tracked back to the robbery and Alan would be looking at a thirty-year sentence, minimum. There was only one thing to do; I had the use of a small flat in Lee Green, South London, that nobody knew about, except the friend who had loaned it to me and, most importantly, there was a garage that came with the flat. As we drove, I told Alan where we were going, and he agreed it was our best chance. I also knew a questionable doctor who might be able to help. The rain was getting heavier, and I drove carefully, until to my great relief, we reached the flat and garage. My heart was racing, and I was praying the wound wasn't too bad. The garage doors were open, and I drove straight inside. I got out and pulled the garage door shut from the inside. I switched the light on. Alan was slumped across the bloodstained rear seat; he couldn't move, and I could see the agony etched over his face. The shotgun blast had scooped a large, ragged circular hole in his thigh. I could see the black pellets embedded in the wound and there was blood gushing everywhere.

I made him as comfortable as I could and said I was shooting over to the flat. I knew a crooked doctor who lived in Brixton; the best bet was to phone him up and get him over. But all I got was the doctor's answerphone. I shook my head in despair and disbelief. Snatching a blanket from the bed and a couple of towels, I rushed back to the garage. Alan's face, now whiter than ever, looked at me enquiringly.

I shook my head. "The doctor wasn't in, but I will try again."

I packed the towels around his thigh and put the blanket around him to keep him warm.

"My feet are cold," he said.

I took his shoes and socks off; his feet were like clumps of ice. The loss of blood and shock were killing him and we were running out of time. The cold seemed to be creeping up to his thighs and his face was pasty-white. I took off my sweater and wrapped it round his feet. I was helpless. A short while later, the breath rattled in his throat and I knew then it was the end. He died. I just sat there; I couldn't believe what had happened. The shock kept me seated for some minutes, staring at his lifeless body. My hands were in my hair; I was numb. I just stared at his body, trying to work out what to do.

Then I moved, reloaded the shotgun and placed it on the roof of the car, within easy reach. I remember thinking, I am in terrible, terrible trouble. But there was no time to hang around feeling sorry for myself or having a mental breakdown. I had a dead body to dispose of and the hottest car in London. The police would go flat-out on this one; they would be kicking doors off left, right and centre, all around the area. Every known robber would get a strong pull, including me.

I opened the boot and wrestled Alan's heavy body into it. I locked the boot and spread the blanket over the rear seat to hide the bloodstains, retrieved the bag of diamonds, locked the car doors, pocketed the keys, hid the shotgun and turned the light out. I closed the garage doors and walked the short distance back to the flat. Once inside, I put the shotgun and the bag on my table and collapsed into the chair, thinking, what the hell should I do? I had been away for a long time, so the police might take a little longer to pull me in; if I was lucky, maybe a week. I had a lot of work to do. Tomorrow, I would have to find a place to bury Alan; that would have to be done tomorrow night. On the second day, I would have to get rid of the car. If I could do all this in forty–eight hours, I stood a chance of coming through alright. If I got pulled in, I would say I had only been home for a month and spin a story, saying why would I go on a robbery so soon after my release? After serving fifteen years, I'd had enough of prison and my bottle had gone from armed robbery. It made sense and they should believe me.

I got up and poured myself a stiff drink. I drank myself into a stupor and looked at the bag, which was soaked in Alan's blood. I shook my head, thinking, what a fucking state to be in. I reached across and opened the bag. There was three grand in cash inside, which was handy. At least I had a few quid to hold me up until I sold the stones. I put the money on the table beside my drink. The diamonds were in a small oblong leather pouch, zippered around the outside. Inside were rows of clear plastic envelopes, containing diamonds of various carats and colours. I shook a few into the palm of my hand, watching them glitter and shine as they caught the light. I had no idea what they were worth. I was sure I would find out in tomorrow's papers. I packed the diamonds away and left the bag on the table. I was hot, sweaty and my clothes were heavily bloodstained. I stripped off and put my bloodstained clothes into a plastic bin liner, ready for disposal in the morning. I took my drink and went into the bathroom for a bath. I sat on the toilet seat with a heavy heart, as my bath was running, planning what to do.

I'd get up early to get the newspapers and see what they said about the robbery and the value of the diamonds. As luck would have it, a pal of mine had a car dealership in Lee High Road, so I would go and see him. Give him two hundred quid and ask for the use of a small van and a decent car for two days. I could use the car to find a burial site, then come back for the van and use it as transport to carry Alan's body to the burial. I had to remember to buy a spade and fork, big enough and strong enough to dig a grave. I stepped into the bath and let the steaming water gush over me. I lay back with a sigh of relief and thought, this is one fucked-up situation.

I got up early, had a large breakfast, thinking that it may have to last me all day. I made my way to the newsagents and got myself three newspapers, which, lo and behold, were filled with the events of the robbery. The police were looking for the getaway car; according to the paper, the diamonds were worth two hundred and eighty thousand pounds. I walked down to Lee High Road to the car front. My pal was buzzing to see me. Especially when I had told him I had come to give him some money. I picked out a transit van and a dark brown Rover for two days. No questions asked.

I decided Kent would be the nearest countryside. It would have to be near a road, as I didn't fancy dragging a dead body too far. I drove towards the Dartford Tunnel; the traffic wasn't too heavy, so it was easy driving. I spotted a sign saying Stone on the left-hand-side. I drove past a small parade of shops, among which I noted was a garden centre. I crossed an arterial road and entered a country lane that looked promising. To my right was a series of flat grassy fields and, to my left, were some dog kennels and a chorus of barking dogs. A railway line ran parallel to the lane. I slowed down and saw a stretch of rough, grassy ground, sloping up towards the tracks of the railway, dotted with clumps of bushes. There was a small stone wall, topped with a single strand of rusty barbed wire, which fenced off the embankment from the public. I stopped the car, got out, jumped over the wall and saw a sprawl of bushes that stood in front of a steel pylon. I walked up the embankment and looked around; at night, this spot couldn't be seen from the lane. It could be seen from the railway, but I could easily duck down behind the bushes if a train approached. I'd found the ideal burial ground.

I returned to the car and drove further down the lane. Again, I was lucky; there was a hard shoulder where I could park the van, just off the lane. I turned round and drove back to Stone, where I stopped at the garden centre to buy the digging tools. Back at Lee High Road, I parked near to the centre and quickly transferred the spade and fork into the van, before handing the keys of the

Rover back to my pal. I drove the van back to my flat; it was about two pm so I had plenty of time. I would be taking Alan's body to Stone, leaving at about eleven-thirty at night. I cleaned and reloaded the shotgun; it would travel under the driver's seat of the van, with extra ammunition. I wasn't going to be caught with a dead body in the van. Any policeman that stopped me would have to lose their life too. In my head, I thought I would have to go all the way, if the worst scenario came about. So, I carried the shotgun under the seat; I had nothing to lose except my freedom and that was more valuable than anything.

The time seemed to drag on; when eleven-thirty came around, knots tied themselves up in my stomach. I was already fully dressed in dark clothes, so I drove to the garage next to the flat and backed the van up to the garage door, as close to it as it would go. I squeezed past the van and opened the boot of the car. Alan lay in the same position, huddled on his side in the foetal position. Taking a deep breath, I bent down, and manhandled his body from the boot of the car into the back of the van. The smell of death wafted around me, and I felt a sense of sadness and great loss. I jumped inside, hauled his body further in and covered him with a blanket. It was still raining as I drove towards Stone and the traffic was light. It was getting on for midnight now, and I knew no one would be on the road soon.

As I drove, I spotted a panda car parked in a lay-by, and all I could think was, I hope he doesn't stop me. If he does, he will be in for a terrible shock. But as I drove by, all I got was a cursory glance. I drove steadily through Stone, crossed the main road and drove down the dark lane. The dogs in the kennels were quiet, most likely fast asleep, and the huge pylon rearing towards the sky guided me in the right direction. When I drew level with the pylon, I stopped the van, leaving the engine running. I opened the back and started to haul Alan's heavy body out.

Suddenly, I saw a flash of light. A car was approaching; I couldn't believe it. I quickly bent down and pretended I was checking the exhaust pipe. I prayed they wouldn't stop and offer assistance, and thankfully the car drove on straight past me. I waited a few moments and then continued to wrestle Alan's body out of the van and over the low stone wall. I tossed the spade and fork after him, closed the van doors, drove quickly to the hard shoulder and parked the van. I hurried back with the shotgun and laid it alongside the tools. Grabbing an ankle in each hand, I began to haul Alan's body up the embankment to the pylon. Leaving him by one of the huge steel legs, I then returned down the slope to retrieve the tools and shotgun, and went to the centre of the pylon. I marked out an area of about six feet by three feet and began to remove the turf. I put the turf to one side, to be replaced when I had finished. During the years I'd spent in prison, I'd heard of too many bodies being discovered because of being buried in shallow graves. I was not going to make the same mistake.

I removed my sweater and began to dig steadily through the earth to the mud and clay below. By now, I was sweating heavily and welcomed the cooling rain, hitting my hot skin. I carried on digging until the ground was level with my shoulders, with earth and clay piled high on each side. As I looked up, I had a sudden irrational fear that it would all collapse on top of me. I sprang out, using the spade as a lever and stood for a while in the rain and darkness, before turning to Alan's body. I dragged him to the edge of the grave and pushed him in. I quickly shovelled about two feet of earth over him. I didn't want the grave to subside, to reveal its outline, so I had to jump into the grave and stamp and tread the earth down over his body. This was the worst part of the job, but I had no choice. I had to keep to the sequence of every layer of earth being carefully packed down. Finally, I replaced the turf as best as best I could and, at last, the job was done.

I was exhausted and mentally drained, but there was still much to do. I brushed bits of earth and clay away from the grave; give it a good six weeks and nobody would ever know the earth had been disturbed. It was not a place where people walked anyway, so it would be unlikely and unfortunate if someone decided to walk this way. But that could be a possibility anywhere, so I had to go with my gut instinct and choose what I thought would be the best burial ground. I was soaked in a mixture of sweat and rain. I pulled my sweater over my head, gathered the tools and the shotgun and headed down the slope to the van. It was now the early hours of the morning, a dangerous time to be out, the time when police would do random checks. I brushed myself down, wiped the earth from my shoes as best I could and set back off to London.

The rain had stopped and the drive to the flat proved uneventful, which was a blessing. Once inside, I breathed a huge sigh of relief and all the anxiety of getting Alan's body buried melted away. I stripped off my soiled clothes, added them to the blood-stained ones in the bin liner and had a well-earnt and needed bath. I was fully wiped out, tired and still in shock, as I had just buried a dead body. I knew I would not sleep, however tired I was, and I wondered If I would ever get a good night's sleep again. I kept seeing his face and the grave, as I shut my eyes in the hot bubbles, soothing my weary body.

Instead of sleeping, I sat in my armchair and watched the new day dawn. I felt I hadn't done badly in the last twenty-four hours, as I knew the gun and clothes could be easily disposed-of. But by now, the car's description would have been circulated to every policeman and their informers would be on the lookout as well. The only edge I had was that the newspaper's description called it light-coloured or white, when in fact it was gold. This was the hottest car in London; if I dumped it, that would give the police a good starting point. The car had to disappear completely and the only thing I could think of was to have it crushed. I decided to contact an old friend of mine, who had been in the scrap metal game all his life, and ask if he could help me. All I would say was that I wanted a motor crushed and could he do it for a few quid. If he refused, my second option was to take it to a quiet spot and burn it. By now it was nearly eight am; without any sleep, I still had a mountain of work to do. I made myself tea and toast, then checked the van for clay and dirt before driving it back to the forecourt. I returned the keys without any issues and went on my next mission, to track my friend down in the scrap metal game. After a bit of searching, I eventually found him at the bar, in a pub in Lewisham. He was happy to see me and, over a couple of drinks, I explained my situation, leaving out some details.

"No problem," he said. "We can get it done today, if you like?" Music to my ears!

He named a scrap metal yard where I should go and that I should bring the car for one-thirty pm. All he would have to do was give the foreman a drink; two hundred quid would do, and the job would be done.

I couldn't believe my luck. I gave him one hundred for his trouble; all I had to do was be there on time. We shook hands and I left there well pleased. I returned to the flat and decided to kill two birds with one stone. I broke the shotgun down, put it in the bag with the clothes and placed the bag in the boot of the car. They would disappear, along with the car. There was nothing I could do about the bloodstained rear seat, except keep it covered with the blanket and make sure nobody got a look at it. It was now approaching one o'clock; time to leave. I drove through the backstreets, only crossing main roads when forced to. My pal was waiting at gates with a tall burly man, whom I took to be the foreman. I was waved straight in and parked near the ginormous crushing machine.

"Everything alright?" I asked.

"Don't worry, John. He is going to do it straight away; he thinks it's an insurance claim."

The foreman waved his hand, and the huge grab was lowered into the compacting machine. Great hydraulic rams effortlessly crushed the car into a neat metal cube. Little did I know, you had to empty the petrol tank before you crushed your car; the whole thing blew up into a ball of fire. The fire brigade was called, causing carnage and some attention on me, people turning to my embarrassed face. But thankfully, the job was done.

If I was pulled over by the police, all I had to do was stick to my story and there was nothing they could do to me. The only thing that was niggling at me was the guy who had set the job up. I was a bit concerned about selling the diamonds to the man who had stuck the work up, for a number of reasons. Could the police be watching him and how much did they know? Also, I thought he might think, due to the shooting, it would be too dangerous to handle the stones and I had a feeling he would not want the heat anywhere near him.

But I had to acknowledge him, as who knows, he might rat me out. So, when I phoned him, I merely asked if he was still interested in our deal, and to my surprise, he said yes. Before the robbery, he said he would be prepared to give a better price than you would normally expect. Which was, for every hundred thousand pounds of stone, you would expect to get twenty grand. I should have got roughly fifty grand from the robbery, but he offered me sixty grand instead. I couldn't say yes quick enough; I wanted rid of the diamonds, and to have all ties of the robbery as far removed and away from me as possible.

I was elated by the offer and thought I would take a short break, due to the tremendous ordeal that I had been through. I thought it best now to keep my head firmly down. I was still under a lot of strain, as I was still uncertain if I had gotten away with it. So far, the police hadn't pulled me in, but they could know more than I thought. I thought the most dangerous time for me was when I was reporting to my probation officer, as it would be an ideal place to take me. So, for a time, I wore a shoulder holster and a gun under my jacket, just in case. As time passed, nothing happened, so I got comfortable with the idea I was safe and the nightmare was over...

CHAPTER 24

WHEN I'M CLEANING WINDOWS

Time passed. Days, weeks and months. I had the itch to get back to earning decent money. I was ready to go back to work, so I decided to start getting out there and look for my next turn-out. It was during this time that I met a young, attractive woman.

A friend of mine had a small family-type pub in Islington and, one day, I thought I would pop in and see him, have a quiet drink and catch up. It was a Wednesday evening, and I was bored and restless. Sometimes, your own company is mind-numbing. When I got there, I learned my friend had taken his wife out for a slap-up meal, so I was going to have a couple of quiet drinks and leave, when I got talking to this girl, who was drinking on her own. She was of medium height, with thick, red curly hair and real good sense of humour. She was easy to talk to and I could sense she was at a loose end. During the conversation, she mentioned she had recently split up with her boyfriend and was trying to move on from the relationship. We seemed to get on well, so I thought, why not pursue her? So I asked if I could see her again and she willingly agreed. I was quite pleased; I had regular female company, but it was normally a one-night affair, after too many drinks and not really knowing each other that well.

This girl and I started to see each other on a regular basis and we formed a blossoming, healthy relationship. She had two children from a previous relationship, who were living with her grandparents in County Durham. She took me to see them, but the travel up there brought back some unwanted memories. Durham, I thought, great. I had only spent time there in the prison. I shuddered at the thought of it, but thankfully, we were only visiting the area. It was great meeting her kids; they were well-mannered and playful. I became part of the family quicky; they welcomed me with open arms and I was happy to be brought into their family fold.

Our whirlwind romance resulted in us being married in Lewisham registry office, after only a few months of dating. I wanted a fresh start and I thought it best to return to South London, so I asked my probation officer if he had any objections. He said he was fine with it. I was now reporting to a new probation officer in Lewisham. He wasn't too bothered about my life outside of prison, so it was a pretty easy meet-and-greet. All he was doing was ticking boxes. I still had a fair amount of money left from the diamond robbery, so we were alright for money. My new wife worked in the city, as a solicitor's clerk, in a firm that specialised in accident claims. Whilst she was out doing a hard day's graft, I used to go out and about, looking for potential robberies. I had acquired several guns, some ammunition and a stolen car in a rented garage, ready to go whenever the opportunity arose.

Of course, it wasn't long until I found an opportunity. On this particular day, a van pulled out in front of me and I decided to follow it to see where it went. I let a couple of cars get between me and the van and followed it slowly to Stratford. Eventually, it drove down a narrow street and came to a halt outside an office block. I liked what I saw and made up my mind to steal the bag of money from the van after collection. I decided I would be working on my own, so I could do it any way I fancied. The bag could be taken quite easily, as the guard came down the steps to the van on his own to collect. The problem was getting to the guard; I had to find somewhere to plot up. I couldn't just stand outside; someone would notice and call the police. I spent a few days wracking my brains; how could I get on with the work and, if anyone did notice me, I wouldn't look suspicious or draw attention to myself?

The answer to my problem came out of the blue. Keeping your eyes wide open and soaking in your environment always sparks new ideas. I was making my way one evening to a McDonalds in Catford, to buy the kids hamburgers and shakes, and I noticed a small blue window-cleaning van, parked in a quiet side road. On the van's roof rack was a small wooden ladder; I went over and peeked through the rear windows and I could see plastic buckets, cloth and squeegees. As I made my way home, I was smiling from ear to ear; I had found my perfect cover. I would disguise myself as a window cleaner; it was as simple as that. I would steal the van just before the robbery and I would be in business. They would never suspect a window cleaner as there were plenty of them floating around. The office block consisted of three-storey windowed offices, looking down on the narrow road, which was lined with small quaint factories and workshops. A small flight of stairs led to a revolving door, beyond which was a wide expanse of shiny tiled floor. There was a small desk facing the entrance with an elderly uniformed guard behind it, whose function was to check and direct all visitors to their required destination. If there was a problem and things did kick off, this guard was incapable of doing anything. I found it odd that they would hire security who were not physically fit to deal with a problem.

Outside, the pavement was wide and lined at intervals with concrete bollards, leaving sufficient space at the entrance for cars and vans. The bottom row of windows was made of frosted glass, shielding the typist and office workers from the gaze of passersby and the glare of the midday sun. The security van used to arrive outside, dead on three o'clock. At around ten to three, I arrived in the window cleaner's van, which I had stolen the day before. Ready to put my window-cleaning act to the test. I parked the van just out of sight from the guard and near enough for me to get to when I needed to escape.

I removed the ladder from the roof rack, hoisted it over my shoulder, crossed the road and placed it gently against the wall by the ground-floor windows. I retraced my steps, opened the rear doors of the van and took out two plastic buckets. One bucket contained a thirty-eight revolver and the other bucket was filled with soapy water and a red plastic squeegee. I had bought myself bright yellow washing-up gloves, which I was wearing as part of the disguise, plus they were perfect to prevent me leaving finger-prints. No one would dream an armed robber would wear gloves of this nature. I was chuffed with the outfit. I closed the van's door, picking up a bucket in each hand and I strolled across the road, past the bollards to the frosted glass windows.

As I was putting the buckets down, four well-built men emerged from the revolving doors, walked down the stairs and stood, waiting for the arrival of the van. An extra security measure had been put in place. They were standing in a line; when the van turned up, I knew they could potentially be a problem. They looked at me briefly, before dismissing me as potential danger and continued chatting amongst themselves, deciding to take no fur-ther notice of me. By this point, I was now busy soaping windows and using the squeegee to dry them. Using my best acting skills as a window cleaner, I thought I was doing quite well. No one batted an eyelid at me; I just blended in with the everyday people.

I glanced at my watch; nearly three o'clock. I thought, I hope the van is here on time. I continued washing the windows, com-pletely ignoring the waiting men. Suddenly, I heard the motor of an approaching van, bang on time. The van turned into the space between the bollards and came to a halt at the bottom of the steps. The four men straightened up, came round and formed a line between me and the guard, completely blocking my way. I couldn't believe it; I had watched the drop for two weeks and, when they were there, they had always stood at the front of the steps, well away from where I was standing. All I thought I had to do was wait until the guard was halfway down the steps, cross the empty steps and the bag was mine. But this week, they were standing directly across the spot I had to cross to get there. This frustrated me greatly; I wasn't about to pull out of the job now. The only good thing was that they had their backs to me. I shook my head in frustration.

But then I thought, now I am here, I am still going to take

the bag. I can't be fucked to allow these people to get in my way. When I make my move, I will shoot one of them straight in the leg. No fucks given.

The guard got out of the van and disappeared through the revolving doors to collect the sack of money. I waited a couple of minutes and edged nearer to the backs of the minders. Suddenly, the heads of the minders turned in unison, watching the guard emerge from inside the building. The guard was carrying a heavy canvas sack in his right hand, and he started to descend the steps. Now was the time to make my move. Bending down, I pulled the revolver from the bucket, and I took a few steps forward.

"Hey!" I shouted.

I saw some startled faces looking towards me, so I just pointed the gun at the nearest minder and pulled the trigger. The force of the bullet threw the minder against the side of the van, before he crashed to the ground, screaming in agony. Blood pumped over his hands like a fountain, as he clutched his thigh, squirming on the floor. The roar of the gun froze everyone on the spot, as if time had suspended; no one had a clue what to do. Before they could recover from their initial shock, I sprang towards the terrified guard. Without any hesitation, the guard tossed the bag towards me. Scooping it up, I turned and ran across the road, leapt into my van and pulled away with a shriek of burning rubber.

One hundred yards down the road, I made a quick right into a block of council flats, drifting to a halt in the middle of a line of dented cars and vans. I ripped my cap off, stuffed it into a holdall with my gloves, closed the door and walked away through the maze of graffiti-decorated walls. I walked past groups of gossiping women and children playing, through the estate, and jumped straight on the tube, disappearing amongst the crowds. Blazing sirens and lights sped past me; the first lot of police were arriving on the scene. I ducked into the tube, down the stairs and out of sight. A tube train soon arrived, so I slipped inside the doors, found a seat and sat with the holdall across my knees. Calm then settled over me, as I knew I had got away, but I had made a huge scene. I didn't like pulling out my gun in front of crowds of people. It wasn't my style, but I wasn't about to walk away from potentially a big sum of money. I had an uneventful ride home; it was only four pm and my wife wouldn't be home for another two hours.

I emptied the bag onto the settee and counted the mountains of cash in front of me. To my surprise, it came to twenty-seven thousand pounds; not a bad day's work for one man. I was delighted with the outcome and just hoped the minder I shot was only wounded. I didn't need another death on my hands. After every job, I always got rid of my clothes and the gun. Never get sloppy and think you can keep any of it. It's all evidence and any job can come back and bite you on the arse. It wasn't as if I didn't have the money to get another gun; I could get one from anywhere. By the time my wife got home, the money was stashed away and she was none the wiser about my shenanigans.

As she came in, she planted a big kiss on me, and quizzed me. "What have you been up to today?"

"Not much." I smiled. "Don't bother cooking tonight. Let's go to a nice restaurant and dine out."

She loved being treated and, after a long day's work, she welcomed a night away from the kitchen and to let her hair down with a slap-up meal and a large glass of vino.

The money would tide me over, so I didn't need to work for a while. Therefore, I could focus my time on my wife and our living arrangements. My wife was keen to be reunited with her children, who at the time were staying with their grandparents in County Durham. The plan was to get them down with us as soon as possible. We decided to rent a shop with living accommodation above it. After a bit of searching, we found a double-fronted shop with a spacious three-bed flat above it, in Hither Green, Lewisham, South East London. We bought the lease and redecorated the property from top to bottom. My wife had always wanted to run a clothes shop and I thought it was a great way to set her up and launder some money through the business. I took the view that, if she was happy, then so was I. We both had a little project we could do together, and it gave me something to focus on, other than robbing. We visited the clothing wholesalers in the commercial road, East London, and stocked up on brightly-coloured dresses, jeans, skirts and tops.

Once the shop was open for business, we travelled to the grandparents and brought the kids back to their new home. They were two bright, cheerful kids, a boy of eleven and a girl of nine, and we all got on well, right from the start. We gelled and I was over the moon that I had my ready-made family. I finally felt like I was complete and was a happy man. I loved my wife dearly and we just clicked from the get-go. Life was finally falling into place for me. The shop was more for her and her passion for fashion; I never had anything to do with the running of it. I soon found out that, when you deal with the public, you must have a great deal of tact and patience, which I didn't have at all. It didn't really suit my character, so I shied away from front-of-house. After all, most of my public dealings were scaring people at gunpoint. I don't think I was cut out for retail.

Initially, the shop did quite well, the kids settled in, and we found a respectable school for them to attend. I was still required to report to my probation officer once a month, which at times was a nuisance, but was something I had to do to keep the law sweet and maintain my freedom. I had a family and a reasonable business, and all the dots started to connect. I felt like I had found my place in society, and I was finally content and at peace with myself. Things were looking up.

CHAPTER 25

GUT INSTINCTS

1979 came around, and we noticed the takings from the shop were falling. I didn't realise at the time how bad the financial economy was. Robbers don't tend to keep up with these sorts of things. I never followed the spread sheets, or the value of the coin. I never normally had to worry about money, so the state of the economy never affected me. The slump of '79 and '80 was creeping around the corner. We tried various ways of attracting customers, but people were being more careful with their money, saving their pennies for a rainy day. The media had scared people, and spending on luxuries was the last thing on their agenda. Everyone thought the worst and survival mode set in. And when all efforts failed, I decided it was time to go back to work and do what I do best.

It was rather ironic really; trying to live an honest life and earn a decent crust, I was now in danger of going skint. This is why a lot of robbers cannot give up the game; it's too lucrative and a normal job does not give you the same quality of life. Normal jobs just pay the bills and maybe a little extra. Treat yourself now and again, or go on holiday once a year, but it was a struggle. I was not going to just survive in the world, I wanted to thrive.

It was 1980 and I went looking for work that I could do on my own. Eventually, I found a bag over in Canning Town. Every Wednesday, two men and a woman collected the wages for a small plastics firm. I watched their routine for two weeks and was satisfied I could pull it off easily. The bank was on the corner and all I had to do was park the ringer outside. Strike as they came out and then lose myself in the maze of small side streets and the hustle and bustle of people going about their daily lives. On the third Wednesday, I arrived there at ten am, parked my car outside the bank, got out, crossed the road and stood by the bus stop until they arrived, which was around ten-twenty. I waited until they entered the bank, pulled a forty-five automatic from my waistband and pointed it straight at one of the minder's heads. In a panic, they couldn't give me the bag quick enough. Once again, a gun pointing in your face will make people do anything you want. I jumped into my car and sped off, dumped the car three hundred yards away in another council estate and blended in with the crowds. So quick and simple, it was like taking candy from a baby.

The bag contained eleven grand; not a lot but it would help me out until I found a bigger job. After the robbery, I went out and stole a car, re-plated it and put it away in a garage, ready for my next robbery. I always liked to get the car way before the next robbery.

Stealing cars wasn't too difficult; years ago, I used to find a quiet car park that was used by commuters. Select the car I needed, then smash the side window, unlock the door and use a sledgehammer, which was normally used to pull dents from the bodywork of cars. I would attach a thin self-taping screw onto the end of the sledgehammer and screw it into the ignition. Then yank the entire ignition out. The next step was to use a small screwdriver, which you poked down the ignition barrel to start and stop the engine. I always had a garage to stash the cars; it was paramount that they were hidden away out of sight. I would go to a motor accessory shop and say I had damaged the front number plate on my car, give the new registration number, then order a new plate. If I was asked for any identification, I'd show a false driving licence. Then I would go to another shop and repeat the same routine for a rear plate. Another trick was to go to a store that sold loose numbers and grey letters and stick the false numbers on the original plates. A touch-up with a bit of paint and no one was any the wiser. The car looked as good as new and was ready to be used when required. It was so simple and easy, I wondered why there weren't more robbers on the streets.

It was about this time, after I had pulled off the eleven grand job, that I came across a man I had known from Hull prison. His name was Don Barrett. We bumped into each other by accident in the Riverdale shopping centre in Lewisham. We exchanged pleasantries and went for a long drink and a catch-up.

He asked me, "Do you fancy teaming up with me?"

I said, "Yeah, if you have any decent work at hand, then yeah, I am up for it."

And that's how our working relationship began. We did a few robberies together, but never earned a great deal of money. It was one of those periods of time when I was turning out, but nothing seemed to be going right. After the last robbery we turned out for, I thought to myself, I am better off on my own. There was something off about him and I felt like I was always on his back to remember the plan and he wasn't too good at finding work. He was becoming a liability and was not much of a good robber either. I preferred my own company; at the end of the day, working alone suited me better. I was skilled enough to work by myself and it meant fewer complications.

But before I could part ways with Don, June 1980 came around and the hammer fell from high in the sky. I had this uneasy feeling, a premonition that something was going to happen to me. The night before I was arrested, I was in bed with my wife and the last thing I said to her was that I felt like I was in great danger. She assured me that it was all in my head and not to worry. If I had been single, I think I would have got out of bed, packed a bag and disappeared for a while. Instead, I ignored my intuition and turned over to go to sleep.

The next morning, I got up bright and early. I was in the kitchen, laying the table for the kids' breakfast, when the doorbell rang, which startled me and made my stomach do a back-flip. I knew instinctively it was the police, as no one knocked on our door. We rarely had any visitors, as we kept ourselves to ourselves. I ran down the stairs, peeked round the door and saw three men standing at the front door. I could also see through the shop windows the figures of armed police, sprawled in the street. I spun round and ran towards the back yard. At the end of the yard was a wooden fence. If I could get over that, I could run across the railway lines down the bank, to the road beyond.

I walked quickly towards the fence but a policeman jumped out from the next-door neighbour's fence and levelled a gun to my head, shouting the words, "Police! Don't move!"

As he said this, armed police popped up from all over the place, like jumping jacks from invisible boxes. They had caught me with great surprise. I was quickly handcuffed and led cautiously to the back door and back inside. Armed police swarmed into the shop.

"Don't frighten my wife and kids," I said. "They are still in bed."

I was taken up into the kitchen, then made to sit down whilst they searched the premises with a fine-tooth comb. Once they were satisfied, I was led outside into a police car, past the horde of spectators and nosy neighbours, then swiftly driven to Walthamstow police station.

I was searched and told to sit down. I still hadn't realised that Barrett had grassed me up. I sat, quietly wracking my brains to think what I have been nicked for. Mind you, I had done so much villainy since leaving prison, it was difficult for me to work out. All I was hoping was that it was not one of my more serious, violent crimes. Alan crossed my mind and I thought, please, don't have found the body.

A CID man came in and opened an old beat-up briefcase. "Here you are, John, this is to show you where you stand." He handed me a picture of myself in a bank with a sawn-off shotgun. I gave it a quick glance.

"That's not me," I said casually. I was quite relieved this was all it was.

He smiled, as if he knew more than he was letting on, and

then handed me a typed statement; it was Barrett, admitting the robbery. He also stuck me up for a total of five other robberies. I kept my face expressionless and tossed the statement on the table. Inside, I was absolutely fuming.

"I don't know what he is talking about, it's got nothing to do with me," I said.

The CID man gave me another smug smile. "I will leave you alone to think things over."

I thought, fuck me. Never in my wildest dreams would I have thought Barrett would grass me up. I was completely blindsided by this one and, at the same time, seething with anger.

I was left alone for a couple of hours, then three CID men came in. "Come with us," the main man in charge said. "We want you to hear something."

I was taken into a small room and there was Barrett, leaning against a mantlepiece, clean-shaven and smartly dressed. He was smiling at his captors, who stood around him in a protective manner.

"Do you know this man?" a CID man asked Barrett.

"Yes, his name is John Hilton."

I thought, you fucking rat. I wanted to rip his smarmy throat out.

"Have you committed any robberies with him?"

"Yes, we have done several bits of work together." He was so brazen; I was embarrassed for him. What sort of man had I been dealing with?

"Are you prepared to say so in court?" the CID man probed.

"Yes, I am," Barrett said with defiance.

The next question was directed at me. "Have you anything to say?"

I merely shook my head before they led me away to my cell. Once the door slammed shut behind me, I shook my head in disbelief; inside, I was seething. My blood was boiling, I paced up and down, thinking furiously, I had been grassed on again! What a fucking bastard. I broke into a sweat of rage and frustration.

Intrusive thoughts started flooding in; I had cars and guns put down and Barrett knew where they were! They had the photo, his statement and God knows what else. I had no chance of getting out of this one and, not only that, I had the life parole hanging over me like a gloomy fucking cloud I would never shift.

Even if I could get out of the robberies, I knew the Home Office would revoke my licence and I would do another ten-to-fifteen stretch, before I would be free again.

Later that day, I was charged with various robberies and made a brief appearance in court, where I was then remanded in custody in wonderful Brixton. A young CID aide told me the Home Office was going mad over me. I had been reclassified as a Category A prisoner and my licence was going to be revoked. My worst fears were confirmed; it wouldn't matter what happened in court, even if I was found not guilty. I would simply be returning to prison as a serving lifer. No matter what happened, I was in deep shit, and I was thoroughly pissed off that I had been betrayed so badly.

In Brixton, I was put into Seg A, which was s special unit for high-risk prisoners, who were awaiting trial for all manner of serious crimes. I was on remand for a long and depressing twelve months. During this time, my wife visited me regularly, bringing me food and clean clothes. She was quite upset by my charges since I had never shared all the details of my criminal life. She was surprised and shocked at my double life, and I could see she looked at me a little differently than before. I couldn't see our marriage lasting, not if I were to be put away for a long stretch. I could see she was already thinking about her options. My solicitor and barrister came to see me, to discuss what line to take for my defence. I had virtually no chance of winning an acquittal. I could possibly get out of four robberies, but was going to be hung out to dry for the other two. The outcome would remain the same; I would get just as much time for two robberies as I would have got for the six. I would still have my licence revoked, so either way, I was going to prison for a long time.

July 1981 came around; a boiling hot summer and I was due

at the Old Bailey. I pleaded guilty to all charges. My barrister did the best he could with a mitigation plea, and I was sentenced to fourteen years of imprisonment. My heart ached; I couldn't believe it. I was taken to Wandsworth prison to serve the beginning of my sentence and was back sewing bloody mailbags again. I was seething for a good while, sitting there, sewing bags, thinking of seeking revenge on Don, as soon as I got the opportunity.

A couple of weeks passed by, and one screw came to me, saying, "The wing governor wants to see you."

I followed him to the Governor's office, knocked lightly on the door and entered. The Governor was reading my record, with deep scrutiny.

He looked at me. "I've got some bad news for you. The parole board have revoked your licence." Which I knew was coming but was still a bitter pill to swallow.

That meant the fourteen years I had been sentenced had little meaning, as the life sentence took precedence over the fourteen years.

"Have you anything to say you'd like to say?"

What was there to say? I thought of several replies I could have made but chose just to say, "No, I understand my position."

I thought, yes, my position is totally fucked. How the hell have I ended back here? I should never have trusted Don, as I felt there was something off with him from the get-go.

He nodded. "Alright, Hilton, you can go."

It was then that I thought about escaping. The urge to escape was stronger than it had ever been, as I could not fathom another life sentence. I was in Wandsworth for about ten months before I was transferred to Long Lartin dispersal prison in Worcestershire. Long Lartin was a tough prison, full of violence and some really nasty men. But I was fortunate enough to know a lot of people and I rarely had any trouble. Shanks were always about in the prisons but were more prevalent once the prison introduced workshops, where scraps of metal were more attainable. You had to always have your wits about you. It was whilst I was in this prison that my marriage broke up, which I can't say was a surprise, as I was likely never to see the light of day again. For me, it was a relief; she was still a young woman and could make her way in the world without me. But a part of my heart ached, as I was now all alone in the world again and pining over the life I had left behind.

During my time in Lartin, I became friends with a Scotsman, Rab Christie. We were in prison together for about four years and we had a lovely, relaxed friendship. When he was discharged, we kept in touch, and he would come and visit me from time to time. Little did he or I know that I would betray our friendship in the most terrible fashion. Out of desperation and fear, I would act terribly towards him. Which is not my usual character, but I was under a lot of pressure. Pressure can make the calmest men do the most irrational things. My actions put him back in prison; because of the fear and terror, I put him under, but this would not happen until some years into the future.

My decision to escape the cold walls of prison was not taken lightly. By the time that moment came, I had completed ten long and painful years. I had thought about it constantly for ten years, dreamt about it and yearned for it. In all that time, though, I did not get the opportunity to do so. I fully realised the terrible price I would pay if I failed, but was willing to give it a go, for my last chance at a life. I had been sentenced to fourteen years, but instead of being released after serving nine years and four months, which at this time was the normal release date after two-thirds of your sentence, I would now serve the full fourteen years. Plus, four more years on top, so I was looking at serving eighteen years. I'd be sixty-eight years old upon my eventual release, but I knew in my heart, if I made no attempt to escape, I would always have the nagging feeling I should have given it a go.

The idea of sitting in prison, doing nothing, rankled with me. My decision was to try and, if I failed, I would die in prison, then so be it. This was not a life; I wanted my freedom.

Over the years in Long Lartin, I became friendly with the Principal Officer. One day, not long into my time there, I asked him to look through my record and tell me where I stood, just to make sure I was on the right track. He kindly agreed to do this for me and, a couple of hours later, he called me to the wing office.

"I have been through your record; do you want the truth?" he asked.

"Yes, I do." I thought this sounded ominous.

"Well, according to your records and the abundance of police reports, you have no chance of being released for a long time. But you do have one thing in your favour."

"What's that?" I asked, with a flutter of hope in my voice.

"Your age." At the time, I was fifty years old. "Every time you are interviewed, plug your age; that is your best bet."

I nodded and thanked him; I never gave much thought to my age and how society would look at me differently, the older I got. But when he mentioned it, it made total sense. It's true, of course; as you get older, people think you haven't got it anymore, no more energy or bottle to commit crime of this nature. Well, I was one old man who would prove them wrong.

The principal officer finished by giving me another piece of advice. "You must never commit another act of violence on anybody in here. You are classed as a very violent man, and they will not believe you have changed if you do the same in here."

I understood what he said, and I took his advice on board. Over the years, there were times where I had to wipe my mouth and walk away and, believe me, it wasn't easy. But I had no choice, if I wanted to get into a prison where I could make a successful escape. It took me ten rotten years, and throughout those years, I plugged my age whenever I had the chance, expressing that I was a finished article. That I had hung up my robbing gloves and shotgun. That I could never return to crime, not just due to my age, but because my bottle had gone, and I couldn't face doing any more bird. Little did they know, I would never change...

CHAPTER 26

THE TRANSFER

I'd served four long and gruelling years in Long Lartin. As you know, they loved to transfer me from one prison to another. All my years in and out of the system, I had the pleasure of staying in every prison in the country.

I was transferred to Blundeston prison in Suffolk; it took me a week or so to realise that to escape from Blundeston was too difficult and far too risky for the people who were willing to spring me. So, I just settled down. I did plenty of weight training and, at fifty-seven, I was still playing football like a pro. I kept plugging my age at every meeting and tried to convince the system I was a reformed character. I did my best to stay out of trouble, thought I found at times it was difficult to avoid conflict and I never enjoyed backing down. But I was ever mindful of the principal officer's advice, so I kept my mouth tightly shut and my hands firmly to myself.

I spent about twenty months in Blundeston before I was transferred to Lewes prison in Sussex, one of my old haunts. I had served about eight years by then, and I could sense it was only a matter of time before my chance came. When I arrived in Lewes, I had the usual interview and was asked where I would like to work. I decided to try for a job in the kitchen; I had an interview with the head cook and was accepted as a diet cook. Like all kitchen workers, we got unlocked earlier than everyone else, around six am, when everything was quiet, except the birds, who were chirping in full song. The vegetable store was outside the back gate, which was always open so you could come and go and, at seven am, the gate would be locked. I used to linger outside, looking at the fence and the wall. I had an hour before the gate was locked. If someone tossed a ladder over the fence, I could be up and over and in Brighton before you knew it. It was roughly eight miles away; it was so tempting, like an itch that needed to be scratched and the scenario of me leaving this way played through my mind every night. I was ready to go; all I needed was someone to keep watch over the yard patrol and mark my card if he appeared. I was now ready to make my move. I had everything arranged. My firm were going to spring me; one day to go and I would be a free man. Everything was in place for the perfect escape.

It was five-thirty in the afternoon and the kitchen workers were standing in small groups, waiting to be let out, back to their wings for showers and association. I was leaning against a wooden table waiting with the others, when I saw three uniformed screws suddenly enter the kitchen.

"Hello, what's going on here?" remarked a nearby con.

"They might be giving us a spin," I replied.

At this, several cons pulled out parcels of food from their waistbands, which they had intended to smuggle onto the wings or pass on to their friends. They tossed them into the nearest pans just in case it was a spin.

I never moved; a terrible premonition swept over me that all was not well. Especially when I saw the screws pause to speak to the cook, then look towards me. My fears were confirmed when the cook beckoned me over to the office. My face gave no indication of concern as I walked past the stainless-steel coppers to the office.

"You want me, Guv?" I Inquired, and the lump in my throat was expanding at a rapid rate.

"Yes, John, you are wanted down the seg unit," replied one of the screws.

I allowed a puzzled look to cross my face. "What's going on?" I asked.

"I'm as wise as you. All I know is, I was ordered to remove you straight to the chokey wing. You can see the Governor in the morning and ask him yourself."

I looked at him with an agreeable expression and allowed myself to be led from the kitchen to the chokey.

Once inside, I was stripped and searched, before being locked in the chokey cell for the day and night. Once on my own, I shook my head in surprise and dismay. How the fuck did they find out I intended to escape in the morning? Only me and the other con knew anything about it. I'd not spoken a word about it, so it must be the other con. He must have told someone else or stuck me up to one of the screws. I'd waited ten fucking years for this chance; if they believed I was going to escape, I'd be put back at least five years. All that hard work for nothing and what about the firm who were going to spring me? They would be walking straight into a trap, and I could do nothing to save them. I paced up and down, wracking my brains, but I was helpless. I didn't fucking believe it. Thoughts, plans, ideas flew through my head, but there was nothing I could do. I was like a caged bird, desperate to fly and the thought of being in this prison for any longer made me feel sick to my stomach.

I lay on my bed brooding, staring at the ceiling, cursing the man who had talked too much. I thought of the saying, 'loose lips, sink ships.' I thought, isn't that the truth? I remember thinking, what will happen when the firm arrive at six-thirty am, all ready to spring me out? All the careful planning and waiting, gone for nothing. I ground my teeth together in pure rage and frustration. If they got nicked, down to that cunt, I would kill him stone fucking dead. The system could do what they liked to me afterwards, I was past giving a fuck. I lay fretting and full of contempt all through the night, watching the morning light grow stronger.

As the new day arrived, the light brought the sound of the early morning flock of seagulls swooping over the prison. They loved to land near the window seals, finding scraps of food flung out by the prisoners. The time dragged on and on; I looked at the time and it was six-twenty am. Getting to my feet, I stood under the open window, straining to hear if they were walking into a ready eye. There would be a terrible row, that was for sure. I should hear whistles, sirens or gunshots, but I could hear nothing, except the sound of early morning traffic from the main road, running past the front of the prison, and the pesky sea birds. At seven am, I gave up trying to listen and returned to my bed, waiting to be unlocked for slopping out and breakfast. The sound of a key unlocking the cell brought me back to my feet once more.

"Morning, John, what are you doing down here?" asked the chokey screw. He was surprised to see me.

"I'm fucked if I know, Guv, I was hoping you could tell me. I was snatched from the kitchen last night and brought down here."

"Maybe someone's complained about your cooking," the screw quipped as he moved to the next cell.

I forced a smile in return; everything seemed to be quite normal to me. I would know straight away if anything unusual had happened. I picked up my plastic chamber pot, went out to recess and emptied in into the sluice bowl. As I passed the officer where the reports were dealt with, the senior officer in charge called my name and said the wing governor would be down to see me later on in the morning.

"Have you any idea why I am down here?" I asked, trying to get as much information as possible, to get my story straight.

The screw shook his head. "All I know is, the wing Governor rang me last night and said we had to bring you down straight away."

"Well, I said, "I think it's a fucking liberty. I've done nearly ten years, I've been here for the best part of two years, working seven days a week to get good reports for my parole application, which is coming up shortly. And for no reason, I am dragged down here." I was laying on the 'woe is me' act as thick as I could.

The screw had a look of empathy about him. "Actually, I think it's a liberty as well, but I'm like you, I have to follow orders, don't I?"

Sensing he was on my side, I immediately replied, "Well, I've done nothing wrong. When I see the Governor, will you put a good word in for me?" I needed as much support as I could get.

"Don't worry, John, I'll do what I can, it's probably all bollocks anyway." With that, he went on about his business and I made my way to collect my breakfast.

I had done a bit of good there, I thought, I might get out of this after all. But still, the nagging worry remained; what had happened to the firm? Were they alright, or had they been nicked? Well, I would soon find out when I saw the Governor.

At about ten am, I heard the sounds of the doors opening and closing; the Governor was doing his rounds. The door to the seg's office next to my cell was unlocked and I could hear the murmur of voices. I grabbed my plastic mug and held one end to the wall, then pressed my ear to the other end, hoping to magnify the sounds. But I couldn't distinguish what was being said; all I could do was return the mug to the table and sit patiently waiting. My cell door was unlocked.

"Come on John," the screw said.

I was led into a large office across the plain brown polished lino to where the Governor was sitting behind the desk. My prison record was in front of him. The screw joined the senior officer, who was standing by the wall. The Governor nodded towards a chair directly in front of the desk.

"Sit down, Hilton." I sat down and tried to compose myself, acting my way through this process. "Well now, I had you removed from the main prison for security reasons," he said. I allowed another puzzled look to cross my face.

"I don't understand," I said, seemingly confused.

The Governor went on. "I've received information that you intended to escape." He looked at me intensely, trying to read my facial expression. But I remained unreadable as ever.

"Escape, you can't be serious, surely."

"No, Hilton, I am quite serious," the Governor retorted.

"May I ask how and when you received this information? As

you quite rightly said, this is a serious allegation. And I feel I am at least entitled to know."

The Governor hesitated before replying, "It was a note we found in the wing letter box."

A wave of sweet relief swept over me; I was in with a chance.

I laughed scornfully. "Someone with a grudge against me puts a note into a box, saying I am going to escape, and you believe it." I was full in flow now. "Do you realise, I have served ten years; I could be out legally in a few years. I have been no trouble and I am expecting to go up for parole soon. Do you honestly believe I would throw all those years and hard work away? If I wanted to escape, I would have tried years ago, at the start of my sentence, but not now."

My speech over, I sat there and thought, I hope he doesn't point out that I'd been a top-security prisoner. He didn't mention it, so I decided to carry on. "Let's have it right, anyone can accuse anyone by slipping a note into a box."

Out of the corner of my eye, I could see the Senior Officer nodding in agreement. I could see my reasoning was having the desired effect on the Governor. Pressing home my advantage, I turned to the senior officer and said, "You have known me for a long time, what do you think?"

The Governor looked inquiringly towards the screw. "Well, sir, I have known Hilton for a long time, and I will say he has been a villain in his day. But I must be inclined to agree with Hilton on this occasion. He has got too much to lose at this stage of his sentence."

I could see I'd won the day, but kept a worried look on my face, as the Governor leaned back in his chair, deep in thought. I could see he was trying to figure out what he was going to do with me.

"Well, Hilton, maybe a mistake has been made. As you say, ten years is a long time to throw away." Once his mind was made up, his face relaxed. "Alright then, you may return to the main prison."

Then he closed my file before dismissing me. The screw took me back to my cell.

"We will come back to you as soon as we can." And he closed the door behind him.

I let out a huge sigh of relief. Fucking hell, you did well there, John boy. I had talked a good one and was convinced I had made them believe the note was a ridiculous accusation and not to be trusted.

When I returned to the main prison, people kept asking me why I'd been taken down to the chokey. I just made a joke about it, saying some mug put a note in the box, saying I was going to escape. It was all bollocks, anyway; I made out it was likely someone who took a dislike to me. When I saw the other con, I hid my anger, although it was extremely difficult. I could see by his manner and the way he was speaking to me, he was the guilty man.

Instead, I smiled in his face and told him, "Not to worry, I've cancelled everything. I've changed my mind about it now, it's too risky," and I left it at that. I kept my distance from this slippery snake from then on.

A couple of weeks passed by and everything was back to normal, until one morning, the cook called me over to say he'd had a phone call. The Governor wanted to see me again. I thought, fuck, now what's wrong? I put down the food I was prepping, washed my hands, the cook let me out of the kitchen and I made my way to the Governor's office. I knocked on the door lightly and entered.

"Morning Governor, do you want to see me?" I was hoping there were no repercussions from the suspected escape.

"Yes, I won't keep you long. A vacancy has come up at Kingston prison. We just had a reception from there and I want to know if you'd like to go there. It's a lifers' prison, and it would be a good move for you. There's no rush; anytime next week will do. Just let me know your answer."

At that time, I had never really fancied Kingston as it was known as a nonces' and domestic lifers' prison and it was in my mind to turn the offer down. I didn't fancy keeping company with those sorts of people.

One evening, I had just had a shower and was in my cell, when I heard someone say, "Excuse me, but are you John Hilton?"

I looked up to see this dark-haired, well-built man standing at my door. "Yes, I am." I looked at him enquiringly, as if asking him to get to the point.

"Are you going to Kingston soon?" he asked.

"I might be," I replied.

"Well, I've just been slung out of there and, if you are going, would you mind taking a message to a pal of mine?" he asked me with some urgency.

"What did you get slung out for?" I questioned. He gave me a sly grin.

"Don't worry, I'm not a funny one. I was crossed by a cunt; he got his wife to write to the Governor saying I was a drug dealer and was trying to force him to buy drugs. What really happened was, I gave him a club around the head, and this was his comeback. Mind you, I was dealing, so they were looking to out me anyway."

I examined the newcomer. He looked alright but, as I have learnt many times over, appearances could be deceptive.

All I said was, "A bit of bad luck there, mate. Anyway, I've got to shoot off now." And with that, I left. I didn't fancy getting mixed up in whatever drama he was involved in.

Next day, I watched who he was mixing with, and they were all decent cons and, from what I could gather, he was a solid man. I had to do my research on him before I made any promises.

A couple of days later, I approached the newcomer. "What do you think of this place, then?"

"It's way more secure here than Kingston was, and the food isn't too clever. Kingston, on the other hand, is very well-run and you're left alone. But I'd sooner be here in Lewes, as there are more decent cons here. No fucking nonces."

My escape radar was firing on all cylinders; less secure? I thought. What a result.

"What's the compound like there?" I asked him, making sure not to sound excited about the security comment.

"Not bad. They have football, cricket, loads of free time, very relaxed, no security at all. Nothing like here," he responded.

"How do you mean, no security?" I was pressing for more information, as I needed to get an idea how lapsed the security was.

"Well, there's no wire fence, just a brick wall with a metal dome on top. In the summer, they all sit with their backs to the wall, not paying much attention to the prisoners. You could get the fuck out of there, especially if you had some good help. I used to work in the kitchen in the morning and the back gate is always open. The back wall is only about twenty feet away and there's never any patrols about." Kingston was sounding more appealing by the minute.

Inside, I was elated, but I stayed nonchalant. "It doesn't sound too bad there," I said. "If I go, I'll take a message to your pal. I'll see you later on then."

As I walked away, I smiled to myself; no fences, no barbed wire. He was right; I would get the fuck out of there and, if he was telling me porky pies or the prison wasn't right for me, I could always come back to Lewes. I had made my mind up and decided to give the Governor a visit. The next day, I once again knocked on the intimidating door of the Governor.

"Morning, Hilton, what can I do for you?" He raised his eyebrows and swung his chair to face me.

"I've decided I'd like to go to Kingston. As you say, it's a good move for me."

The Governor nodded in agreement. "Good," he said. "Just a minute and I'll tell you when you can go." He started to shuffle fresh papers on his desk. "Here we are; you're in luck, you could go in three weeks' time."

I thanked him and made my way back to the kitchen and straight to the cook's office, as I wanted to give him my news straight away.

"I've just been told I'm going to Kingston in three weeks' time."

"Oh, well done, John," the cook replied. "I'm pleased for you."

"Could you do me a favour, Guv? I wonder if you could phone the kitchen at Kingston for me and explain I've worked under you for nearly two years, and could the cook give me a job because you know I couldn't stand the shops anymore and you know how boring they are." Obviously, I was eager to get to the kitchen, as the ideal escape route.

"That's no problem, John you've been a good worker. Don't worry, I'll give you a good reference and I'll tell him I'm sorry to lose you." I had faith he would do just that, as we had a good working relationship and he was right, I was a good worker.

"Thanks, Governor, you're a gentleman." And with that, I returned to my work, thinking I'd better get a quick visit in with the firm, to tell them the good news and also find out why they never turned up for the last attempt. I arranged a VO and got them in the nick of time before the transfer.

"Hilton you've got a visit." I followed the screw to the visiting room and sat down at the small table.

The sounds of women's and children's voices filled the room. I stepped in and straight away smelt the familiar stench of perfume, wafting through the air, blown by the breeze from the open windows. I had not smelt women's perfume for quite some time and it evoked mixed feelings. I smiled as I saw a large figure I knew all too well, making his way past the crowded tables, filled with relatives and children.

"Am I pleased to see you," I beamed. "I thought you were nicked or something, I spent all night worrying about you."

"No, John, nothing happened. Listen to this, you ain't going to believe this, but we had a puncture on the van, carrying the ladders. When we nicked the van, no one thought about if it had a spare wheel or not, so we had to leave it off the main road, tear back to London and get a spare wheel for the poxy van. Return and change it, so we could get it back, and by that point, it was too late. We missed our chance. All this aggro over a fucking wheel. You were worried about us, John boy, but you weren't on your own. Anyway, everything's alright now and we'll have another go when you're ready."

I was greatly relieved. Out of sheer embarrassment, I decided to say nothing of my problems inside. I talked instead about my transfer to Kingston and the chances I had of going over the wall...

CHAPTER 27

THE GREAT ESCAPE

I was taken to Kingston by taxi. I remember looking out of the window, watching the world go by and thinking that, with a bit of luck, I should be out before too long. I was over the moon and could see a sliver of light at the end of the longest tunnel. Kingston, at that time, had about one hundred and thirty convicts. It was an exceptionally clean and tidy prison, with all the facilities you could ask for and the staff overall were quite reasonable. I remember, on my first day, I made my way to the dining hall and joined the queue of convicts waiting for tea to be served. I stopped and looked them over and I can't say I was too impressed. They all looked peculiar indeed, like rejects from society that never found their place in the world. I couldn't see any robbers, that's for sure; it was the first time in my life I'd ever been to prison where I didn't know a soul, and in fact, as time went on, I felt I was the odd man out. I felt completely alone and unable to relate to anyone. If I hadn't intended to escape, I would have asked to go back to Lewes in a heartbeat.

I remember a screw saying to me, "You have done well getting here, especially with your record."

I merely said, "All that was years ago. I'm sixty-one now, everyone slows down as you get older." I stuck to that story, every time anyone questioned my past.

The first time I walked out into the exercise yard, I was quite surprised, as it was exactly as I'd been told; no fence, no barbed wire or cameras. Just a large red brick wall, topped with a large metal dome. Just as the other convict had described.

I estimated that a twenty-five-foot ladder would get me over the wall, no trouble at all. I had another stroke of luck when the cook came to see me and said he'd had a phone call from Lewes prison.

"I was told you're a good worker, and we are short a diet cook, so would you like the job?"

Of course, I said yes and I was told to report for work the next day. My starting time was at six-thirty am and, since we were in constant need of plenty of vegetables, the cook was in the habit of leaving the back gates open. You could leave the kitchen and get what you needed from the veg store, pretty much whenever you liked. Every morning, the cook would sit in his office, writing out the day's menu while drinking a mug of tea. He seemed to have a lot of trust in me, and I could go and come as I pleased. Once out of the gate, the wall was only twenty-five feet away, so all I had to do was get the ball rolling and I would get the fuck out of Kingston. I got in touch with my pals and asked them to scout around outside to check if an escape was visible and safe, especially for them. They had to get word to me without visiting me. That would focus attention on them after the escape, so I arranged to have a third party visit me, and all I had to do was tell them the exact spot to put the ladders up against the wall. I decided the best time to make any move would be six-forty-five am. I had to wait a few weeks before getting the messages through and arranging the day for when I wanted to make the move. Things were looking good.

It was a chilly October morning; a blustery wind drove gusts of rain against the cell window, bringing a cold damp air into the sparsely furnished cell. I awoke way before the cell door opened and began getting ready slowly with excitement and angst. I sat waiting for the night patrols to come round and unlock the kitchen workers out of their cells. I glanced at my watch, which was hanging from a nail driven into the cell's wall. It was six o'clock in the morning. It won't be too long now, I thought. My stomach gave a lurch in anticipation. I threw the blankets back and stood over the plastic bucket, watching the yellow stream of urine splashing in. I smiled. Last time, John boy, I thought. I dressed quickly in my white kitchen trousers and pulled an old short-sleeved sweatshirt on. I thrust my feet into a battered pair of trainers, spotted with oil and fat from the kitchen ovens. I tied the laces up tightly, buckled my watch on and unwrapped two slices of bread, thickly spread with honey. I ate them, washed down with tepid tea left over the remains of my flask from the night before. I thought I would save it for the escape day, as it would give me some quick energy when I needed it. I sat quietly in the dim light, waiting for my cell door to be opened. The wait was unbearable, then suddenly I heard the clattering of keys and the heavy footsteps of the approaching night patrol. The door was quietly opened, revealing the tall, bearded figure of a man, the night screw.

"Morning, John."

"Morning, Governor." Last good morning to these fuckers, I thought!

"It's a bit cold this morning isn't it?" I said, acting like I normally would.

Small talk over. The screw nodded and smiled. He left to continue unlocking the other kitchen workers. I glanced at my watch again; six-fifteen am, bang on time as usual. I gave a final look back at my cell, before pushing the door shut. I turned left along the landing, down the iron stairs and left again into the passage leading to the kitchen. Looking through the windows, I saw yellow lights gleaming with the fine rain, shimmering against the glare of the beams, illuminating the tall brick wall, topped with a grey metal dome. As I entered the kitchen, I could see the kitchen screw sitting in his glass-fronted office, drinking tea from a white china mug. Every morning in nick was like Groundhog Day. Same pattern, same structure.

"Morning, John."

"Morning." And what a fine morning it is, I thought.

I glanced over at the back door; it was open, leading to the wire mesh vegetable store and I saw the outline of the rain-washed wall looming in the background. I started dipping bread into a box of oil and laying them on the large metal trays, ready to put them into the baker's oven. That morning, it was fried bread and beans for breakfast. I turned to the mini board to see what vegetables I needed for dinner.

"Morning, John," shouted the bakers as they came through the door.

"Morning, there's a fresh tea on the go," I said.

"Later on, mate, we've got to get this ready." He nodded towards the large metal bowl containing the dough mixture.

I went on studying the menu. The screw in his glass-fronted office was hunched over his desk, writing out the day's menu. The clock on the wall said it was time. Time to make the move.

Nobody took any notice as I walked casually past the office, through the gate and out towards the vegetable store outside. There was a row of black plastic rubbish bins; I lifted the lid of the middle one and took out three empty glass jars. I walked towards the wall, peeked towards the glass sentry box; as usual, it was empty. I breathed a sigh of relief; the night screw had left early and was lingering near the front gate, waiting for his relief to come on duty. I ran to the wall and threw the jars one by one over the wall. I heard one of them smash on the narrow path that ran under the wall. A dull thump echoed softly, and I saw the top of a wooden ladder hit the top of the wall with a small thud, pointing towards the early morning sky, followed by a bobbing, black balaclava'd head. Then the scraping sound of another ladder being hauled up over the wall, then swinging down towards me. In my eagerness, I jumped up to grab it before it reached the ground. The instant it was ready, I climbed rapidly up to the top, and sat straddling the metal dome. I pulled the ladder up behind me, lowering it down towards another masked figure in the lane outside. I took one last glance over my shoulder, back at the prison, before scrambling down the ladder to freedom, laying the ladder down quietly beside the other one.

"This way, John."

I followed the other two down a grass slope to the railway lines, along the track, then up the bank.

I pushed my way through a wire mesh fence into the rear of a hospital's grounds. A Ford Granda was waiting, driven by a third man, so I jumped into the rear seat and was immediately driven away. Through the rear window, I saw the other two men who had been waiting for me, making their escape in a light-coloured Volvo. The Granda turned left into the main road, and I ducked down as we passed the studded wooden gates of the prison, to avoid being seen by two blue-raincoated screws walking towards the main gates. The morning shift was arriving, and the driver grinned over his shoulder at me.

"Alright, John, all your gear's on the back seat."

I wriggled out of my white trousers and pulled on a pair of dark grey tracksuit bottoms. There was a leather shoulder holster resting on the top of a blue zip-up bomber jacket. I slipped my arms through the strap, shrugging my shoulders until the harness fitted comfortably. The driver looked through the rear-view driving mirror.

"Under the jacket," he said.

I lifted the jacket to reveal a forty-five revolver. I checked it was fully loaded and slipped it into the holster, pulled the jacket on and zipped it up.

"Where's the other two?" I asked.

"Don't worry, we will see them in a couple of days."

I sat in silence, watching the passing scenery. "There will be murders when they find out you're gone, John."

"Fuck them," I replied. "I'm out and that's the main thing. Where are we going?"

"We're going to The Stow for breakfast."

I started laughing. "Egg and bacon will go down very well right now."

"How do you feel?" asked the driver.

"I'm OK now, sweet as a fucking nut."

I was driven to London, had some breakfast and then got dropped off at King's Cross. We shook hands; his involvement in the escape was now over. I made my way to the station and phoned an old friend from South London. I explained I'd just gone over the wall from Kingston, and I needed some help. He told me to be outside WH Smith's in one hour and he'd be there. I passed the time by going for a walk along the Marylebone streets before waiting outside the shop. Sure enough, I saw my friend approaching. It was good to see him again. We went to a nearby pub for a drink and I told him I wanted to go to work as soon as possible. I had given myself a three-month period to steal as much as I could, then I intended to leave the country for good. He agreed it was the best thing to do. He suggested I stay in a hotel in King's Cross for a couple of days, until he could fix me up with a flat in South London. He gave me some money and said he had a couple of guns I could have when I needed them. I was well pleased at the help he was giving me. I rented a small room for two days and waited for my friend to return.

After two days went by, he returned and took me to a council flat in Walworth. He gave me two guns, ammunition and a ringer and I said I wanted to turn out as soon as I could. I couldn't get any of the firm that had sprung me to work with me. They said I was too well-known and too badly wanted. Instead, they would fit me up with a man they knew, who was eager to turn out. He also wouldn't know my true identity. Which suited me fine.

In the meantime, I scouted around the South Coast and eventually found a small jeweller's shop in The Lanes, Brighton. It wouldn't come to much, but it was a start. I examined the window and thought it might come to twenty grand my way. It would hold me up until I could find some better work. I returned to London and arranged to meet this guy I had been set up with. I explained I had this bit of work in Brighton. I would hold everyone up in the shop and mind his back, while he cleared the window. In and out in ninety seconds, top whack. I would park my car about seventy feet away from the shop's entrance. It would be easy to get back to dump the car and then take a quiet stroll along the sea front to a restaurant near the palace pier and spend an hour having a meal. And when the fuss died down, we could make our way to Brighton station and return to Victoria by train. I took him to Brighton and showed him the getaway route and the jeweller's. He said he was satisfied with the plan, and he agreed to turn out with me.

We split up after agreeing to do it on Tuesday morning. I picked him up at Elephant and Castle at eight am on the Monday and we spent the day preparing for the robbery. I bought a seven-pound hammer so he could smash his way into the window. I also made a trip to the theatrical outfitters of Charles Fox in Covent Garden to buy a stick-on beard to disguise my accomplice. All I would wear was a hat; if I was recognised, it didn't matter very much because I was already serving a life sentence. The day of the robbery was bright and sunny, and we had a pleasant trip down the motorway from London. When we arrived in Brighton, I drove straight to the covered car park, just off West Street and parked in a quiet corner, while my accomplice put the disguise on and the rest of his robbing attire. The hammer was concealed inside a plastic bag. When all was ready, I drove to the lanes and parked the car a short distance from the shop.

It was about eleven o'clock and there were shoppers and pedestrians about, but it wasn't too crowded. As we walked towards the shop, we slipped our gloves on, and we had a stroke of luck; a young couple with a baby in a small pram were entering the shop and were forced to open both doors to gain entry. I waited until they were inside, then we followed them in. I remember a young female shop assistant was rather concerned about the doors being left open. It's not good practice to be slack when there is so much money in the shop.

At this point, I pulled out my forty-five, stuck it in her face and shouted, "Anyone move and I'll shoot her."

Everybody froze in panic; my accomplice drew the hammer from the bag and, with one blow, smashed his way into the window, snatching all the jewellery on display.

"Don't shoot the baby," shouted the shop owner.

I couldn't believe what he was saying, "I won't shoot the baby," I replied, "but I'll shoot you if you don't behave yourself."

The window was cleared in seconds; we ran to the car and tore away. Sharp right, then left into a quiet side street. He ripped the beard off, stuffing it into his pocket, I put a fawn camel-hair overcoat on and left my hat in the car. Then we strolled along the sea front towards the old Steine gardens. There was a white-painted public toilet just by the gardens, and we ducked inside. He went into a cubicle to take the jewellery out of the bag and into his pockets. I stayed a while, then went upstairs to wait for him outside. Immediately, I saw two young plain-clothed policemen standing outside the toilets. One was carrying a portable radio.

As I walked by them, I heard one saying into the radio, "There's nothing happening here."

I strolled to a park bench and sat down, watching and waiting. Suddenly, the policemen went down into the toilets. I loosened my gun in its holster; if the policemen came out with my accomplice, I intended to shoot the two of them, stop a car and drag the driver out. I had to do what I could, as I had no time to fuck around with policemen. I knew Brighton like the back of my hand, and I was quite certain we could get away. Suddenly, the policemen reappeared, empty-handed, and strolled away, obviously happy there was nothing amiss. I watched them waddle off and thought, you'll never know how lucky you've been. My accomplice had heard the radio as they came down the stairs and pulled his trousers down. He sat quietly, hoping for the best. Once they had disappeared from sight, I slipped down the stairs and banged on the cubicle door.

I said, "Look lively, let's go, now they are gone."

We walked up the stairs and made our way to a restaurant on the sea front to have a meal until things had quietened down.

We ordered a roast lamb lunch with a bottle of wine. We stayed about an hour, casually enjoying the meal and the view. We then went into the toilet where he passed me half of the jewellery, as his pockets were overfilled. We finished the wine, paid the bill and walked to Brighton railway station, bought two tickets to Victoria and, as far as I was concerned, that was the end of the Brighton work. So easy.

Once back in London, we made our way by underground to his house. The first thing I did was to empty my pockets of the jewellery, then turn them inside out to show that they were empty. He too emptied his pockets. I looked at the jewellery on the table.

"Is that the lot?" I asked.

"Yes," he said, but I had a feeling he was lying.

"Turn your pockets out," I said, "just to make sure."

He did as I asked and three rings fell out.

He said, "They must have got caught in the lining of my pocket."

But I could see by his face and manner that he had tried to fuck me over. I didn't say anything but, as far as I was concerned, he couldn't be trusted.

I put all the jewellery into a bag and said, "We can sell these tomorrow and I will give you your share." He agreed and that was that.

The next day, I went over to North London with the jewellery. The buyer weighed and examined each article and offered me sixteen grand, which I accepted. I was paid in full an hour later. I immediately phoned my accomplice and arranged to meet him at King's Cross, where I gave him his eight-grand share. He appeared pleased and said, if I ever needed him again, he would turn out with me. I felt like telling him he was lucky I didn't put a bullet in him, but I said nothing and departed back to South London.

CHAPTER 28

BURLINGTON GARDENS

I now had eight grand to hold me up, but that wouldn't last long and, if I wanted to leave the country, I would need a lot more money than eight grand. So, I had to find some more work and a partner I could trust implicitly. I bought a reasonable second-hand car for two grand and, every day, I travelled down to Guildford, Maidenhead, Oxford, Winchester, and all the coastal towns, cruising the roads, trying to find something decent to rob. I saw plenty of potential work but nothing I really fancied. I was looking for a good tom-shop, which is a jewellery shop, ideally with about half a million in the window, which should fetch me roughly ninety grand at street value. Eventually, I decided to look in London. I knew it was more dangerous working in London, especially being on the run, but that's where the money was. I had to accept that I had no other choice; it was a great risk, but I was confident I could pull it off. I thought I'd take a walk around the West End, giving my eyes a chance. I saw some lovely, glimmering windows, but the getaways were difficult, if not impossible. Anyway, I persevered for a while, almost giving up hope, until l I came upon a shop in Burlington Gardens, near Old Bond Street. It looked like an easy window to take out. By the looks of the jewellery on show, I thought it was worth about four hundred grand, give or take. It should fetch me about eighty grand, but again, the getaway was difficult, due to the one-way system.

Then a bright idea came to mind; the alternative was to use Burlington Arcade as a passageway for a getaway on foot. I walked through the arcade several times; if I walked quickly, it would take me about seventy seconds to get through. I could then lose myself in the crowds, walk the short distance to Piccadilly Circus and disappear down the underground. I spent a long time walking around the immediate area and discovered, once the workers arrived in the morning, there was a short lull between nine-thirty and ten-fifteen, when there was a noticeable lack of pedestrians before the shoppers and tourists arrived. During this lull, I would be able to get through the arcade quicker and I thought I would have an excellent chance of getting away. So here I was; I had found the work I wanted. However, I was in a predicament. I was desperate and, when you are desperate for money and on the run, you start making rash decisions. What I needed was someone to work with, as I could not do this job on my own, but unfortunately, I was hot property and anyone with a sane mind wouldn't touch me with a barge pole. I knew lots of robbers, but I couldn't approach any of them, in case I got stuck up. I needed someone to work with, but who?

As the days passed, I was getting more worried, anxious, frustrated and I am not proud to say, angrier at the position I was in. If I wasn't careful, I'd find myself a deep shit. My mind was not right; looking back, I realise that now, but you do not see the fog until you are out of it.

I went back and forth in my mind, trying to figure out a potential partner, preferably one who was not known in London. Finally, one day, as I was wracking my brains for a solution to my problem, a name came to mind; Rab Christie. Over the years we spent in prison together, I'd found out quite a lot about his personal life. And I knew the village he lived in and his local pub. I remember he sent me a cutting from his local newspaper, of himself outside a pub, during a fundraising event for charity. Rab's birthday was December the third and I thought there would be a good chance he would go for a lunchtime drink on his birthday. I took the view that I would see him there, without fail. So, I drove down to St Alban's to his local, the Camp pub. I was eager to get down there, so I arrived just before opening time, parked outside and waited by a bus stop, just opposite the pub. About twenty-five minutes later, I saw Rab walking towards the pub. As he crossed the car park, I called out to him. I could see he was extremely surprised to see me. I even think he looked slightly nervous; he walked over to me. I tossed him the keys to my car and nodded towards it.

"Get in," I demanded. "I want you to drive to London, because I want to show you something which may interest you." I didn't even ask how he was; I was so wrapped up in my situation.

"I'm sorry, John, but I can't come with you. It's my birthday and I have some friends waiting for me inside," he responded.

Not for a moment did I consider he would say no. He was messing with my plans and I had one goal; nothing would take me off my target.

My patience snapped; I opened my jacket showed him my gun and said, "Do as I say. It won't take long."

I could see he had a worried look on his face; he seemed confused and shocked that I was threatening him. He opened his mouth to say something, then looked at my face and, with a sigh, reluctantly got into the car and drove us back to London. The first point of call was to go and see the Burlington Gardens shop.

On the way to London, I decided to make small-talk. After all, he was meant to be my pal. "How are you doing, Rab?"

He looked at me like I was totally nuts. "My wife has health problems and money is tight, as it always is. Why are you making me drive to London?" He looked at me with great concern and I felt a slight pang of guilt.

"Don't worry, Rab," I answered. "I may have a solution for your lack of money. Just be patient and I'll tell you when we get there."

After what I'd heard, I was one hundred per cent sure he would take part in the robbery. I took him to the shop window, showed him the jewellery on display and spun a story about how the owner wanted me to rob him, so he could claim more insurance than the window was worth. I went on to explain that there would be no resistance from anyone; it was just a matter of walking in, taking the jewellery and away we go through the arcade. I was so convincing, I had even convinced myself that it would be easy.

Rab's reaction was total disbelief; he started to laugh and retorted, "You must be joking!"

He refused point blank to help me. I couldn't believe what I was hearing and I didn't want to accept his answer. I was in no mood to be told no. Just by the entrance to Burlington Arcade was a row of telephone boxes.

I nodded towards him, saying, "Let's go over there, so we can talk in private."

We walked over to one of the grimy and beaten-up phone boxes. I opened the door and pushed Rab inside, with some force.

"What's up with you? The money is good, your wife is ill and you've got no money, plus it's easy work. What's the problem?" I couldn't make sense of his lack of enthusiasm to do this job.

He still refused, with a determined no and laughed at the idea, as if I was crazy. At this, I lost control and flew into a furious rage. I started cursing and swearing. Normally, I have the self-control of a saint, but I could feel myself unravelling and I noticed I was becoming unhinged. I was desperate; I had to have someone to help me. I needed the money to get out of the country; my brain was going haywire at the thought of not doing the job. Rab may have had his problems, but as far as I was concerned, they were nothing compared to mine. With sheer desperation and running out of ideas, I did the worst thing I could do to a friend. I opened my jacket and pulled my gun out, thrusting it into his bulging belly.

"If you won't come with me, I'll kill you here and now. I can't let you go, as you know too much already."

His face turned ashen white with fear. I could see he was absolutely terrified of me and, rightly so, as I was acting bonkers.

"Alright, alright, I'll do as you say. Just put the gun away."

I knew I had won the battle, but not quite the war. I also knew he would be hoping to slip away, the first time the opportunity presented itself. He suggested that he return home and promised he would come with me whenever I asked. No way was that going to happen. I intended to see the job through the next day and, in the meantime, I wasn't going to let Rab out of my sight.

I decided to take Rab to my flat for the night. After the robbery, I would move away and change my car, just to make sure that, if Rab decided to say anything, I'd be long gone. On the way to Woolworth, I made Rab stop at a chemist. I took him inside and bought some hair dye, dark brown in colour. Rab had a distinctive look and you could spot him a mile off. He had a thick head of silver hair; witnesses would remember the bright, glossy silver, so it had to be dyed. And after the robbery, all Rab had to do was get his hair dyed back to its normal colour, return home and no one would be any the wiser.

During the night, I explained all this to Rab, in an effort to win him over. He nodded in agreement, but I could see he was nervous and did not want to be anywhere near me or involved in this situation. I ignored his defiance and his feelings; instead, I helped him dye his hair. I also had some spare false beards and fixing glue. With his hair dyed and a false beard, he never would be recognised. After a while, we fell silent and Rab slept on the sofa, while I cat-napped in the armchair. The day of the robbery was a crisp sunny one; I was dressed in a dark blue suit, white shirt and a red tie. Under my jacket, I carried my gun. Rab wore a sports coat and jeans; he carried a large bag. Our hands were covered with long strips of Elastoplast down each finger and thumb and a square patch covered the palm of each hand. At a casual glance, you would never notice the plaster.

If you were to walk into a tom-shop wearing gloves, they'd be instantly suspicious and someone's fingers would be near the alarm just in case you were a robber. But if you walked in with apparently bare hands, it gave you that extra few seconds to stick a gun in their face and stop them hitting the alarm.

On the morning of December the fourth, we travelled by tube to Piccadilly Circus and, in the same telephone box where I threatened him, Rab put on the full outfit and he was ready. As he walked to the shop, I could see a resigned look on his face; he looked like he was about to throw up. But I had no time for wobbles, or backing out; that was not an option. We stood looking at the window for a couple of seconds.

"Remember, take as much as possible, as quickly as you can."

Rab nodded and gulped. His heart was not in it. So, I rang the doorbell and walked straight into the shop.

I stood facing the counter, pulled out my gun and shouted, "Don't move and no one gets hurt."

Everyone froze; the normal and universal look of people with guns in their faces appeared and I could see the gun once again had the desired effect. As they stood dead on the spot, I could hear the sound of the window partition being torn open. A few seconds elapsed and I saw Rab run from the shop, clutching the bag, brimming with jewellery from the window display. Everything was going to plan. I spun round and followed Rab out of the shop. Turning left and left again into Burlington Arcade, I walked quickly, trying to avoid attention.

Out of nowhere, I heard shots behind me. I glanced back and I could see two men sprinting, coming after me with determination. I turned and fired; they both ducked into the nearest doorway. I resumed walking faster but they still followed me, so I fired again and began to run. As I passed a shop, I saw a uniformed policeman standing by the door. I pointed the gun at him and he never moved; I'm sure he was happy to let me go. As I passed him, the two men no doubt were spurred on by the sight of the nearby policeman and started shouting at the top of their lungs. I turned to fire another shot, wounding one of them in the thigh. By now, the shouting and sounds of gunshots had alerted the shoppers, who were all coming out in their drove to see the commotion. Making it impossible to pass, they were like a wall of people. Interlinking, doing their care-of-the-community bullshit. At that moment, I knew I was in deep shit, as there was nowhere to turn. An off-duty policeman and one of the jewellers rushed at me, and others joined in. I was overpowered and disarmed. Rab had disappeared, but others took up the chase. It was no use. I had fucked this up, never considering the might of the general public. Who would have thought they would have been so brave as to try and catch an armed robber?

I was handcuffed, put into a police van and taken to West End central police station, searched once more and stripped of all of my clothing, then given a one-piece paper suit to wear. They threw me an old pair of slippers and made me sit on my own. No one had yet asked my name or questioned me.

CHAPTER 29

THE FINAL CAPTURE

I was seated behind a small desk, waiting to be processed. I remember looking at a policeman walking back and forth with a spring in his step. He was clutching pieces of paper, chatting away frantically on a phone, throwing an occasional glance my way. I sat quietly for a while until eventually a detective approached me. He was polite, which was a vast contrast to the detectives of the seventies; they had a tough no-nonsense manner, whereas this detective seemed wet behind the ears. Care-of-the-community kind of fella. As I have experienced before, though, not all is what it seems and I was not going to be tricked by this officer. For all I know, he was probably playing the role the system had told him to do.

"Can I have your name?" he asked.

"Mickey Mouse," I replied.

To which he smiled and nodded. He didn't find me amusing, but I thought my response was hilarious. I could not believe how things had turned out.

"Look," he said. "This is obviously not your first time in a police station, so you know how this goes. We will just hold you down and take your prints by force, if we must."

I had to check my behaviour and thought for a moment. I didn't fancy rolling around on the floor with several burly police-men. Them on top of me, beating the shit out of me for some simple information. Which they were going to get, one way or another. So, I gave him my date of birth, 19/ 08/29. He looked happy he had been able to change my defiant mood. Like he had won half the battle already. He scurried away, leaving me to run my birthday through the computer, which would give him all he needed to know. Then they would be revelling in the glory of catching me.

A short time later, a door opened, and several suited men entered the room.

One came over and said, "Hello, John, we knew you were back on the streets again. We were lucky to get you so quick, as we knew you would eventually go on a rampage to get money. Anyway, you're nicked, that's the main thing."

The way he spoke to me was more matter-of-fact than nasty, and he smiled at me. For a moment, I thought he seemed quite sympathetic to my predicament. All the men left me alone for a short while, leaving me with gloom and hopelessness setting in. After which, my clothes were removed, and I was given a white paper suit. In all cases where shots are fired, this is the custom clothing given, whilst your clothes are being forensically examined. Once they were taken way, I was taken to a cell. The door slammed shut and I was left to sit on the hard bed, staring aimlessly at grubby walls.

I thought, fuck me, John, you're in deep shit. When you're in terrible trouble, it's no use pacing up and down, wishing this and that; you have to accept what is done is done. There is no changing the course of events. It's what's called the hazards of the profession. I lay on the bed and the immortal words of Fagin came to mind: 'I started to review the situation.' The more I considered the situation and the various outcomes, the worse it looked. I'd escaped from prison, which made me unlawfully at large; that alone was enough reason to give me life and lock me up and throw away the key, as I was a lifer on the run. Especially one like myself; they can act in a vindictive manner towards criminals like me, when caught. I was not only on the run, I had also committed an armed robbery, with a gun, where shots had been fired in a public place. And you can't get more public than Burlington Arcade. Doing the calculations in my head, I was looking at least eighteen years, with probably another five on top, just to rub salt into my sore wound.

The Home Office would make me serve the full eighteen years, possibly twenty-three, so doing the math, I would be eighty-three before I hit the streets again. I must confess, it wasn't a pleasant thought. I felt sick to my stomach that, quite possibly, I could end up dying an old man in prison. A couple of hours had passed and the door opened, all uniformed policemen this time.

"Come with me," one ordered.

He led me through a corridor into a room where the desk Sergeant was there, with quite a few plain-clothed detectives standing around. I was led to his desk and listened intently whilst he read off my list of charges.

"Armed robbery, discharging a gun in a public place whilst unlawfully at large." And so it went on, his words becoming one big string of jumbled sounds. When he finished, he looked at me and asked me if there was anything I wanted to say.

"Yes," I replied. "Could I have a cup of tea, I am gasping for one."

There were a few smiles that darted across the room, and the Sergeant looked at me with a glint in his eye. "I will see what I can do."

They seemed to admire my tenacity and fighting spirit, but admiration was not going to get me out of this mess. And with that, I was led back to my bed and locked away for the night. I spent an uncomfortable night in the cell, as I couldn't sleep much. I had a lot on my mind; my freedom was soon to be taken away from me and, this time, I knew it would be impossible to ever leave a prison again. The night dragged on and, eventually, the morning came. Daylight crept into the cell in small staggered stages, and as I watched the shimmer of light appear around me, I couldn't feel any joy for a new day. At around ten am, my door was unlocked and I was told I was on the move. Meaning I was taken to reception, handcuffed to be processed, and then led to a police car by plain-clothed officers. I didn't have the energy to ask where I was going. It didn't matter to me where I was going; I had lost all ability to care. I would soon find out what shitty HMP hotel I would be in.

As we were driving through the West End, I looked longingly out the window at the shoppers and the hustle and bustle of everyday life. We stopped at the traffic lights, and I thought to myself, it will be a long time before I see any of this again. If ever. The impending doom of the situation set in; I sat quietly wondering which prison I was bound for. Anywhere, please, I thought, anywhere but Wandsworth; it was a terrible prison, like hell on earth, but worse, I was no longer cut out for that place. We drove over the water and into South London; my worst fears were confirmed when we eventually turned left at Neal's Nursery, drove a little further and came to a halt. Outside were massive wooden doors; my heart dropped as the doors creaked open. Wandsworth. We drove slowly inside and were greeted by two large steel gates that led to the prison. I didn't think I could feel any worse than that moment.

The policeman at the gate took my paperwork, studied it for a few seconds and then opened the steel gates for us to enter. We turned left and rolled up to the reception. The reception screw greeted us with, "What do you want?" He seemed a little pissed off.

"We have a prisoner for you."

The screw looked annoyed; he glanced at me before reading my paperwork. His face dropped slightly as he was reading my record and he said, "We don't want him."

This was music to my ears; my heart leapt in a little dance of happiness. The feeling was mutual.

"What do you mean, you don't want him?" the policeman inquired.

"We don't want him. He is a lifer, he's a Cat A escapee, and on top of that, he is a fucking nuisance!"

I tried to conceal my smile, but I just couldn't help it; my lips curled up with pure delight. I thought, what a result.

The policeman I had come with was a bit dumbfounded. He said, "What do we do with him?"

The reception screw unlocked the gate and ushered us to leave, with no care for the policeman's predicament. He retorted, "That's not our problem." And proceeded to turn his back on us.

We both stood outside, as if suspended in mid-air, none the wiser as to what to do. I thought I would cut the tension looming over us and make a helpful suggestion.

"Why don't you try Pentonville?" In my cunning and calculating mind, I thought, if I could get to Ville, I could have a chance of getting over the wall again.

Anyway, the policeman started making frantic phone calls, until it was finally agreed I was going to Wormwood Scrubs, which wasn't too bad; a hundred times better than Wandsworth, at least. We got back in the car for another drive, and I got another glance of the streets. South London didn't have all the glitzy shops like that of West London; it seemed drearier and wearier. Life was a little tougher in the south, and we were now venturing to the West. In the car, the officer was still in a state of shock.

"That's the first time to our knowledge that a prisoner has been refused entry to a prison."

It felt like quite an achievement, I thought. It was only a fleeting moment of smugness, which then melted away at the thought of my situation. I felt completely isolated. I was completely fucked, as there was no getting out of this one.

We came to a halt and finally reached Wormwood Scrubs. The walls and building brought back memories of when I first entered it as a young sixteen-year-old Borstal boy and now I was back here, as a sixty-year-old man. Looking at the longest stretch, it felt like such an anti-climax to my life story.

We passed into the prison and the usual procedure followed; the paperwork was examined and signed. The cuffs were removed, and the policeman left me, wishing me good luck, before he departed back to his station. One of the screws beckoned me over and the normal formalities were completed.

He leaned in and said, "I was told you are an escape risk, which means you will have to wear these trousers."

They had a yellow stripe down the leg and a jacket to match, with a yellow patch on it. The same outfit I had worn many a time before. He told me I would be in Cat A and would have to wait a while before they put me in my cell. Marvellous; another long wait.

This reception block I was in was lively. There was a lot of noise and commotion; some of the new prisoners couldn't speak any English and there were junkies, going cold turkey in the waiting room, being sick all over the floor. Shaking and sweating out, having terrible withdrawal symptoms. The carnage and mess were a sight to behold. One screw was talking to an African man; from what I could make out, he had come straight from Heathrow. He was in traditional dress and couldn't speak any English.

The screw was asking, "Do you know where you are?"

The African looked at him blankly; he was confused and had no idea how to respond. The screw shook his head and walked off, telling the African to stay there. Leaving him standing there, with the reception screw not knowing how to deal with the language barrier either. The screw that walked off eventually came back and told me and the African we were in Cat A, even though I knew that already. I was then escorted across the yard to A Wing and stood, waiting to be allocated a cell.

I made a head gesture to the African and said to the screw, "Do you think he thinks he is in a hotel?"

The screw laughed and said, "Some hotel!"

Yes, I thought, five-star treatment here. He is in for a shock being in Wormwood and I wondered how he had ended up in this place.

Lots of lifers lived in A wing; I looked around at the convicts leaning over the rails, looking down, seeing if they knew any of the newcomers. There were others seated at tables, drinking their teas and coffees and rolling cigarettes. They were all chatting and were loud; as far as I could tell, I didn't know anyone. I just ignored them.

"Hilton," the screw barked.

"Yes," I replied.

"You're up on landing two in cell number twenty-one."

I grabbed my bedding and went up to my cell. The door was open and, to my surprise, the cell was quite clean. I dumped my stuff on the bed and took the jug to go and get some fresh water. I was parched.

As I came out of the cell, I heard a voice call, "John Boy." I looked up and saw a couple of guys I knew; I was with them in a prison many moons ago.

"Where are you, cell 21?" one called Mark asked. "I will be down in a minute."

I returned to my cell and started to make my bed. Making a bed is the first thing any convict does upon entering a new cell. Suddenly, three more convicts appeared at the doorway. I was pleased to see people I knew; we shook hands like old friends.

"We heard you got nicked in Burlington Arcade and didn't you go over the wall in Kingston prison? I laughed when I found out. You haven't changed one bit, mate."

I smiled. "Yes, it's all true." I seemingly had a reputation and pretty much everybody knew about my antics.

"How much trouble are you in?" Mark asked me, with curiosity.

"Deep shit. I went on an armed robbery and let three shots go. I went over the wall in Kingston prison and there will be hefty charges to come. I'm looking at an eighteen-to-twenty stretch, at least."

Mark pulled a face, as if to say he was sorry for me. "I don't know what to say." He shook his head and looked at me, disgruntled on my behalf.

"Don't worry. I can cope with anything they throw at me."

Just then the bell rang; it was time for roll check, and everyone had to return to their cells.

Mark said, "I'll see you later," and swiftly departed.

For the next few days, nothing much really happened; various cons I knew came to see me, bringing toiletries and tins of food.

I was soon fully stocked up. On the third night, I think it was a Saturday, Mark and Gary appeared at my door.

"Do you fancy a drink?"

Of course I did; my eyes lit up with glee. Anything to take me out of reality; after all, drinking and smoking weed are a form of escapism and all I wanted was to escape, more than anything.

Gary produced a little bottle of vodka and coke; I couldn't believe it.

Mark said, "We have got the storeman straightened up. He brings us food and drink in." All the cons seemed to have the storeman straightened up, he must be making a fortune! Mark grinned. "Do you fancy a puff on a joint?"

"Come in properly," I said, and we shut the cell door.

Mark rolled up a large joint and gave it to me. He said, "You go first."

I lit up and took a couple of large puffs; it was a pure moment of pleasure and relief, all the pressure of life seemed to slip off my shoulders. Like heavy armour had been removed after a bloody and lengthy battle. I was suddenly intoxicated. Gary poured me another drink and we sat around, sipping vodka and smoking hash, before the bell went for the end of association.

Before Mark left, he said, "Tomorrow, we have some more booze coming in. Take this." He gave me a nice lump of hash.

As soon as they left, I shut my cell door and waited for the screws to do their nightly rounds and checks. Once I knew the coast was clear, I excitedly skinned up another joint and drank the rest of the vodka, before lying on my bed in a pleasant haze and fully buzzed. That's all I remember, until the sun cracked through the sky and the morning came. For me, it was a much-needed release and it felt good to escape the dreariness and mundane routine of prison life and the torture and turmoil in my mind.

I soon slipped back into the prison regime, like a duck to water. I was back, living the prison life, trying my best to forget about the outside world. I got myself a little cleaning job, which kept me busy and got me out of my cell. I was getting regular supplies of booze and hash, so I was sorted for the evenings. When my thoughts would wander into darkness, drink and hash were the only things to give me comfort.

I decided to concentrate on my fitness, keep the mind and body sharp. I did a circuit in my cell, press-ups, sit-ups, squats, trying to keep as fit as possible. There was no point in losing hope; I had to stay positive and make the best out of a bad situation. Falling into complete darkness wouldn't do anyone any good and I kept reminding myself of that every day. It's easy to slip into a routine of laziness, which again can cause depression. In prison, especially, you must stay mentally alert and physically strong. I always found strength within myself; however bad things were, I never gave up on hope. I chose happiness. It didn't choose me.

CHAPTER 30

DISPERSAL PRISON

A few weeks slipped by and I was told to expect to be moved to a dispersal prison. A dispersal prison houses Category A prisoners. After some notorious prison escapes, it was decided that special secure units should be built to enable the allocation of Cat A prisoners, which meant high security and more screws, which of course I didn't want. I always thought I had a chance of making an escape in Scrubs and, one day, my chance came.

One of my pals, Mark, said to me, "The storeman is willing to bring a small hydraulic jack in. We can get a jack delivered to the prison and he can get it to us within a matter of weeks. Now, if it comes in, you must do nothing. We will arrange for the bars in recess to be sprung."

The bars in the prison were the old-fashioned bars, which could be sprung without too much trouble. Once I got out into the yard, there were dozens of wooden pallets and building materials by the wall. All I had to do was pile them up high enough to reach the top of the wall to clamber up and I needed a rope made from sheets to securely lower me down. Tie one end onto something heavy, climb a makeshift ladder over onto the top, throw the sheets over the wall and slide down. A couple of guys promised to wait outside the prison with a car and have some fresh clothes and a bit of money for me to get by with.

I couldn't believe my good fortune. I was lucky to have such good people inside with me and many criminal friends, both inside and out. The plan was, once I was out, I would drive to South London and hide undercover there. Over the years, I had plenty of good help to call upon, especially in South London, which I had always considered home. Most of my good pals were in South London too, so it seemed the best place to go. If all went well and I succeeded in the escape, I would have a good plan in place. I started to imagine the screws' faces when they realised I had escaped again, which gave me an overwhelming buzz and a great 'fuck the system' moment. I tried not to ponder too long on the promise of being sprung. The thought of escape can be all-consuming, so in the meantime, I increased my workouts to maintain good stamina and strength and waited patiently for the day to arrive.

Mark came up to me and said, "The storeman has gone on holiday for two weeks. On his return, the jack will be brought in."

Which was slightly aggravating, but I thought, two weeks isn't much of a wait. When the two weeks were up, Mark came with weed and booze, but nothing else. The storeman had only brought the drug and drink supplies. The seed of doubt had set in and I thought the storeman had got cold feet. Of course, I was right; they were no longer able to get the jack, as the storeman knew it would be used for an escape. Mark explained the storeman was worried that all traces could be led back to him; he didn't want the police tracing our escape back to him as then he would be an accomplice.

Obviously, I was disappointed. I had a great plan in place and was ready to go, but I understood the storeman's predicament. People never want to get involved in anything too heavy, especially if you are an average citizen, without a criminal mind. All I could do now was sit back and wait to be transferred to a dispersal prison. About a month later, two screws came for me and said I was being transferred. I didn't ask where I was going; a lot of them took joy and pleasure out of not telling you and I didn't want to give them the satisfaction. So, I kept my mouth firmly closed.

I was taken to the reception stripped, searched, handcuffed and led outside, where a prison van awaited me. The van had four small compartments, with benches for seats, which were hard, small and uncomfortable. The small compartment was claustrophobic and I was struggling to fit in it. I was placed into one and the doors were bolted. I felt like cattle being taken off to market to be slaughtered, hung, drawn and quartered. We were on the move. At the steel gates, we suddenly came to a sharp halt. A senior officer waved down the van, asking it to stop before departure. The van doors were pulled wide open, the senior officer came up to me and made sure my cuffs were secure, double-checking I was not able to escape or have an opportunity to do so. Once he was fully satisfied, the compartment was bolted back up and the van locked; then we were off.

I did find their suspicion of me escaping highly amusing. After all, I had done it so many times, it was almost becoming something of joke. They would be idiotic not to double-check. Now back on the road, I got to once again gaze upon the free world. I had no idea where I was going, so I enjoyed the ride, looking outside the window at the life passing me by. Lots of new shops had sprung up, places I didn't recognise, and I noticed some new-style vehicles on the road, which I took some interest in. When moving from one prison to another, you realise how disengaged you are from society. Even though you are part of the makeup and fabric of it, you don't get to be fully immersed in the real world anymore and reality really hits you when you see society again with your own eyes. It unsettles you, as you know this life is now fully out of your grasp, yet you long for the life you once knew, with all your heart.

After about an hour, I rumbled the route; we were on our way to the Isle of Wight! So, Parkhurst was my final destination. The last time I was in Parkhurst was in 1969, when I took part in the Parkhurst riots and, suddenly now, I was being transported back there in 1991, as if no time had passed at all. The wheel of prison life had come full circle. We drove onto the ferry and sailed across the channel to Parkhurst prison. I had this gut-wrenching thought; this is it, this is my final resting place. The last time I was on the ferry was in 1978, when I was in the company of a small group of friends. We were on our way to a hotel, for a lovely holiday; this time, it was more like a death sentence than a vacation. We eventually arrived at the main gate and had to wait for the all-too-familiar gates to be opened, once again driving up to the greeting area of reception. I went inside, the cuffs were removed and I was told to sit on a bench, whilst my paperwork was being examined. I had done enough sitting for one day, cooped up in that van, but I obliged, so as not to irritate the screw.

A couple of screws looked at me and asked me with surprise, "You are sixty-one?"

"Yeah," I replied.

"You're a bit old now for prison, but it looks like you're in plenty of trouble, with your escape especially."

I made no reply. I just thought, bollocks to the lot of you. I sat there until I was called to see the doctor. With most prisons, there is a medical team on site, including a dentist, a nurse and a doctor. On standby for your so-called care. Prisoners are meant to get the same healthcare and treatment as anyone outside of prison. But this is arguably questionable. The doctor told me to sit down and asked my name and date of birth. He then proceeded to look at my medical record. Taking his time to flick through the pages.

"Any complaints?" he asked.

"No," I replied. I was as fit as a fiddle.

"Alright, you can go to the main prison."

I turned and followed the screw outside. And that, my friends, was my medical check. Quite outrageous, if you think about it. One question and then, 'Off you go, see you later.' They didn't give a shit; my arm could be hanging off and they would give me a plaster to slap on it. Again, another reason why the system was laughable and totally incompetent.

Back outside, I planted myself on the uncomfortable and bum-numbing bench, waiting to collect my bedding. It had been a long, tiring journey and I was fed up of waiting around. Finally, I was taken to the main prison. All in all, it took around an hour and I was escorted to B wing and handed over to the staff. I was given a cell on the twos landing; it was just a normal, basic cell. It had been cleaned out, which was a bonus, as sometimes you can go into a cell and it's disgustingly filthy, filled with the previous occupant's grime and their lingering smell. So, I was thankful I had a clean place to rest my weary bones.

I was unpacking my bed when a couple of Lewes lads came into my cell. "Alright, John," one of them said.

"I'm alright. What's it like here?" I inquired.

"It's not too bad. A couple of bad screws here, but overall, it's not too bad. Leave your unpacking, come downstairs and meet a few pals of yours."

So, I reluctantly followed them downstairs. By this point, the travel had taken all my energy and I would much have preferred the peace of my cell. I saw quite a few lads I knew from previous prisons. I sat down and a mug of tea was produced, which I was grateful for. I was parched and I loved a sweet tea after a long journey. We exchanged news and had a good catch-up, which made me feel a little better. I realised, if you didn't have any friends in prison, the whole experience would be difficult. Thankfully, I always knew someone, so it made it much easier to integrate in any prison I ended up in. Being a well-known criminal can sometimes end up paying off. In this situation, it did me many favours to be a notorious inmate.

I've seen lots of newbies in my time come into prison, who didn't know a soul, and no one would chat to them, because they didn't know anything about them. For all the convicts knew, they could be anyone; nonces, grasses, lowlifes. So, cons were reluctant to approach you, without any background checks. You always had to be cautious of new faces. Until they were vouched for, they were on their own.

So, once again, I was in the old routine of pumping iron down in the gym, which would be a daily activity of mine. Every chance I got, I took all the fresh air and exercised as much as they would allow me to. I would play lots of sports and loved a bit of tennis out in the courts and even worked out in my cell. I tried to remain focused and upbeat, and exercise was a perfect distraction. My only wish was that I had a couple of joints of hash to unwind and relax, the same way people like to unwind with some scotch or a couple of drinks. Weed was my pleasure, my down-time. But unfortunately, it was not as readily available in this prison. I just survived the best way I could, keeping active to the point where I was so tired by bedtime, I was asleep in seconds when my head hit the pillow.

Parkhurst was an old prison, which had a lot of building work going on, as they were refurbishing a wing right next to the wing I was in. Whilst I was there, I would often fantasise about a way out. I was always looking for an exit. If I could find a way into where the refurbishing was taking place, there would be an easy exit, a soft spot in the matrix to take advantage of. There were quite a few ladders and tools left unchained. I knew, with these tools and equipment, I could easily get over the fence and make a swift escape. The thought of it made my body pump with adrenaline and desire and would send my mind into a frenzy. I had managed to get in touch with a friend of mine and arranged to have a car and money for me when the escape took place. All I had to do was find a way over that poxy fence. I told a couple of close friends about my plan, and they agreed that it could be done. I fancied cutting a bar in my cell wing, as I was on the ground floor. Again, all I needed was rope from sheets, and a makeshift hook and I would fly over that fence with ease. I also needed a hacksaw blade to cut through the bars. Getting to the fence, however, would be a little tricky. Being a dispersal prison, it had extremely stringent security in place. Up until the day of the escape, I would have to keep a low profile and see if I could execute my plan.

Little did I know that there were three other cons, planning their own escape. One of them was clever with his hands, a highly skilled man. He was able, with great accuracy, to replicate the key to the gymnasium, the door that led to the compound. Once out, they would cut a hole in the wire fence. Then with a homemade rope and a hook, they could get over. Then it was a simple matter of clambering up the rope and over the wall. Their plan seemed to coincide with mine, so I needed to get out before their attempt, otherwise there would be no chance of leaving. The place would be on lockdown. If I did make it over, I would have to do a couple of robberies and get out of the country as quickly as I could.

Anyway, I carried on as normal, keeping my head down, waiting for the word that the escape was on. When the word came, it appeared the con getting the blade couldn't get his hands on one. He decided to steal one from the prison workshop. But the prison suddenly changed the routine regarding the use of the tools and it became impossible to get hold of a blade. Another failed attempt at escaping. You had to bide your time and wait for the right opportunity. Sometime in the future, our luck might change, but all our avenues to break out of this prison were exhausted. We needed to be patient and I had somehow mastered the art of that; after all, I had all the time in the world and then some.

CHAPTER 31

NO REGRETS

It was at this time, in 1991, that my past came back to haunt me. Of course, I had never forgotten the death of my friend, Alan, how I had accidentally killed him, killed the jeweller, dug my friend's grave and buried him under the earth, as if he never existed. I confessed to both murders, not too long after my arrest for the robbery on the jewellery store in Piccadilly. For me, it was the end of the road; there was little chance of me ever escaping prison again, especially in a dispersal prison. I knew it was time to accept my fate, that I would die in prison.

One day, I was called out for a solicitor's visit, who informed me that I would go on trial in September. He started to talk about what we could put forward as plea of mitigation.

I retorted, "Are you serious? What possible plea of mitigation could be put forward to have any effect on my sentence? I would mug myself off in front of the judge. I want no plea. I'm just going to plead guilty, and he can do as he likes."

There was no point in trying to wriggle my way out of this one. My brief nodded in agreement and said, "You are right, John," before hastily leaving. I knew he was trying to get the best out of the case, but there was no hope. I returned to my wing and told my pals what had transpired.

Tony agreed with my decision. He said, "You're right, there is nothing you can do. How do you feel, mate?"

"I could do with a stiff drink, if I am honest."

"Don't worry, I will get you a bottle of booze tonight."

Sure as the day is long, I was enjoying my coping mechanism.

Later, when I was locked up for the night, I smoked some hash and had a good drink and my last thought before bed was, fuck them, they can do what they want. They will never beat me. My fate was now in their hands and, as far as I knew, they would lock me up and throw away the key.

Anyway, September soon came around. I shook hands with the firm and was escorted to the reception, where I went through the usual routine of searching me for contraband. After which, I sat on a bench, watching who was being transferred to other prisons and the lucky ones who were being discharged.

One of the screws shouted, "Hilton!"

I got up and went over to the desk, where my name and number were checked against the list of people going for trial.

"What court are you going to?" he asked.

"The Old Bailey," I replied.

He beckoned two screws over. One of my escorting officers handcuffed me to him and led me to the yard, then placed me in a cellular van. We jolted off and lurched forwards towards the front gate. The car came to a halt, where the usual formalities went underway. Handcuffs were checked, paperwork examined with a fine-tooth comb. The van door was locked, and we drove out into Heathfield Road, on our way to the Old Bailey. I looked out of the small window at the passing scenery; pretty women passed me by, suited businessmen and parents holding hands with their children. No one gave us a second glance; I felt like I was in an invisible bubble, a forgotten member of society and most likely never to be walking the streets again.

We arrived; a policeman held the traffic back and waved us through the narrow tunnel that led down to the cells below. The court van stopped, and I was removed and placed into one of the dimly-lit cells. The cuffs were removed, and the cell door was slammed shut. In the early 90s, the holding cell was grubby, full of graffiti left by the previous occupants, who had scratched their names deep into the walls and various comments, cursing the judge and slagging off the institution we were all caught up in.

Telling people who had grassed on who and the sweet declarations of love to their partners or their love for their children. I studied the walls, but I did not recognise any of the names. After intently studying the wall to kill time, covering every etching on there, I began to pace up and down and, when I became tired, I was quite resigned to my fate and would be pleased when it was all over.

After a couple of hours, the door was unlocked, and I was told to hold my hands out and handcuffs were placed on my wrists. I was taken to number four court and waited patiently until I was called in. The door opened and I was led to the felon's door and stood there, handcuffed to the screw. The judge was seated high up in the court and gave me a piercing glare. I cannot say I was too intimidated; I'd had plenty of judicial glares in my life. The prosecution was to my right and the jury was just in front. To my left was the public gallery; I glanced up but didn't recognise anyone. I looked to my right and watched the prosecution get to his feet; he looked in my direction before the questions started.

He first went through my past criminal record, so the jury could obviously be biased against the evidence I was about to give. Considering my criminal record was the length of my arm and then some, I had no chance of winning the jury over. I was at court for the robbery of the jewellery store in Burlington Arcade. Rab was on up charges and I only thought it fair to try and help him. He also decided the best angle to take for his defence was one of duress, that I had forced him under pain of death to commit the robbery. A defence of duress means you must be certain that the person who is threatening you would follow through on his threats, which was to kill him. Hence my confession to Alan's and the jeweller's murder, to show the court that I could kill. I portrayed myself as a desperate, callous robber, who was on the run from prison. No one would work with me, as I was badly wanted by the police and presented a constant danger to anyone involved with me. That's why I was desperate to find someone to work with.

At the end of the day, I did the best I could for him, even to the extent of confessing to two murders, to prove how dangerous I was. But I am afraid, by a vote of ten to two, the jury found him guilty. I glanced towards Rab; I was gutted for him, but could do nothing. The charges against me were read out.

"How do you plead?" the judge asked me.

"Guilty," I replied.

"Have you anything to say?"

"No," I replied. I thought, what was there to say? What was done was done and I didn't want to pretend like I felt any remorse, because I didn't.

The judge looked at me before saying, "Is there nothing that I can say to you?"

No, it's all been said before, I thought. I really wanted to give the judge a volley of abuse, but refrained from doing so, mainly for Rab's sake. I didn't want to rock the boat and tick the judge off. If I upset the judge, they could drop a bigger sentence. Unfortunately, he was out for blood that day and passed life times two, with the recommendation that I never be released. Another heavy blow.

To hear those words uttered sent me into an out-of-body experience. I was overwhelmed and, dare I say it, shocked. I was escorted down the steps, but from there to the cell was a complete blur. The screw led me from the court to the cell below, my cuffs were removed, and the door shut; my fate was now sealed. I sat down, thinking of the judge's words. Fuck me, I thought, this is the end of the road for you. All I could do was carry on and do the best I could and, when the day came, I could do no more than try and make amends for my sins. But one thing I knew was that I would die a brave man; they would get no tears or emotion from me. I had to accept that whatever you do in life will eventually catch up with you. Nothing stays a secret forever, and a part of me was pleased I no longer had to carry the heavy secret of Alan's death with me anymore.

I was sent to Whitemoor for sixteen lengthy years of my life. I made no attempt to escape, I settled into the world of prison and accepted I would see the rest of my days out within Her Majesty's hotel. I would often reflect over the time I had spent being a robber. I was never fortunate enough to have committed a big robbery, where millions were stolen. Out of all the robbers I knew, few were lucky enough to make a big score or pull off a major heist. I had met a couple of people along the way that were this fortunate; for example, being inside with some of the Great Train Robbers. I would describe myself as a bread-and-butter robber. If I was working two-handed, as I was in later years, and we nicked, say, a twenty to twenty-five grand bag, then it was ten or twelve grand each. Which, at the end of the day, wasn't too bad for a minute's work, but was never going to change your life significantly.

I had always dreamed of a big robbery, getting millions and emigrating to a hot, exotic land. Spending my days with my family and the kids. But things just never worked out that way. I did alright for money, especially for a man with no job skills or any education. If you could turn out well once a month, as far as I was concerned, I was getting a fairly good living. Of course, if you got nicked, well, that was too bad; it's a risk all robbers take and accept. In total, I counted up all the years I had been behind bars, and it was forty-five years! It's quite a long time, but I am fortunate enough to still be here at ninety-four. When I received my last sentence in 1991, I think the total amount of cash and jewellery I had gained from my robberies was in the region of four hundred thousand pounds. But not all my robberies were successful; sometimes I turned out and things went wrong and I came away empty-handed. This would be every robber's nightmare, but again, part and parcel of the job. Sometimes, we would have dry spells that could go on for weeks, risking your freedom to have nothing to show for it.

I suppose, during my career, I've sold about a million in cash and jewellery; not as much as some but, as I've said, I was a bread-and-butter man. I met many a notorious East End gangster, both in and out of the nick. The only time I ever came into close contact with one of the Kray brothers was when I was in Lewes prison in 1998. Reggie Kray was there but I had nothing to do with him, as he wasn't my kind of person. Also, he was involved in the killing of two of my friends in the 60s, who as far as I was concerned, were two good men. I didn't much like their methods too much or how they conducted themselves. I gave them a wide birth. It was a fortunate thing that I was totally focused on my impending escape and I didn't want to rock the boat when it came to getting revenge for my friends. I was too wrapped up in securing my own freedom to do anything that would jeopardise that.

Life in prison dragged on and I became weary and obedient to the regime; the system had won the war with me. I was never going to escape again, as it would be near-on impossible. Especially when they started putting secure systems in place. Prisons became a fortress and I had given up trying to outsmart them and beat the system.

One day, I received a letter from the Minister of Justice. I started to read the beginning of the letter; it was all negative and I ended up not reading the rest of it, throwing it casually in the bin. I thought the letter was just a load of nonsense and didn't want to get irate reading it before my lunch. It was only my friend, who decided to retrieve it from the trash and read the full contents of the letter.

The letter informed me that one of my whole life sentences was to be squashed, cast aside and that I would only serve twenty-five years. Meaning I had around six years left; I would be eighty-three on release and I had hope that I would live out my days, able to walk the streets again one last time.

I suppose you are wondering how I felt about being released and did I have any regrets? I can't say I felt great elation on my release; all I had done was exchange one set of concerns for another. When I finally walked out of those prison gates, the world had changed dramatically. I had missed a whole era; laptops, mobile phones, computers, it was all alien for me. I just ignored the new world and carried on my business.

Most people wonder and question what gives a normal human being the urge to take what belongs to someone else. What drives someone to live a life where they hold a gun to someone's face, or beat them with a cosh? Then you are asking the wrong question entirely. You are making the assumption that robbers have the capacity to have empathy, have remorse or care about anyone's individual feelings. We don't care, we have no regard for anyone, we are not normal people. We live on the outskirts of society, doing what we want, when we want, and take whatever we like. It is as simple as that. We don't show remorse for the death of anyone; it is part and parcel of the job. Things go wrong and lives are lost. We know what we are getting into and know the consequences can lead to jail-time. We don't feel bad for taking anyone's money, we don't have bouts of regret or shame. We just don't give a fuck. We do the bird and get on with it. No conscience, and certainly no regrets. This may be hard for people to understand, but I believe telling the real truth of the mindset of a robber is far better than pretending we have a conscience.

On my release, I knew my robbing days were firmly behind me, as I was too long in the tooth. All I could do now was enjoy the rest of life. I settled down on the Isle of Sheppy; the pace of life is slow and tranquil and I have always gravitated to the sea, as the coast is such a peaceful place.

Do I regret any of my life choices? Would I have done things differently? I can honestly say no. Maybe this makes me callous and void of human emotion. But, for me, it is what it is. I served forty- five years in total in prison; a long time, but prison came with the nature of the job. It has always been in my nature to be a robber; I enjoyed the thrill, the chase and the money. I believe it was in my blood to be a criminal; robbing was all I knew and loved. I never felt the need to change my ways. I do wish some parts of my life had played out differently. I would be a happier man if no one had died at my hands, but the nature of the job inevitably leads to trouble and sometimes people getting hurt. I don't regret being a robber. In fact, I enjoyed it considerably, but it was a different time, and the world we are in now does not suit that criminal way of life anymore.

When I am with my thoughts, I think back to what that lovely Irish nurse said to me: "God must have kept you alive for a reason." I think she was right; he saved me to live a colourful life, reap the rewards that were ready for the taking and to share my story with you and maybe someone out there, who can learn from my lifetime of crime. Maybe they can take something from it. Good or bad, you decide...

If you have enjoyed this book, we appreciate your Amazon reviews and check out John's podcast interviews on Shaun Attwood's YouTube channel: 45 Years in EVERY UK Prison: John Hilton

OTHER BOOKS BY GADFLY PRESS

By John G Sutton:
HMP Manchester Prison Officer: I Survived Terrorists, Murderers, Rapists and Freemason Officer Attacks in Strangeways and Wormwood Scrubs

By Lee Marvin Hitchman:
How I Survived Shootings, Stabbings, Prison, Crack Addiction, Manchester Gangs and Dog Attacks

By William Rodríguez Abadía:
Son of the Cali Cartel: The Narcos Who Wiped Out Pablo Escobar and the Medellín Cartel

By Chet Sandhu:
Self-Made, Dues Paid: An Asian Kid Who Became an International Drug-Smuggling Gangster

By Kaz B:
Confessions of a Dominatrix: My Secret BDSM Life

By Peter McAleese:
Killing Escobar and Soldier Stories

By Joe Egan:
Big Joe Egan: The Toughest White Man on the Planet

By Anthony Valentine:

Britain's No. 1 Art Forger Max Brandrett: The Life of a Cheeky Faker

By Johnnyboy Steele:

Scotland's Johnnyboy: The Bird That Never Flew

By Ian 'Blink' MacDonald:

Scotland's Wildest Bank Robber: Guns, Bombs and Mayhem in Glasgow's Gangland

By Michael Sheridan:

The Murder of Sophie: How I Hunted and Haunted the West Cork Killer

By Steve Wraith:

The Krays' Final Years: My Time with London's Most Iconic Gangsters

By Natalie Welsh:

Escape from Venezuela's Deadliest Prison

By Shaun Attwood:
English Shaun Trilogy

Party Time
Hard Time
Prison Time

War on Drugs Series

Pablo Escobar: Beyond Narcos
American Made: Who Killed Barry Seal? Pablo Escobar or George HW Bush
The Cali Cartel: Beyond Narcos
Clinton Bush and CIA Conspiracies: From the Boys on the Tracks to Jeffrey Epstein
Who Killed Epstein? Prince Andrew or Bill Clinton

Un–Making a Murderer: The Framing of Steven Avery and Brendan Dassey
The Mafia Philosopher: Two Tonys
Life Lessons

Pablo Escobar's Story (4-book series)

By Johnnyboy Steele:

Scotland's Johnnyboy: The Bird That Never Flew

"A cross between *Shawshank Redemption* and *Escape from Alcatraz*!" – Shaun Attwood, YouTuber and Author

All his life, 'Johnnyboy' Steele has been running. Firstly, from an abusive father, then from the rigours of an approved school and a young offenders jail, and, finally, from the harshness of adult prison. This book details how the Steele brothers staged the most daring breakout that Glasgow's Barlinnie prison had ever seen and recounts what happened when their younger brother, Joseph, was falsely accused of the greatest mass murder in Scottish legal history.

If Johnnyboy had wings, he would have flown to help his family, but he would have to wait for freedom to use his expertise to publicise young Joe's miscarriage of justice.

This is a compelling, often shocking and uncompromisingly honest account of how the human spirit can survive against almost crushing odds. It is a story of family love, friendship and, ultimately, a desire for justice.

By Ian 'Blink' MacDonald:

Scotland's Wildest Bank Robber: Guns, Bombs and Mayhem in Glasgow's Gangland

As a young man in Glasgow's underworld, Ian 'Blink' MacDonald earned a reputation for fighting and stabbing his enemies. After refusing to work for Arthur "The Godfather" Thompson, he attempted to steal £6 million in a high-risk armed bank robbery. While serving 16 years, Blink met the torture-gang boss Eddie Richardson, the serial killer Archie Hall, notorious lifer Charles Bronson and members of the Krays.

After his release, his drug-fuelled violent lifestyle created conflict with the police and rival gangsters. Rearrested several times, he was the target of a gruesome assassination attempt. During filming for Danny Dyer's Deadliest Men, a bomb was discovered under Blink's car and the terrified camera crew members fled from Scotland.

In *Scotland's Wildest Bank Robber*, Blink provides an eye-opening account of how he survived gangland warfare, prisons, stabbings and bombs.

By Michael Sheridan:

The Murder of Sophie: How I Hunted and Haunted the West Cork Killer

Just before Christmas, 1996, a beautiful French woman – the wife of a movie mogul – was brutally murdered outside of her holiday home in a remote region of West Cork, Ireland. The crime was reported by a local journalist, Ian Bailey, who was at the forefront of the case until he became the prime murder suspect. Arrested twice, he was released without charge.

This was the start of a saga lasting decades with twists and turns and a battle for justice in two countries, which culminated in the 2019 conviction of Bailey – in his absence – by the French Criminal court in Paris. But it was up to the Irish courts to decide whether he would be extradited to serve a 25-year prison sentence.

With the unrivalled co-operation of major investigation sources and the backing of the victim's family, the author unravels the shocking facts of a unique murder case.

By Steve Wraith:

The Krays' Final Years: My Time with London's Most Iconic Gangsters

Britain's most notorious twins – Ron and Reg Kray – ascended the underworld to become the most feared and legendary gangsters in London. Their escalating mayhem culminated in murder, for which they received life sentences in 1969.

While incarcerated, they received letters from a schoolboy from Tyneside, Steve Wraith, who was mesmerised by their story. Eventually, Steve visited them in prison and a friendship formed. The Twins hired Steve as an unofficial advisor, which brought him into contact with other members of their crime family. At Ron's funeral, Steve was Charlie Kray's right-hand man.

Steve documents Ron's time in Broadmoor – a high-security psychiatric hospital – where he was battling insanity and heavily medicated. Steve details visiting Reg, who served almost 30 years in a variety of prisons, where the gangster was treated with the utmost respect by the staff and the inmates.

By Natalie Welsh:

Escape from Venezuela's Deadliest Prison

After getting arrested at a Venezuelan airport with a suitcase of cocaine, Natalie was clueless about the danger she was facing. Sentenced to 10 years, she arrived at a prison with armed men on the roof, whom she mistakenly believed were the guards, only to find out they were homicidal gang members. Immediately, she was plunged into a world of unimaginable horror and escalating violence, where murder, rape and all-out gang warfare were carried out with the complicity of corrupt guards. Male prisoners often entered the women's housing area, bringing gunfire with them and leaving corpses behind. After 4.5 years, Natalie risked everything to escape and flee through Colombia, with the help of a guard who had fallen deeply in love with her.

By Shaun Attwood:

Pablo Escobar: Beyond Narcos

War on Drugs Series Book 1

The mind-blowing true story of Pablo Escobar and the Medellín Cartel, beyond their portrayal on Netflix.

Colombian drug lord Pablo Escobar was a devoted family man and a psychopathic killer; a terrible enemy, yet a wonderful friend. While donating millions to the poor, he bombed and tortured his enemies – some had their eyeballs removed with hot spoons. Through ruthless cunning and America's insatiable appetite for cocaine, he became a multi-billionaire, who lived in a $100-million house with its own zoo.

Pablo Escobar: Beyond Narcos demolishes the standard good versus evil telling of his story. The authorities were not hunting Pablo down to stop his cocaine business. They were taking it over.

American Made: Who Killed Barry Seal?
Pablo Escobar or George HW Bush

War on Drugs Series Book 2

Set in a world where crime and government coexist, *American Made* is the jaw-dropping true story of CIA pilot Barry Seal that the Hollywood movie starring Tom Cruise is afraid to tell.

Barry Seal flew cocaine and weapons worth billions of dollars into and out of America in the 1980s. After he became a government informant, Pablo Escobar's Medellin Cartel offered a million for him alive and half a million dead. But his real trouble began after he threatened to expose the dirty dealings of George HW Bush.

American Made rips the roof off Bush and Clinton's complicity in cocaine trafficking in Mena, Arkansas.

"A conspiracy of the grandest magnitude." Congressman Bill Alexander on the Mena affair.

The Cali Cartel: Beyond Narcos

War on Drugs Series Book 3

An electrifying account of the Cali Cartel, beyond its portrayal on Netflix.

From the ashes of Pablo Escobar's empire rose an even bigger and more malevolent cartel. A new breed of sophisticated mobsters became the kings of cocaine. Their leader was Gilberto Rodríguez Orejuela – known as the Chess Player, due to his foresight and calculated cunning.

Gilberto and his terrifying brother, Miguel, ran a multi-billion-dollar drug empire like a corporation. They employed a politically astute brand of thuggery and spent $10 million to put a president in power. Although the godfathers from Cali preferred bribery over violence, their many loyal torturers and hitmen were never idle.

Clinton, Bush and CIA Conspiracies: From the Boys on the Tracks to Jeffrey Epstein

War on Drugs Series Book 4

In the 1980s, George HW Bush imported cocaine to finance an illegal war in Nicaragua. Governor Bill Clinton's Arkansas state police provided security for the drug drops. For assisting the CIA, the Clinton Crime Family was awarded the White House. The #clintonbodycount continues to this day, with the deceased including Jeffrey Epstein.

This book features harrowing true stories that reveal the insanity of the drug war. A mother receives the worst news about her son. A journalist gets a tip that endangers his life. An unemployed man becomes California's biggest crack dealer. A DEA agent in Mexico is sacrificed for going after the big players.

The lives of Linda Ives, Gary Webb, Freeway Rick Ross and Kiki Camarena are shattered by brutal experiences. Not all of them will survive.

Pablo Escobar's Story (4-book series)

"Finally, the definitive book about Escobar, original and up-to-date." – UNILAD

"The most comprehensive account ever written." – True Geordie

Pablo Escobar was a mama's boy, who cherished his family and sang in the shower, yet he bombed a passenger plane and formed a death squad that used genital electrocution.

Most Escobar biographies only provide a few pieces of the puzzle, but this action-packed 1000-page book reveals everything about the king of cocaine.

Mostly translated from Spanish, Part 1 contains stories untold in the English-speaking world, including:

The tragic death of his youngest brother, Fernando.

The fate of his pregnant mistress.

The shocking details of his affair with a TV celebrity.

The presidential candidate who encouraged him to eliminate their rivals.

The Mafia Philosopher

"A fast-paced true-crime memoir with all of the action of Goodfellas." – UNILAD

"Sopranos v Sons of Anarchy with an Alaskan-snow backdrop." – True Geordie Podcast

Breaking bones, burying bodies and planting bombs became second nature to Two Tonys, while working for the Bonanno Crime Family, whose exploits inspired The Godfather.

After a dispute with an outlaw motorcycle club, Two Tonys left a trail of corpses from Arizona to Alaska. On the run, he was pursued by bikers and a neo-Nazi gang, blood-thirsty for revenge, while a homicide detective launched a nationwide manhunt.

As the mist from his smoking gun fades, readers are left with an unexpected portrait of a stoic philosopher with a wealth of charm, a glorious turn of phrase and a fanatical devotion to his daughter.

Party Time

An action-packed roller-coaster account of a life spiralling out of control, featuring wild women, gangsters and a mountain of drugs.

Shaun Attwood arrived in Phoenix, Arizona, a penniless business graduate from a small industrial town in England. Within a decade, he became a stock-market millionaire. But he was leading a double life.

After taking his first ecstasy pill at a rave in Manchester as a shy student, Shaun became intoxicated by the party lifestyle that would change his fortune. Years later, in the Arizona desert, he became submerged in a criminal underworld, throwing parties for thousands of ravers and running an ecstasy ring in competition with the Mafia mass murderer, Sammy 'The Bull' Gravano.

As greed and excess tore through his life, Shaun had eye-watering encounters with Mafia hitmen and crystal-meth addicts, enjoyed extravagant debauchery with superstar DJs and glitter girls, and ingested enough drugs to kill a herd of elephants. This is his story.

Hard Time

"Makes the Shawshank Redemption look like a holiday camp." – NOTW

After a SWAT team smashed down stock-market millionaire Shaun Attwood's door, he found himself inside Arizona's deadliest jail and locked into a brutal struggle for survival.

Shaun's hope of living the American Dream turned into a nightmare of violence and chaos, when he had a run-in with Sammy "the Bull" Gravano, an Italian Mafia mass murderer.

In jail, Shaun was forced to endure cockroaches crawling in his ears at night, dead rats in the food and the sound of skulls getting cracked against toilets. He meticulously documented the conditions and smuggled out his message.

Join Shaun on a harrowing voyage into the darkest recesses of human existence.

Hard Time provides a revealing glimpse into the tragedy, brutality, dark comedy and eccentricity of prison life.

Featured worldwide on Nat Geo Channel's Locked-Up/Banged-Up Abroad Raving Arizona.

Prison Time

Sentenced to 9½ years in Arizona's state prison for distributing ecstasy, Shaun finds himself living among gang members, sexual predators and drug-crazed psychopaths. After being attacked by a Californian biker, in for stabbing a girlfriend, Shaun writes about the prisoners who befriend, protect and inspire him. They include T-Bone, a massive African American ex-Marine, who risks his life saving vulnerable inmates from rape, and Two Tonys, an old-school Mafia murderer, who left the corpses of his rivals from Arizona to Alaska. They teach Shaun how to turn incarceration to his advantage, and to learn from his mistakes.

Shaun is no stranger to love and lust in the heterosexual world, but the tables are turned on him inside. Sexual advances come at him from all directions, some cleverly disguised, others more sinister – making Shaun question his sexual identity.

Resigned to living alongside violent, mentally ill and drug-addicted inmates, Shaun immerses himself in psychology and philosophy, to try to make sense of his past behaviour, and begins applying what he learns, as he adapts to prison life. Encouraged by Two Tonys to explore fiction as well, Shaun reads over 1000 books which, with support from a brilliant psychotherapist, Dr Owen, speed along his personal development. As his ability to deflect daily threats improves, Shaun begins to look forward to his release with optimism and a new love waiting for him. Yet the words of Aristotle from one of Shaun's books will prove prophetic: "We cannot learn without pain."

Un-Making a Murderer: The Framing of Steven Avery and Brendan Dassey

Innocent people do go to jail. Sometimes mistakes are made. But even more terrifying is when the authorities conspire to frame them. That's what happened to Steven Avery and Brendan Dassey, who were convicted of murder and are serving life sentences.

Un-Making a Murderer is an explosive book, which uncovers the illegal, devious and covert tactics used by Wisconsin officials, including:

– Concealing Other Suspects

– Paying Expert Witnesses to Lie

– Planting Evidence

– Jury Tampering

The art of framing innocent people has been in practice for centuries and will continue until the perpetrators are held accountable. Turning conventional assumptions and beliefs in the justice system upside down, *Un-Making a Murderer* takes you on that journey.

HARD TIME BY SHAUN ATTWOOD

CHAPTER 1

Sleep deprived and scanning for danger, I enter a dark cell on the second floor of the maximum-security Madison Street jail in Phoenix, Arizona, where guards and gang members are murdering prisoners. Behind me, the metal door slams heavily. Light slants into the cell through oblong gaps in the door, illuminating a prisoner cocooned in a white sheet, snoring lightly on the top bunk about two thirds of the way up the back wall. Relieved there is no immediate threat, I place my mattress on the grimy floor. Desperate to rest, I notice movement on the cement-block walls. *Am I hallucinating?* I blink several times. The walls appear to ripple. Stepping closer, I see the walls are alive with insects. I flinch. So many are swarming, I wonder if they're a colony of ants on the move. To get a better look, I put my eyes right up to them. They are mostly the size of almonds and have antennae. American cockroaches. I've seen them in the holding cells downstairs in smaller numbers, but nothing like this. A chill spread over my body. I back away.

Something alive falls from the ceiling and bounces off the base of my neck. I jump. With my night vision improving, I spot cockroaches weaving in and out of the base of the fluorescent strip light. Every so often one drops onto the concrete and resumes crawling. Examining the bottom bunk, I realise why my cellmate is sleeping at a higher elevation: cockroaches are pouring from gaps in the decrepit wall at the level of my bunk. The area is thick with them. Placing my mattress on the bottom bunk scatters them. I walk towards the toilet, crunching a few under my shower sandals. I urinate and grab the toilet roll. A cockroach darts from the centre of the roll onto my hand, tickling my fingers. My arm jerks as if it has a mind of its own, losing the cockroach and the toilet roll. Using a towel, I wipe the bulk of them off the bottom bunk, stopping only to shake the odd one off my hand. I unroll my mattress. They begin to regroup and inhabit my mattress. My adrenaline is pumping so much, I lose my fatigue.

Nauseated, I sit on a tiny metal stool bolted to the wall. *How will I sleep? How's my cellmate sleeping through the infestation and my arrival?* Copying his technique, I cocoon myself in a sheet and lie down, crushing more cockroaches. The only way they can access me now is through the breathing hole I've left in the sheet by the lower half of my face. Inhaling their strange musty odour, I close my eyes. I can't sleep. I feel them crawling on the sheet around my feet. *Am I imagining things?* Frightened of them infiltrating my breathing hole, I keep opening my eyes. Cramps cause me to rotate onto my other side. Facing the wall, I'm repulsed by so many of them just inches away. I return to my original side.

The sheet traps the heat of the Sonoran Desert to my body, soaking me in sweat. Sweat tickles my body, tricking my mind into thinking the cockroaches are infiltrating and crawling on me. The trapped heat aggravates my bleeding skin infections and bedsores. I want to scratch myself, but I know better. The outer layers of my skin have turned soggy from sweating constantly in this concrete oven. Squirming on the bunk fails to stop the relentless itchiness of my skin. Eventually, I scratch myself. Clumps of moist skin detach under my nails. Every now and then I become so uncomfortable, I must open my cocoon to waft the heat out, which allows the cockroaches in. It takes hours to drift to sleep. I only manage a few hours. I awake stuck to the soaked sheet, disgusted by the cockroach carcasses compressed against the mattress.

The cockroaches plague my new home until dawn appears at the dots in the metal grid over a begrimed strip of four-inch-thick bullet-proof glass at the top of the back wall – the cell's only source of outdoor light. They disappear into the cracks in the walls, like vampire mist retreating from sunlight. But not all of them. There were so many on the night shift that even their vastly reduced number is too many to dispose of. And they act like they know it. They roam around my feet with attitude, as if to make it clear that I'm trespassing on their turf.

My next set of challenges will arise not from the insect world, but from my neighbours. I'm the new arrival, subject to scrutiny about my charges just like when I'd run into the Aryan Brotherhood prison gang on my first day at the medium-security Towers jail a year ago. I wish my cellmate would wake up, brief me on the mood of the locals and introduce me to the head of the white gang. No such luck. Chow is announced over a speaker system in a crackly robotic voice, but he doesn't stir.

I emerge into the day room for breakfast. Prisoners in black-and-white bee-striped uniforms gather under the metal-grid stairs and tip dead cockroaches into a trash bin from plastic peanut-butter containers they'd set as traps during the night. All eyes are on me in the chow line. Watching who sits where, I hold my head up, put on a solid stare and pretend to be as at home in this environment as the cockroaches. It's all an act. I'm lonely and afraid. I loathe having to explain myself to the head of the white race, who I assume is the toughest murderer. I've been in jail long enough to know that taking my breakfast to my cell will imply that I have something to hide.

The gang punishes criminals with certain charges. The most serious are sex offenders, who are KOS: Kill On Sight. Other charges are punishable by SOS – Smash On Sight – such as drive-by shootings because women and kids sometimes get killed. It's called convict justice. Gang members are constantly looking for people to beat up because that's how they earn their reputations and tattoos. The most serious acts of violence earn the highest-ranking tattoos. To be a full gang member requires murder. I've observed the body language and techniques inmates trying to integrate employ. An inmate with a spring in his step and an air of confidence is likely to be accepted. A person who avoids eye contact and fails to introduce himself to the gang is likely to be preyed on. Some of the failed attempts I saw ended up with heads getting cracked against toilets, a sound I've grown familiar with. I've seen prisoners being extracted on stretchers who looked dead – one had yellow fluid leaking from his head. The constant violence gives me nightmares, but the reality is that I put myself in here, so I force myself to accept it as a part of my punishment.

It's time to apply my knowledge. With a self-assured stride, I take my breakfast bag to the table of white inmates covered in neo-Nazi tattoos, allowing them to question me.

"Mind if I sit with you guys?" I ask, glad exhaustion has deepened my voice.

"These seats are taken. But you can stand at the corner of the table."

The man who answered is probably the head of the gang. I size him up. Cropped brown hair. A dangerous glint in Nordic-blue eyes. Tiny pupils that suggest he's on heroin. Weightlifter-type veins bulging from a sturdy neck. Political ink on arms crisscrossed with scars. About the same age as me, thirty-three.

"Thanks. I'm Shaun from England." I volunteer my origin to show I'm different from them but not in a way that might get me smashed.

"I'm Bullet, the head of the whites." He offers me his fist to bump. "Where you roll in from, wood?"

Addressing me as wood is a good sign. It's what white gang members on a friendly basis call each other.

"Towers jail. They increased my bond and re-classified me to maximum security."

"What's your bond at?"

"I've got two $750,000 bonds," I say in a monotone. This is no place to brag about bonds.

"How many people you kill, brother?" His eyes drill into mine, checking whether my body language supports my story. My body language so far is spot on.

"None. I threw rave parties. They got us talking about drugs on wiretaps." Discussing drugs on the phone does not warrant a $1.5 million bond. I know and beat him to his next question. "Here's my charges." I show him my charge sheet, which includes conspiracy and leading a crime syndicate – both from running an Ecstasy ring.

Bullet snatches the paper and scrutinises it. Attempting to pre-empt his verdict, the other whites study his face. On edge, I wait for him to respond. Whatever he says next will determine whether I'll be accepted or victimised.

"Are you some kind of jailhouse attorney?" Bullet asks. "I want someone to read through my case paperwork." During our few minutes of conversation, Bullet has seen through my act and concluded that I'm educated – a possible resource to him.

I appreciate that he'll accept me if I take the time to read his case. "I'm no jailhouse attorney, but I'll look through it and help you however I can."

"Good. I'll stop by your cell later on, wood."

After breakfast, I seal as many of the cracks in the walls as I can with toothpaste. The cell smells minty, but the cockroaches still find their way in. Their day shift appears to be collecting information on the brown paper bags under my bunk, containing a few items of food that I purchased from the commissary; bags that I tied off with rubber bands in the hope of keeping the cockroaches out. Relentlessly, the cockroaches explore the bags for entry points, pausing over and probing the most worn and vulnerable regions. *Will the nightly swarm eat right through the paper?* I read all morning, wondering whether my cellmate has died in his cocoon, his occasional breathing sounds reassuring me.

Bullet stops by late afternoon and drops his case paperwork off. He's been charged with Class 3 felonies and less, not serious crimes, but is facing a double-digit sentence because of his prior convictions and Security Threat Group status in the prison system. The proposed sentencing range seems disproportionate. I'll advise him to reject the plea bargain – on the assumption he already knows to do so, but is just seeking the comfort of a second opinion, like many un-sentenced inmates. When he returns for his paperwork, our conversation disturbs my cellmate – the cocoon shuffles – so we go upstairs to his cell. I tell Bullet what I think. He is excitable, a different man from earlier, his pupils almost non-existent.

"This case ain't shit. But my prosecutor knows I done other shit, all kinds of heavy shit, but can't prove it. I'd do anything to get that sorry bitch off my fucking ass. She's asking for something bad to happen to her. Man, if I ever get bonded out, I'm gonna chop that bitch into pieces. Kill her slowly though. Like to work her over with a blowtorch."

Such talk can get us both charged with conspiring to murder a prosecutor, so I try to steer him elsewhere. "It's crazy how they can catch you doing one thing, yet try to sentence you for all of the things they think you've ever done."

"Done plenty. Shot some dude in the stomach once. Rolled him up in a blanket and threw him in a dumpster."

Discussing past murders is as unsettling as future ones. "So, what's all your tattoos mean, Bullet? Like that eagle on your chest?"

"Why you wanna know?" Bullet's eyes probe mine.

My eyes hold their ground. "Just curious."

"It's a war bird. The AB patch."

"AB patch?"

"What the Aryan Brotherhood gives you when you've put enough work in."

"How long does it take to earn a patch?"

"Depends how quickly you put your work in. You have to earn your lightning bolts first."

"Why you got red and black lightning bolts?"

"You get SS bolts for beating someone down or for being an enforcer for the family. Red lightning bolts for killing someone. I was sent down as a youngster. They gave me steel and told me who to handle and I handled it. You don't ask questions. You just get blood on your steel. Dudes who get these tats without putting work in are told to cover them up or leave the yard."

"What if they refuse?"

"They're held down and we carve the ink off them."

Imagining them carving a chunk of flesh to remove a tattoo, I cringe. He's really enjoying telling me this now. His volatile nature is clear and frightening. *He's accepted me too much. He's trying to impress me before making demands.*

At night, I'm unable to sleep. Cocooned in heat, surrounded by cockroaches, I hear the swamp-cooler vent – a metal grid at the top of a wall – hissing out tepid air. Giving up on sleep, I put my earphones on and tune into National Public Radio. Listening to a Vivaldi violin concerto, I close my eyes and press my tailbone down to straighten my back as if I'm doing a yogic relaxation. The playful allegro thrills me, lifting my spirits, but the wistful adagio provokes sad emotions and tears. I open my eyes and gaze into the gloom. Due to lack of sleep, I start hallucinating and hearing voices over the music whispering threats. I'm at breaking point. Although I have accepted that I committed crimes and deserve to be punished, no one should have to live like this. I'm furious at myself for making the series of reckless decisions that put me in here and for losing absolutely everything. As violins crescendo in my ears, I remember what my life used to be like.

Printed in Great Britain
by Amazon

44434326R00165